Table of Contents

LIST OF TABLES

LIST OF FIGURES

Prologue

This book is the product of a confluence of experiences from both of us as professional consultants in the for-profit arena, as leadership trainers, spiritual formators, parish administrators, clergy (we are both permanent deacons), and as parish-life consultants for a combined total of more than 60 parishes throughout the U.S. This book is also considered a rare genre, a unique combination of what has been developed in leadership theory in the secular world along with what is expected to be accomplished as leaders in the pastoral setting. The book relies on formal research and recent scholarly findings from the leadership discipline, yet it also brings forward what these models may be lacking in terms of pastoral values. In simpler terms, this book is the product of what would occur if there were a group of leadership scholars, experienced leadership practitioners, pastoral experts and theologians in the same room who were asked, "What do you all have in common?"

The ten-year journey to compose and finalize this book exposed us to many other ongoing efforts to bridge the divide between secular leadership and pastoral demands. Yet in most cases, spiritual dynamics were either a supplement or an added appendix to secular modeling. We even heard comments such as, "Any leadership model will work in the pastoral setting, as long as you add prayer…"

We disagree. Leaving this divide up to each pastoral leader to resolve has not worked well so far. We found pastoral leaders—especially pastors—spending large amounts of energy reconciling the goal of "becoming an effective executive" using the training and coaching along secular models and trying to continue living a deep spiritual life. In some cases, we saw successes, but we also saw failures. Regardless of success levels, priests from both the successful side and the failed side confided in different ways that "I don't want to be a CEO... I want to be a pastor, a priest." It was the sacrifice of these pastors in offering the best they could to reconcile these opposites that we discovered and later shared with them a powerful insight, one that drives the flow and core of this book—that of *leadership being a spiritual practice.* When we mentioned to these pastors (and priests as well) in one-on-one coaching sessions or informal gatherings that leadership is a spiritual practice, the reaction was unmistakable: eyes wide open, a hesitation, and then a smile. *Eyes wide open* because it's a language much easier to understand than "*CEO speak.*" A *hesitation* while the connections are made between "leading" and his spiritual development. And finally, a *smile*, that signals the more comfortable—and better aligned with vocation growth—approach to leadership in the pastoral setting.

From these experiences you can easily see how we felt compelled to structure our approach to pastoral leadership and the mantra of "*leadership is a spiritual practice.*" Leadership is about "influences," and the academic circles that study leadership emphasize the two most common forms of influences: *rational* and *emotional.* Yet in recognizing the strength of spiritual formation in the pastoral setting, we decided to add a third form of influence—that of spiritual influence—and make it the cornerstone of pastoral leadership modeling while at the same time never losing the insights and developments on leadership theory that are evolving from academic disciplines. To the question of whether pastoral leadership is a specialized role or an *influence* (spiritual, in our case), we suggest the role speaks to the spiritual influence and the spiritual influence speaks to the role. This is also a conclusion derived from the pastors we have worked with over the years. Why would it not apply to any pastoral leader?

For these reasons we opted to work together in collecting the experiences, research and best leadership practices we have seen in parish life since 1999, with even more emphasis after *"Collaborate leadership: Moving towards relational paradigms in lay ministry development"* was published (Rojas, 2003, Bloomington, IN: Authorhouse). Although the outcomes of these experiences could be presented in a variety of ways, given the interlocking nature of these spiritual topics, having to find a linear path for these ideas in a manuscript format for publication drove the order of the topics.

The first chapter sets the stage to recognize some of the value in using secular leadership models within the pastoral domain, but it also attempts to create awareness about some of their shortcomings. Leadership models are *social constructions* and *culturally bound*, so through a series of examples we challenge the "wholesale" application in Church. Rather than adapting Church and parish ministries to social constructions and cultural bounding, should not it be the other way around? Challenging the assumptions and capability levels of secular leadership models is a proper first step in understanding the fundamental challenges of pastoral leadership and is foundational in beginning a more detailed look at the "forms of leader influence" that offer a better fit with Church (rather than secular) objectives—especially those related to personal and community spiritual growth. Leading teams is one thing; leading a spiritual community is more than just leading a team.

Once a keener sensitivity of the potential shortfalls of secular leadership models in Church is presented, what follows is a refocusing on the fundamental concepts of leadership. In Chapter 2, drawing from the discoveries and research of the leadership academic discipline, leadership is defined in terms of its hard (task orientation) and soft (relationships) sides, where the dynamics of leading is based upon various forms of influence (e.g., rational, emotional, situational) rather than on "power." In fact, Chapter 2 introduces another form of influence—that of *spiritual influence*—as a category better fit for pastoral ministry. Chapter 2 goes on to pronounce *leadership as a spiritual practice*, which then becomes the cornerstone for defining different forms of *spiritual influences* available to the pastoral leader. Specifically, personal calling, character strength, the primacy of relationships, spiritual community and envisioning are defined and become the topics for the chapters that follow (Chapters 3-7).

Chapter 8 addresses the topic of *discernment* as the integrating force of all these spiritual influences, and presents a simple yet profound methodology of discernment we have used in clergy and lay leader formation, what we call *discernment of voices*. In exercising spiritual influences that are guided by discernment processes, the pastoral leadership becomes a "stewardship of God's laborers."

After the strong emphasis on the "leader" himself or herself, the focus in Chapter 9 shifts toward the situational realities of the team (or ministry). Here we introduce pastoral team (group) life-cycles, where regularities that seem to occur over time in ministry are segmented into discrete states of organizational development. Out of the experiences of working as parish consultants and drawing from the academic research on life-cycles within small businesses and non-profit organizations, seven stages of development are presented. Each stage of this model is discussed, and best observed spiritual practices are paired with each stage. The combination of the life-cycle model and what was presented earlier on leadership as a spiritual practice provide a wider landscape of possibilities and options, all embedded within parish life.

In the final chapter, we recount some of our experiences since 1999 in developing and validating much of what is presented here on pastoral leadership, and how our experiences point to discernment skills as the starting point and portal to access the other spiritual practices. We suggest a catalog course description and syllabus for a graduate-level pastoral leadership course, and we encourage academics, researchers, consultants and other professionals to continue exploring pastoral leadership under the mantra of "leadership is a spiritual practice."

Note that each chapter is structured to not only address the intellectual understanding of these concepts but also to facilitate the integration of these spiritual influences into ongoing formation processes individually and within a group setting. Each chapter has a case study with discussion questions and exercises that can be conducted in a group setting, as well as personal reflective questions that can be used for spiritual journaling or as subjects of dialogue with spiritual directors. At the end of the book are two additional resources, a sample syllabus for a graduate course (elective) on pastoral leadership and the leadership pre-assessment survey we use as a tool to determine the priority of topics as we get ready for a workshop.

To suggest this is a definitive work on pastoral leadership is to not fully understand the dynamics of Church and Spirit. By no means are we suggesting this is a static model. In applying spiritual influences to the exercise of leadership in the pastoral setting—and without negating the value that some secular models already add to ministry growth—we realize there are many more influences that could have been included in this edition. Leadership—at least in practice—is more than just a simple recipe: it seems to depend more on a repertoire of influences that are exercised in different degrees, depending on the internal and external urgencies of the group, team or community.

Yet we are not comfortable at this point, because in presenting all the spiritual influences observed upon the crafting of this manuscript, we have decided we need more time to formulate many of the influences we observe from a "grounded theory" approach rather than just as a theoretical contribution. We also realize the need to publish and promote the spiritual-influences approach to pastoral leadership. That was our guidance to present only five spiritual influences (practices) in this current edition. For now, our other observations require more time to mature before we start writing on them.

There are some cautions that need to be explicitly expressed as you go through the content and suggestions of this book. First of all we want to present a comment (and disclaimer) regarding the case studies illustrated in this book as supplemental materials for reflection and discussion. Our intent is to use real scenarios of parish life as much as possible as a discussion platform for the different concepts and models we use on pastoral leadership. These cases are hardly the unique domain of any single parish, but very likely reflect scenarios that have occurred— and we have seen— in many parishes we have observed, worked with or consulted with in the past. Individual names, places and parish statistics in these cases are either products of our imagination or are used fictiously to stress a point for discussion, a controversy or a special scenario. Any resemblance to actual events, locales or persons, living or dead, is entirely coincidental.

Next, there is a fundamental assumption underlying the effectiveness of any form of spiritual influence, and that is the presumption of a healthy and growing spiritual life. In other words, these practices are not intended as stand-alone techniques to improve leadership stature short term. The best examples of pastoral leaders we have seen exercising the spiritual influences presented in this book happen also to be women and men with a profound value for continued spiritual growth. This is perhaps the audience that will most easily capture the significance of "leadership as a spiritual practice" and provide the role-modeling for much of what we have to say of these topics. But we are also hopeful that any type of leader who is inspired toward forms of spiritual influence would be enticed to continue exploring and advancing in spiritual maturity.

Another aspect of this book that needs to be addressed is the strong focus on spirituality and less emphasis on theology, scripture and tradition. This was a difficult but necessary choice, because it simplifies our attempts to effectively integrate and track the evolution of academic (secular) research within the leadership discipline as foundational to our pastoral leadership modeling. Again, being able to draw the best practices from the secular leadership experience (for-profit, non-profit) and use them as a foundation for pastoral leadership represents a unique feature of this book. Suffice it to say that we do believe that theology, scripture and Church teachings are relevant to the emerging forms of effective pastoral leadership, yet we are quick to point out these were not the primary focus as we began researching the assortment of possible influences germane to the pastoral setting. This consideration alone illustrates the preliminary nature of much of what is said in this book. Nevertheless, we encourage pastoral theologians, scripture scholars and parish consultants to continue what this book and others like it have already started. Whether this was an effective approach or not still needs to be fully discerned.

Here is another stipulation worth presenting that addresses the value and intent of this book. We realize that not everyone in ministry would be excited about understanding multiple forms of pastoral leadership and spiritual influences in more depth. There are a number of leaders who are fine with their current level of leadership skills in ministry. Yet there is also another group of leaders that aspires to higher levels of proficiency and performance, either because they are driven by personal ideals or by community needs. In other words, it is one thing to be able to "ride a bike." But just because you can "ride a bike" doesn't mean you are ready to compete in the *Tour de France*. Similarly, just because you know how to swim does not mean you are ready for an Olympic event. Just because you can "run" does not mean you are ready for the *Boston Marathon*. There are those ministry leaders who are content with basic skills, and truthfully are performing well under those conditions.

The fact that they are volunteering to assume parish leadership roles is itself quite admirable. But there are also those within the pastoral setting who strive for more depth, higher levels and more intensity. To those seeking *Pastoral Excellence,* we dedicate this book and the variety of workshops and retreats that have resulted from the topics of this book.

We also have approached the subject of spiritual influences in leadership with an open mind and open heart, not preferring any particular school of spirituality within the Church, but at the same time trying to remain open to all traditional and post Vatican II worldviews of spirituality. Of course, we will draw insights and examples from the Benedictine, Franciscan, Dominican, Ignatian, Carmelite, Redemptorist, Monfortian or any of the post-Vatican lay movement spiritualties (e.g., Charismatic, Schoesntatt, Opus Dei, Focolare, Taize, etc.). We even recognize and attempt to be respectful of different spiritual styles or expressions of spirituality, such as the word-centered approach, the emotional approach, the art or symbol approach, as well as the action-centered approach, or the communal approaches. If any examples are used, they are intended as illustrations, not as prescriptions.

Of course a project of this nature depends on suggestions, comments and corrections from direct contributors as well as from others preferring to have a say in more indirect ways. First of all, the official readers for this project are among those that we owe our deepest gratitude. Here we are grateful to Dr. Marti Jewell, Msgr. Harry Bumpus, and Fr. Carlos Rojas for their time, effort, and inputs to the final manuscript. We also want to acknowledge the comments and encouragement of the many pastors, priests, deacons, women religious, and lay ministers from all the parishes and dioceses that we served in the capacity of parish consultants or as their formators during the past ten years. Especially we are grateful to Fr. Maina Waithaka the parish staff of St Catherine Labouré in Glenview (Illinois), Fr. Paul Stein and the leadership team of St Sylvester (Chicago), Fr. Ron Aubin and Deacon Dennis Snyder (Our

Lady of the Rosary in Land O' Lakes, Florida), Father Ralph Argentino (Director of Deacons in the Diocese of St Petersburg, Sr. María Palmer, Sr. María Isabel Bracero and the leaders of the Schoenstatt Movement in Puerto Rico. All of them allowed us to conduct and learn from the leadership workshops offered to them during past years. We are also grateful to Daniel Gast, the Director of the INSPIRE Project, his staff, and fellow parish consultants for allowing us to gather hands-on experience in sharing leadership development experiences that nurtured this project. We are grateful to the doctoral students of B7777 (Doctoral in Business Administration, Argosy University-Tampa) for their validation on how many of the elements presented here can also be applied as a complement to the Spirit at Work movement. We would like to also thank Dr. Ryan Niemiec (VIA Institute on Character) for crafting the correct wording and for use of the VIA-Me Character assessment tool, and to Dave Fiore for editing services. Finally, we are grateful for the patience and love of our spouses Isabel Rojas and Julie Alvarez. They continue to be for each of use a source of inspiration and joy in fulfilling this as well as past projects.

All in all, our hopes are that what is expressed in this book would resonate with leaders seeking to use their spiritual strengths as the proscenium for the leadership functions. We hope that our experiences and insights will continue to motivate others to explore and disseminate in theory and in practice a trend that *leadership is a spiritual practice*.

Deacon (Dr.) Ronald R. Rojas
ronrojas@aol.com

Deacon John R. Alvarez
JAlvarez@stpaulchurch.com

"The Church is not an organization or a corporation, but an entity of an entirely different class..."

Pope Benedict XVI
Vatican City, December 10, 2008

2

CHAPTER 1

The Fundamental Challenges

A fact about the nature of the leadership construct that is frequently underestimated— yet central to the pastoral sector— is that *leadership* is related to *spirituality*.

The demand for true leadership is traditionally said to arise from an expectation that "effectiveness" of group performance is resolved in large part by the leader (Borgatta, Bales, & Couch, 1954). But in looking deeper at the dynamics that drives the collective yearning for a "leader role" there is a more fundamental purpose, one that reaches into the soul. In many ways the need for a "leader role" is tied to a journey rooted in the soul, a sort of spiritual quest for direction where there is chaos, for transcending worldviews where there is inconsequentiality, for assurance where there is uncertainty, and for worth where there is uselessness.

It's quite intuitive in nature to accept how a leader attends to some of the basic needs of the soul. Leaders are visionaries, meaning-makers and guides. Leaders offer a sense of accomplishment and provide inspiration and consolation, boundaries and priorities, comfort and hope. But what becomes more difficult is for the leadership discipline in general to recognize that it is also navigating side by side among the dis-

3

3

ciplines that study soul. Of course the leadership discipline draws from psychology, sociology, management and education but what about the other scholarly disciplines that have more experience in understanding the dynamics of the soul? Isn't leadership also related to fields of philosophy, theology and spirituality? Every major discipline has some level of discourse related to leadership topics within its own boundaries. But the leadership discipline has yet to fully reach out and benefit from the centuries of knowledge accumulated by schools of philosophy, religion, and spirituality.

If the maxim *from St. Augustine (Lib 1,1-2,2.5,5: CSEL 33, 1-5) "You have made us for yourself, O Lord, and our heart is restless until it rests in you."* holds true, then it could be only a matter of time in which leadership— just as many other disciplines—would eventually drift into the dynamics of the heart and soul. So it is no surprise that after close to 100 years of empirical focus of behaviors, use of power, traits, skills, and leader situational contexts, some prominent authors and scholars within the leadership field have asserted spirituality as a missing element within the leadership field of study (Dent, Higgins, & Wharff, 2005: Fairhom, 1997; Fry, 2003; Korak-Kakabadse, Kouzmin, & Kakabadse, 2002; Vail 1998).

Yet this interest is spirituality and leadership is not without its opponents. Unsurprisingly, spirituality in leadership has the *business sector* as its toughest adversary and critic. In fact the separation of spirituality and business was considered the norm for most of the twentieth century (Crossman, 2010). The "profit motive" and the sacred were though as two separate domains, one dealing primarily with action the other with contemplation (Durkeim, 1968). The business sector was too enamored with rationalist and scientific approaches to leadership and organizational culture. But towards the beginning of the twenty first century, failures in major corporations such as Enron and more than 20 others named on the Forbes Corporate scandal list (Patsuris, 2002) prompted scholars, consultants, and the media to re-evaluate the effectiveness of leadership training (Hannah & Zatzick, 2007). What had been missing

4

from all these years of leadership education that would result in these moral failures? Consequently, the business sector became more willing to allow values oriented forms of leadership which provided a gateway for moral, ethical, relational, emotional and eventually even spiritual perspectives of leadership modeling as the remedy to the wave of scandals.

Given this evolution of leaders, how has the evolution of the leadership discipline affected the way the leadership function is exercised within ministry? Have some of the leadership education flaws that triggered a rash of ethical misbehaviors in the business sector also latent within the ministry sector? And is the emerging interest in spirituality from the secular sector compatible with the understanding of spirituality in the ministry or pastoral setting?

These are important questions that do not have a simple answer. In order to answer these questions fully, it is necessary to analyze the evolution of leadership theory, the underlying assumptions of secular leadership models, to explore the assumptions and limitations inherent in these models and to demonstrate the circumstances in which it is appropriate to use them. By exploring how the nonprofit, education, government, social service and even the military sectors have reacted to the flaws inherent in current leadership models, we will be able to develop a clearer understanding of the severe limitations of these same models for ministry endeavors. An analysis of differences will illustrate the limits of secular leadership models in the ministry sector, and highlight the unique dimensions of pastoral leadership as a discipline in its own right.

The Imperfections of Secular Models

As benign as this may seem, two of the most common assumptions made about leadership models, which are responsible for their broad popular appeal, are the assumptions of *universality* and *guaranteed success.* As a result, when a new leadership model becomes publicly available, the implicit promises of universal applicability and success lead to a seemingly blinding eagerness to implement the model every-where and anywhere a quick and cheap approach to excellent leadership is required.

The tendency to adopt leadership models unquestionably and un-challenged is frightening and dangerous. Current research clearly demonstrates that there are no grounds for accepting the assumptions of universality and guaranteed success of leadership models. There are no valid grounds to assume that a leadership model, which originated in the private sector, would work just as effectively in other sectors such as nonprofit, educational, government, social service or the military. Addi-tionally, the eagerness to apply a leadership model is many times more powerful than the desire to understand whether this model will be effec-tive or not under circumstances different than originally intended. De-spite the eagerness to apply new leadership models across sectors, the assumptions of u*niversality* and *guaranteed success* have no scientific validity whatsoever.

These two assumptions alone have been a significant cause of popular leadership models being forced into situations and environments for which they were never intended. Granted, using any leadership mod-el consistently in a sector that is in need of leadership improvement will result in some benefits to the organization. Yet, more to the point, each sector, including ministry, has its own unique needs and qualities, which, if ignored, will result in at best a short-lived improvement. In fact, if commercialized secular leadership models had to include appro-priate warning labels, they would have to state in bold letters *"May be hazardous to your organization. Use at own risk."*

Warning labels or not, many sectors are already re-evaluating the limits, depth and applicability of leadership models imported from other sectors. One example of this cross-sector skepticism is the application of the "boot camp" training model in the business sector. Although partici-pating executives of some corporations acknowledge the value of lead-ership "boot camps" as a corporate skills builder (Brown, 1998), military leadership models are still better for basic training than for the boardroom. In an article on the value of military leadership models applied to the business sector, Brandt (2003) observes: "Although there's an enormous amount to admire in the U.S. military—from professionalism to willingness to sacrifice for freedom—it's not a viable model for your business."

Using commercially available leadership models doesn't seem to work well in the military either. For example, an author critiques the Air Force's apparent fascination with off-the-shelf leadership programs: "As a former facilitator of Covey's Seven Habits series, I must admit that I really enjoyed the material. It's principled, concise, and well-focused. But it's not focused on the Air Force and the unique problems that we encounter." (Thirtle, 2002).

Another way to demonstrate the incompatibilities of leadership models across disciplines is to look at the effectiveness of leaders who have been formed in American corporations and later sought opportunities to apply their skills to the nonprofit sector. On the surface it seems reasonable to assume that skilled leaders in the business sector would also be effective in the nonprofit sector. Yet many seasoned corporate CEOs and business leaders who end up volunteering in leadership positions of non-profit organizations are also quick to recognize subtle, but crucial differences, and caution others to be sensitive to these differences (Schweitzer, 1998). Leading an organization in the direction of optimizing financial performance requires a different skill set than optimizing a social-service organization that is focused more on providing a service than on generating a return for the shareholders. The leadership experience in corporate America is based on employees as human resources, whose successes or failures are measured through performance appraisals. But how can one validly insist that a volunteer be measured in the same or similar manner when one of the major aims of the organization is to attract and encourage volunteers to give generously of their time, talent and even their treasure? And how can we ignore that a key purpose of any corporation is to sustain its growth, where the objective of a nonprofit organization is to make a difference in society? Although there are some fundamental skills that experienced corporate, American executives can bring to the nonprofit sector, there are still significant realities in this sector that are incongruent with business skills alone.

The educational sector presents another example of how leadership models can be incompatible with the realities of the sector. For example, although participatory leadership models seem to have become a standard among colleges and universities, some research is suggesting that the models are adversely affecting organizational performance (Kezar, 2001). Important questions to consider in this regard include: Are learning processes primarily participatory in nature? How much learning can be achieved through participation? If participatory styles are emphasized in education, what may be lost or undermined?

Given this evolving sensitivity and healthy skepticism in applying leadership models in different sectors, to what degree is pastoral leadership aware of the boundaries and limitations of secular leadership models?

There already seems to be some noticeable dissatisfaction coming from the pastoral sector. One study on parish pastoral leadership addresses some of the essential sector attributes that are put at risk when business models are applied to ministry. The survey notes that "specific intangibles unique to Catholic ministry, such as building a true sense of community, growing within an ecclesiastical communion, and the inclusion of spirituality, are just some of the aspects clearly not addressed in secular leadership models, yet paramount to managing a successful Catholic ministry" (Rojas, 2002a). A document on U.S. Hispanic Catholics poses an interesting question when looking at the inability of many secular models to embrace cultural diversity in the Church: "What model of leadership will Hispanic Catholics offer as they become the majority group?" and "How will this model strengthen the unity of the body of Christ in increasingly culturally diverse communities?" (Donovan, 2002). Secular leadership models can only remain silent when confronted with these types of questions.

8

To validate our suspicions that some kind of "gap" existed between what secular models offer and what may be better tailored to parish pastoral work, we conducted an exploration of Catholic publisher listings, books and other materials, as well as training programs offered throughout the United States. Here we attempted to assess the current status and content of "leadership" resources currently being used for the formation of pastoral leaders at different levels within the Church. Without wanting to be overly critical, yet needing to make a statement, we reviewed the "major topics" listed from more than 70 Catholic publishers in the United States and found that only a handful of them stated "leadership" as a major topic of interest. We also reviewed the six most popular leadership training programs being offered at parish and diocesan level throughout the United States, and discovered a heavy dose of secular models with slight modifications to accommodate pastoral distinctiveness. At least for the both of us, these discoveries accentuated the scarcity of research, modeling and attention to this gap between "secular models" and what would be better tailored to "ministry activities". Yet on the other hand, we were encouraged by the recent initiatives of a few Catholic universities that were either developing a certificate program or a graduate specialty in "pastoral leadership."

Another example should further illustrate our concerns regarding a tendency to adopt leadership models without question and unchallenged. In an article titled "Diocesan Bureaucracy," McDonough notes: "A model of diocesan leadership that has been familiar to three generations of Catholics is proving to be less effective than had been hoped" (McDonough, 1997). What went wrong? Did the short-term successes of leadership models overshadow more profound long-term realities? Does this form of leadership set ministries and leaders on a collision course with the realities and needs of a parish?

> If there are tensions in the future, they will probably be between the more educated, older lay ministers and the younger priests. As the number of lay ministers increases and the num-

9

ber of priests decreases, some priests will feel that their turf is being encroached upon" (Feuerherd, 2002).

It appears that if Catholic lay leaders continue incorporating—with minimal discernment—business models of leadership in their ministries, they will be on a collision course with the clergy, since such models do not address the complexities of a hierarchy of roles, among other issues.

There is little doubt that business models have various degrees of effectiveness in the ministry sector. Yet a majority of the underlying assumptions of secular leadership models emerge primarily from empirical observations made on and for business organizations, whereas the assumptions inherent in pastoral leadership emerge from Church teachings and traditions, Sacred Scripture and a rich spiritual heritage. The secular leadership paradigm is based on objectives that are primarily financial in nature, whereas leadership for ministry is based on achieving goals that affect life processes and sacramental realities within a Catholic worldview. The vocabulary and fundamental constructs of business leadership deliberately exclude realities that lie within the core of Catholic ministry, such as mystery, solidarity, faith, grace, forgiveness, prayer, discernment, divine providence, communion and the Holy Trinity, to mention only a few. Finally, the parameters of secular leadership are about tangibles, such as efficiency, optimization, metrics and organization building. Pastoral leadership is mostly about intangible life issues and faith-based community skills, which demand "techniques of the heart," a set of skills so evidently absent from secular models. Given these facts, it seems curious that parish and diocesan leaders still seem eager to use secular leadership models in their ministries. If we are to continue to foster appropriate and active involvement of the laity in the life of the Church, it seems critical to the success of that endeavor to recognize the limits of leadership models that are imported from other sectors. This can occur only when we realize that pastoral leadership is unique enough to be considered a leadership discipline in its own right.

This is the fundamental challenge of pastoral leadership. Without a broader understanding of the context, assumptions and limitations of secular leadership models, many of us will continue to learn and apply (many times incorrectly) the leadership model "de jour" in hopes of becoming better leaders, but to the potential detriment of ministry and the Church and the meaningful involvement of the laity in the life of the Church.

As a starting point, it is imperative to canvas the landscape of leadership models and assess the implications of secular leadership models for the formation of pastoral leadership. In that way we will implement leadership models that are true to form, fit, and function for the ministry sector.

The Flawed Journey of Leadership

The evolution of leadership models is far from being a perfect process. For those of us interested in the evolution of leadership theory and practice and how these models relate to the pastoral sector, we find that a crucial part of human nature has been overlooked since the discipline was formalized. A majority of leadership theories have been originating primarily from the observation of social behaviors, and until recently, with minimal consideration to spiritual realities. In other words, most of what we know about leadership today was developed on the basis of an incomplete human foundation, by observing the interactions of power and influence among individuals and groups, but without consideration for the spiritual realities that surround them.

To illustrate this omission, consider one of the most widely known compendiums of leadership theory by J. Thomas Wren. In his works, J. Thomas Wren argues that the concept of leadership is an essential activity that embraces the totality of human endeavor, and that the study of leadership "...should be as all-embracing as the human experience itself" (Wren, 1995). This "Leader's Companion," as he titles his work, consists of an impressive collection of leadership perspectives produced throughout the ages that gives the reader a structured tour of the evolution of leadership trends up to the modern day. Yet despite J. Thomas Wren's appeal that leadership become an "all embracing activity of human endeavor," the spiritual dimension of the person is excluded for the leadership models. It seems persuasive that as long as the *spiritual component* is excluded from the evolution of leadership models, something crucial to our understanding of the person and leadership remains unaddressed.

Another, more recent, demonstration of the effects of a leadership without the spiritual dimension of the person is the work by Ian Mitroff and Elizabeth Denton. After conducting more than 90 in-depth interviews with executives and managers, Mitroff and Denton observe:

> We believe that today's organizations are impoverished spiritually, and that many of their most important problems are due to this impoverishment. In other words, today's organizations are suffering from a deep, spiritual emptiness. (Mitroff & Denton, 1999).

As long as leadership theory and practice continues to ignore the dynamics of the soul, leadership models will remain underdeveloped for the secular sectors and certainly for the pastoral ministry sector.

A natural reaction to the "absence of the spirit" in leadership theory and practice is to "Christianize" secular models. Examples of this movement include Hyperion's "Jesus CEO: Using ancient wisdom for visionary leadership" (1995) by L. Jones, "In the Name of Jesus: Reflections on Christian Leadership" (1989) by Henri J. M. Nouwen, and Berrett-Koehler's "The Leadership Wisdom of Jesus: Practical Lessons for Today" (1998) by C.C. Manz.

Many of these attempts were originally classified as fads because the scholars and practitioners paid no attention to the dynamics of the soul as a factor of leadership. Many scholars even argued that neither spirituality nor religion had any place at all in how leadership evolved. Consequently, religion became a "user" of leadership theory and was never considered as having any role in the development of original models that would be useful. To make matters worse, it became difficult to find scholars with expertise in both fields who would challenge the practice of developing leadership models that totally excluded the spiritual dimension of the person.

Yet interestingly enough, a more rigorous, scientific study of spirituality in leadership and organizational development emerged during the second half of the past decade, as academics, practitioners and consultants came to realize that spirituality and leadership were inextricably related. Toward the end of the decade, writings such as "A Corporate Audit of Corporate America" (Jossey-Bass, 1999) by I. Mitroff and E. Denton and "Spirited Leading and Learning" by Peter Vail (Jossey-Bass, 1998) set the pace for texts published with much more scientific rigor. One of the more successful cases is the *servant leadership* model, published by Robert Greenleaf (Berrett-Koehler, 1998). An increase in studies relating spirituality leadership and management, especially in doctoral dissertations, became another indication that spirituality actually offered the leadership disciplines a promising new territory to explore.

Such developments illustrate the evolving landscape of secular leadership theories. In recent times, the fact that leadership and spirituality can be discussed concurrently in the secular world without being ridiculed is in fact a significant breakthrough. Furthermore, this awakening is considered a welcomed trend, particularly for those voices that have protested for so long about the schizoid separation of public life and the spiritual. Yet it appears that another "caution label" may be appropriate for this emerging trend.

It would be reckless to assert that the developing models of leadership that include spirituality sufficiently meet Catholic pastoral needs. The excitement generated by the opportunity to finally apply concepts of spirituality to the day-to-day practice of leadership must not overwhelm prudence (Allen, 2003). In reality, and despite their lure, there are at least three aspects of their theoretical framework that diverge from acceptable pastoral practice in the Catholic Church. These areas of concern include the definitions of spirituality commonly used for these models, the individualistic nature of the spirituality praxis suggested and the strong association of leadership roles with position power within in an organization or hierarchy. We believe these three elements of secular leadership models that acknowledge the spirituality dimension of the person often misrepresent Catholic tradition and teachings.

First of all, the most frequent definitions of spirituality used in scholarly circles are composed in total isolation from a religious context (Mitroff & Denton, 1999). In other words, spirituality has nothing to do with religion. For these researchers, religion is associated with a sense of belonging and the practice of a tradition, whereas the spirituality definitions concentrate on a personal commitment to a holistic inner development separate from religion (Reiss, 1999). Essentially, these definitions of spirituality are disconnected from any religious and therefore theological richness.

This separation of spirituality and religion may be just an artificial, academic convenience, yet it has started to foster some "spiritualities without religion" (Rooney, 2003) and has led to movements promoting a separation between institutions and individuals (Pargament, 1997). We are starting to see an emergence of spiritualities without a church community, spiritualities without a meaningful theology and spiritualities without a substantial tradition. Clearly, the leadership models encouraging spirituality in isolation from religion are inappropriate and hence a threat to the varied and rich spiritual traditions that are an integral part of what it means to be Catholic.

A second observation of these emerging "spiritual" leadership models is the individualistic focus of the spirituality. Catholic theologian Lawrence Cunningham notes: "Much spirituality ... is highly narcissistic and not easily distinguished from old self-improvement schemes" (quoted in *Christian Century*, 2002). This "me-first" spirituality is already a well-established and controversial issue in colleges and universities (Schaper, 2000). Not only is this newly identified American spirituality individualistic in nature, but it is also characterized as driven by consensus, thereby suggesting a spirituality that is fundamentally "democratic" in its praxis (Lesser, 1999). Individualistic spiritualities and democratic Churches may be appealing to the American pluralistic society at large, but they hardly resonate with the notions of community, communion, collaboration and hierarchical authority and communion.

A third aspect of spiritual leadership that leads away from acceptable pastoral practice is the notion of the individual or leader as the center of attention and activity. In this model, spiritual leadership is still commonly understood in relation to a "position" in the organization rather than as a function among equals. Such a model erroneously implies that the leader is in some way an extension of the hierarchy, and that the leader is the "keeper" of spirituality. This implicit attribute of early leadership theory is a common thread running across many leadership models (Kezar, 2000) and is incongruent with Church teachings on the nature and functions of lay ministry (Christifideles Laici, n. 23).

The concerns over the separation of spirituality and religion, individualistic spirituality and a focus on hierarchical status are just a few reasons to exercise caution when applying the secular models of spiritual leadership to pastoral praxis. On the surface, these models seem appealing, but upon further evaluation these leadership concepts should be looked at with a healthy dose of skepticism. In other words, the awakening of the "soul" in the discipline of leadership is thus far more about the "spirituality of leadership" and less on the "leadership of spirituality." So even in this promising development, the warning label "*May be hazardous to your organization*" still applies.

Nevertheless, the fact that spirituality has become an item of interest in the recent evolution of secular leadership models is encouraging, to say the least. It is encouraging to know that formalized research in leadership and spirituality may lead to new career fields, expanded professional disciplines, and a more holistic approach to research with

15

human subjects. It is even more encouraging to see how this trend may promote a wider acceptance of spirituality in leadership discourse and day-to-day organizational activities across the business, non-profit, government and Church sectors.

But along with the excitement of new leadership developments and innovative practices come challenges that we should remain aware of, and even to a certain degree, anticipate (Allen, 2003). Although the direct application of many leadership models to pastoral settings may certainly produce initial benefits, the question of long-term impacts remains to be explored. Specific intangibles unique to Catholic ministry, such as building a true sense of community, growing within an ecclesiastical context (traditions, hierarchy, teachings), sacramental animation and the inclusion of traditional schools of spirituality, are just some of the aspects clearly not addressed in secular leadership models yet are paramount to leading a successful Catholic ministry. While secular models seek to optimize "organizational performance" through "process improvements," ministerial leadership must seek to "build nurturing communities" by focusing on "relational" more than "structural" activities. The "how to" of these secular models must be toned down, and the "whom to" must take center stage again (Blackaby & Blackaby, 2001).

The Wake-up Call

The ability to differentiate between useful and harmful consequences of secular leadership models in lay pastoral development is the most fundamental challenge of pastoral leadership. By definition, leadership concepts are socially constructed and culturally bound (Mellahi, 2000), so the application of any secular leadership model to the pastoral sector requires constant and careful examination against the culture and framework of the Catholic Church. Models coming from the business, non-profit, government, military or industry sectors are built primarily for their respective sectors. Although their coherence may lead to a temptation to adopt them, their indiscriminant use, particularly in sectors for which they were never intended, has already proven to be deeply problematic. Evaluating the underlying assumptions of these models and correlating their definitional components to a healthy understanding of the pastoral sector represents a significant first step in acknowledging the unique nature of pastoral leadership. Said differently, a leadership expert or successful practitioner in one sector will not guarantee success in another sector.

Challenging the assumptions and fit of secular leadership models is a proper first step in understanding the fundamental challenge to pastoral leadership, but other steps are necessary if lay ministry leadership is to evolve along genuine Church traditions. In the next chapter, a more detailed look at the theoretical foundations leading to a set of core principles for pastoral leadership is constructed.

Case Study

A few months ago, Cindy Cunningham was designated by Father Ed (the Pastor) as the head of Religious Education. Cindy helps the parish part time, and is also a full-time supervisor at a local software company, Calamity Software Inc. Recently, Calamity Software sent Cindy on an eight-day training session on transformational leadership. As she discovered, transformational leadership refers to the process of building commitment to the organization's objectives while empowering others to accomplish basic business objectives in ways that are good for the organization and the people. Cindy was most attracted to transformational leadership's appeals to a person's "higher level" of morality, ethics and values. Transformational leadership aims to elevate self and others from their "everyday selves" to their "better selves." Needless to say, Cindy is ready to apply transformational leadership in the parish because it is "empowering." The parish is large; there are over 350 elementary-school children and 42 volunteer teachers in the religious education program.

Father Ed is thrilled with the idea, since the start of the new CCD class coincides with Lent. Father Ed exclaimed, "Transformation is what education and the Church is all about…"

DISCUSSION:

1. Assume you are a member of the parish council. As a consultant to the Pastor, you are a bit skeptical about the value of transformational leadership in ministry work. What steps would you take before presenting your case to the Pastor?

2. Search the academic literature for the true meaning of transformational leadership. What does transformational leadership have to offer as a model for lay ministry leadership? What is questionable about transformational leadership for lay ministry?

3. What is the true definition of "empowerment" and what risks could it present to pastoral leadership?

4. Discuss ways in which secular leadership "fads" can migrate into the ministry setting, and ways to prevent them from being misused.

Workshop Activities

1. In small group format (or as an individual reflective), formulate your own definition of *leadership*.

2. How does the definition of leadership formulated in the first question fit the needs of pastoral leadership? For instance, how did the definition above include discerning God's will in performing leadership responsi-

bilities? Are there other pastoral values that may be missing from these definitions?

3. How would you state the *fundamental challenge of pastoral leadership* in your own words? What are the challenges you have experienced? Share these experiences with others in the group.

4. In comparing different models of secular leadership (transformational leadership, servant leadership, situational leadership, value leadership, ethical leadership, etc.), what elements seem to work for the pastoral setting and what elements seem missing?

5. Using the previous discussion on leadership definitions, now formulate a definition of *"leadership effectiveness."* What makes leaders effective or ineffective?

6. It could be argued that just as business, government, nonprofit, military and industry-specific sectors have their own leadership models, pastoral leadership is a discipline of its own and should have its own sector-specific model of leadership, called of course, *pastoral leadership*. How would you defend this position? What arguments would you use to state that pastoral leadership should have its own models?

7. What is the difference between "management" and "leadership?" Are they the same? Are they different? And how do these terms apply to the pastoral setting?

8. If leaders play a significant role in developing and maintaining organizational culture and values, what are the expectations of pastoral leaders in affecting ministry group culture and values?

9. If leadership is about "influence tactics," what forms of influence would be appropriate for the pastoral setting? What types would be inappropriate?

Personal Reflective

1. Conduct an inventory of all the significant spiritual practices you currently have in place. Which spiritual practices directly support you in performing the leadership function? What spiritual practice would you consider adding to your repertoire that would improve both your spiritual life as well as your leadership abilities?

2. Leadership is always associated with use of "power," yet "power" is a strange word to use within the context of Church work and parish life. What are some consequences of taking this "power" approach to leadership in ministry?

3. Write down your own definitions of leadership. Also write down your own definitions of spirituality. What kind of "connections" do you see between spirituality and the leadership functions?

4. Find and complete a leadership self-assessment on the web. Reflect on the value of the self-assessment in helping you become a better pastoral leader. Does it help or do you suspect certain relevant areas of assessment may be missing?

5. If you already have a journal that guides your spiritual life, should you not also journaling about the effectiveness of your leadership roles within ministry?

6. Leadership focuses of influencing others. Make a list of the forms of influence you exercise as a pastoral leader. Which of these forms of influence seem best for the pastoral setting? Which have the risk of doing harm?

The Challenges of Pastoral Leadership

Chapter References

Allen, J.L. Jr. (2003). Vatican looks at 'New Age,' issues 'appeal to discernment.' *National Catholic Reporter*, 39(16), 12-13.

Anonymous (2002). Less support for lay ministry reported among young priests. *America*, 187(8), 5.

Anonymous (2003). State of the profession. *Partner's report*, 4, 4.

Blackaby, H., & Blackaby, R. (2001). *Spiritual Leadership: Moving people to God's agenda*. Nashville, TN: Broadman & Holman.

Benjamin, P., & Looby, J. (1998). Defining the nature of spirituality in the context of Maslow's and Roger's theories. *Counseling & Values*, 42, 92-100.

Boadella, D. (1998). Essence and ground: Toward the understanding of spirituality in psychotherapy. *Journal of Psychotherapy*, 3, 29-51.

Bolman, L., & Deal, T. (1995). *Leading with Soul: An Uncommon Journey of Spirit*. San Francisco, CA: Jossey-Bass.

Borgatta, E.F., Bales, R.F., & Couch, A.S. (1954). Some findings relevant to the Great Man Theory of leadership. American Sociological Review, 19(6), 755-759.

Brandt, E. (1996). Corporate pioneers explore spirituality. *HR Magazine*, 41, 82-87.

Bristow-Braitman, A. (1995). Addiction recovery: 12 step programs and cognitive-behavioral psychology. *Journal of Counseling & Development*, 73, 414-418.

Brown, E. (1998). War games to make you better at business. *Fortune*, 138(6), 291-296.

Conger, J. A. (1994). *Spirit at Work: Discovering the Spirituality in Leadership*. San Francisco, CA: Jossey-Bass.

Chaffee, M.W., & Arthur, D.C. (2002). Failure: Lessons for health care leaders. *Nursing Economics*, 20, 225-229.

Crossman, J. (2010). Conceptualizing spiritual leadership in secular organizational contexts and its relation to transformational, servant and environmental leadership. *Leadership and Organizational Development Journal, 31*(7), 596-608.

Cunningham, L. (2002). In *Christian Century*, 119(24), 7. (Extracted from *Notre Dame Magazine*, Autumn).

Davis, K.G. (2002). Architects of success. *America*, 186(14), 6-8.

Delbecq A.L. (1999). Christian spirituality and contemporary business leadership. *Journal of Organizational Change Management*, 12, 345-354.

Dent, E.B., Higgins, M.E., & Wharf, D.M. (2005). Spirituality and leadership: An empirical review of definitions, distinctions, and embedded assumptions. *The Leadership Quarterly, 16*(5), 625-653.

Dillion, K.M., & Tait, J.L. (2000). Spirituality and being in the zone in team sports: A relationship? *Journal of Sport Behavior*, 23, 91-100.

Donovan, G.D. (2002). Bishops to consider document on Hispanic ministry priorities. *National Catholic Reporter*, 39(3), 6.

Duvall, N. S. (1998). From soul to self and back again. *Journal of Psychology and Theology*, 26, 6-15.

Elkins, D.N. (1995). Psychotherapy and spirituality: Toward a theory of the soul. *Journal of Humanistic Psychology*, 35, 78-99.

Elkins, D.N. (1999). Spirituality. *Psychology Today*, 5, 45-48.

Fairholm, G. W. (1996). Spiritual leadership: Fulfilling whole-self needs at work. *Leadership and Organizational Development*, 17(5), 11-17.

Fairhlom, G.W. (2002). *Capturing the heart of leadership: Spirituality and community in the New American workplace.* Westport, CT: Praeger.

Feuerherd, J. (2002). Study shows priestly generation gap stirs tension. *National Catholic Reporter*, 38(40), 13.

Fry, L.W. (2003). Towards a theory of spiritual leadership. *The Leadership Quarterly, 14*(6), 693-727.

Garret, M.T., & Wilbur, M.P. (1999). Does the worm live in the ground? Reflections on native American spirituality. *Journal of Multicultural Counseling & Development*, 27, 193-210.

Greenleaf, R. (1977). *Servant Leadership.* New York, NY: Paulist Press.

Goldfarb, L.M., & Galanter, M. (1996). Medical student and patient attitudes toward religion and spirituality in the recovery process. *American Journal of Drug & Alcohol Abuse*, 22, 549-561.

Gunther, M. (2001). God & business. Fortune, 144(1), 58-70.

Hamilton, D.M., & Jackson, M.H. (1998). Spiritual development: Paths and processes. *Journal of Instructional Psychology*, 25, 262-271.

Hart, A.W. (1995). Reconceiving school leadership: Emergent views. *Elementary School Journal*, 96, 9-28.

Hannah, D.R., & Zatzick, C.D. (2007). An examination of leader portrayals in the US business press following the landmark scandals of the early 21st century. *Journal of Business Ethics, 79*, 361-377.

Hogg, M.A. (2001). A social identity theory of leadership. *Personality and Social Psychology Review*, 5(3), 184-200.

Howard, B.S., & Howard, J.R. (1997). Occupation as spiritual activity. *American Journal of Occupational Therapy*, 51, 181-185.

Iannone, R.V., & Obenauf, P.A. (1999). Toward spirituality in curriculum and teaching. *Education*, 119, 737-745.

Jarusiewicz, B. P. (1999). Spirituality and addiction: Relationship to religion, abuse, gender and multichemical use. *Dissertation Abstracts International*, B59/11, 5781.

Johnsen, E. (1993). The role of spirituality in recovery from chemical dependency. *Journal of Addictions & Offender Counseling*, 13, 58-61.

Karasu, T.B. Johnsen, E. (1993). The role of spirituality in recovery from chemical dependency. *Journal of Addictions & Offender Counseling*, 13, 58-61.

Kezar, A. (2001). Investigating organizational fit in a participatory leadership environment. *Journal of Higher Education Policy and Management*, 23, 85-101.

Korak-Kakabadse, N., Kouzmin, A., & Kakabadse, A. (2002). *Journal of Managerial Psychology, 17*(3), 165-182.

Lesser, E. (1999). *The New American Spirituality: A Seeker's Guide*. Random. c.352p. LC 98-50310. ISBN 0375-50010-3.

Mack, M.L. (1994). Understanding spirituality in counseling psychology: Considerations for research, training and practice. *Counseling & Values*, 39, 15-32.

Mahoney, M.J., & Graci, G.M. (1999). The meaning and correlates of spirituality: Suggestions from an exploratory survey of experts. *Death Studies*, 23, 521-527.

Meraviglia, M.G. (1999). Critical analysis of spirituality and its empirical indicators. *Journal of Holistic Nursing*, 17, 18-34.

Miller, W.R. (1998). Researching the spiritual dimensions of alcohol and other drug problems. *Addiction*, 93, 979-990.

McDonough, K.M. (1997). Diocesan bureaucracy. *America*, 177(10), 9-13.

Mellahi, K. (2000). "The teaching of leadership on UK MBA programmes." *Journal of Management Development*, 19, 297-308.

Mitroff, I.I., & Denton, E.A. (1999). *A spiritual audit of corporate America*. San Francisco, CA: Jossey-Bass.

Nino, A.G. (1997). Assessment of spiritual quests in clinical practice. *International Journal of Psychotherapy*, 2, 193-212.

Okundaye, J.N., & Gray, C. (1999). Re-imaging field instruction from a spiritually sensitive perspective: An alternative approach. *Social Work*, 44, 371-384.

Pargament; K. I. (1997): *Theory, research, practice. The psychology of religion and coping*. New York: Guilford.

Parker, R.J., Horton, J.R., & Shelton, H. (1997). Sarah's story: Using ritual therapy to address psychospiritual issues in treating survivors of childhood sexual abuse. *Counseling & Values*, 42, 41-54.

Patsuris, P. (2002, July 26). The corporate scandal sheet. *Forbes Magazine*.

Porter, G. (1995). Exploring the meaning of spirituality and its implications for counselors. *Counseling & Values*, 40, 69-80.

Prest, L.A., & Keller, J.F. (1993). Spirituality and family therapy: Spiritual beliefs, myths, and metaphors. *Journal of Marital & Family Therapy*, 19, 137-148.

Quick, J.C., Quick, J.D., Nelson, D.I., & Hurrell, J.J. (1997*). Preventive stress management in organizations* (pp. 243-244). Washington DC: American Psychological Association.

Rainey, H.G., & Steinbauer, P. (1999). "Galloping elephants: Developing elements of a theory of effective government organizations." *Journal of Public Administration Research and Theory*, 9, 1.

Reiss, J. (1999). The mystical heart of discovering a universal spirituality in the world's religions. *Publishers Weekly*, 29, 68.

Renesch, J (Ed.). *New traditions in business: Spirit and leadership in the 21st century* (Ed.). San Francisco, CA: Berrett-Koehler.

Roof, W.C. (1993). Toward the year 2000: Reconstruction of religious space. *Annals of the American Academy of Political & Social Science*, 527, 155-171.

Rooney, M. (2003). Spiritualism at What Cost? One Campus Movement Promises Self- Awareness, but Some Question Its Approach. *The Chronicle of Higher Education*, 49(18), A31-32.

Rojas, R.R. (2002a). Comparing secular and ministry leadership. *Deacon Digest*, 19(3), 16-17.

Rojas, R.R. (2002b). Management theory and spirituality: A framework and validation of the Independent Spirituality Assessment Scale. *Dissertation Abstracts International*, DAI-A 63/02, p. 668.

Schaper, D. (2000). Me-first 'spirituality' is a sorry substitute for organized religion on campuses. *The Chronicle of Higher Education*, 46(50), A56.

Schweitzer, C. (1998). Corporate assets: Corporate CEOs serving as volunteer leaders. *Association Management*, 50(1), 30-36.

Slife, B.D., Hope, C., & Nebeker, R.S. (1999). Examining the relationship between religious spirituality and psychological science. *Journal of Humanistic Psychology*, 39, 51-85.

Teasdale, W. (1997). The interspiritual age: Practical mysticism for the third millennium. *Journal of Ecumenical Studies*, 34, 74-92.

Thirtle, M. (2002). Toward defining Air Force leadership. *Aerospace Power Journal*, 16(4), 9-15

Vaill, P. (1998). *Spirited leading and learning: Process wisdom for a new age*. San Francisco, CA: Jossey-Bass

Westgate, C. E. (1996). Spiritual wellness and depression. *Journal of Counseling & Development*, 75, 26-35.

Wren, J.T. (1995). *The leader's companion: Insights on leadership throughout the ages*. New York, NY: The Free Press.

Zinn, L.M. (1997). Spirituality in adult education. *Adult Learning*, 8, 26-30.

Zinnbauer, B.J., Pargament, K.I., & Scott, A.B. (1999). The emerging meanings of religiousness and spirituality: Problems and prospects. *Journal of Personality*, 67, 889-919

.

"For Christian leadership to be truly fruitful in the future, a movement from the moral to the mystical is required."

Henri Nouwen

CHAPTER 2

as Spiritual Practice

In the previous chapter, we presented the fundamental challenge of pastoral leadership, which is developing the skill to recognize the strengths and weaknesses of secular leadership models across different sectors. More specifically, we indicated how these models, when indiscriminately used in the pastoral sector, will eventually lead to various degrees of inconsistencies and unhealthy tensions with the Catholic way of thinking and acting, despite their initial promise of significant benefits. This led us to a crucial conclusion that speaks to the premise of this book – pastoral leadership is a sector on its own merits and thus requires careful adaptation of leadership models developed in and for other sectors.

Another implication of this conclusion is that it inevitably leads to an important reversal of perspective in how leadership models are designed and put into practice. Rather than just searching for secular models that may be adapted to the pastoral sector, we should also consider what unique contributions the pastoral sector can offer the leadership discipline. In other words, we consider what the disciple of pastoral leadership can contribute to the broader body of leadership knowledge. For example, what are the unique realties of the pastoral sector, and what might the insights gained from a study of these unique realities contribute to the discipline of leadership? More boldly, what does pastoral leadership have to offer the secular world that might be of benefit to the leaders in those sectors?

Currently, there exists a substantial divide between the leadership disciplines in the secular and pastoral sectors. To illustrate this divide, consider the following scenario. We convene in the same room a group of leadership scholars, consultants and business leaders with a group of theologians. We pose to them a seemingly straightforward question: *"What do you all have in common?"* After some initial uneasiness, we can plausibly see the scholars, consultants and business leaders, religious differences aside, seeking guidance from the theologians on how to restore a meaningful connection between the work of the organization and what is most fundamental about a person. We can also imagine the theologians seeking guidance on how to effectively mobilize large groups of modern people around a single, well-defined mission. Such a contrived situation characterizes the current state and key needs of leadership theory and practice. There is an urgent need to recognize the power of the human spirit in the exercise of leadership in the secular sectors, while at the same time, there is a need for effective leadership models and practices that are compatible with the unique mission and demands of the pastoral sector.

This book addresses the gap created by the unmet leadership needs of both secular and pastoral sectors. Leadership as an academic discipline is not only about tasks and goals, but also about the total person and therefore about the human spirit and the dynamics of spiritual growth. This is a topic on which the Church in general and the pastoral sector in particular has a lot to offer. We believe that the bridge connecting both sides of the gap is *spirituality*. Our contention throughout this book is that when leadership is seen as a means of cultivating spirituality, as a way to grow and connect with others on a meaningful level, the gap between these two sectors is reduced and the long-term effectiveness of leadership practices is increased. For Catholic leaders, this effort becomes largely a matter of converting our worldview into a day-to-day application of the discipline of leadership.

Interestingly, some of the world's greatest practitioners of lead ership have benefited from understanding leadership as a spiritual pra tice. For example, it is not unusual for world leaders to pray when fa with agonizingly difficult decisions. Abraham Lincoln stated, "I l been driven many times upon my knees by the overwhelming convi that I had nowhere else to go. My own wisdom, and that of all abo seemed insufficient. . . . One stormy night I tossed on my bed, unabl . sleep as I thought of the terrible sufferings of our soldiers and sailors. I spent an hour in agonizing prayer." Mahatma Gandhi also understood the relationship of prayer and leadership: "Prayer is not an old woman's idle amusement. Properly understood and applied, it is the most potent instrument of action. Prayer is a confession of one's own unworthiness and weakness."

But why only pray when the decision at hand pushes the leader over his or her human capabilities? Why do leaders only pray when prompted by situations in which the boundaries of their humanity are tested? And more importantly, why is it that when a leader speaks to God it's called prayer, but when God speaks to the leader it's a mental illness? Should not all important decisions include an appropriate dialogue with God as well as a substantial investment in prayerful discernment?

Leadership is not a spiritual practice only in difficult times, but a spiritual practice all of the time. Leadership is not only a means for accomplishing worthwhile goals; it is also a way of elevating others. An analogy used by Ken Blanchard in "Whale Done" (2002, Free Press)

31

describes how leadership is a spiritual practice that continuously elevates others.

> How do they train killer whales to jump over the rope at Sea World? Do they hang a rope 20 feet over the pool and then shout to the whale "Up, up, up!" No. They start with the rope under the water. When the whale swims over the rope, it gets rewarded. Then the rope is gradually raised. Each time the whale swims over it, again, a reward is given.

As a leader, "elevating the rope" to higher levels is in itself a task, a goal, a mission. But it is also akin to a vision, to an internal purpose, to a series of consequences tied to spiritual growth. Is pastoral leadership not also a calling to pursue a deeper spirituality for the leader and "elevate the rope" for those entrusted to the pastoral leader? The notion of linking organizational goals with personal spirituality is a key concept toward a fuller understanding of the uniqueness of pastoral leadership.

The *task-sprit connection* is usually not difficult to recognize for those engaged in pastoral leadership. This important connection is also becoming more evident to those involved in the evolution of secular leadership theory and practice. Leadership as a spiritual practice is a "natural" idea for the pastoral leadership sector; that principle is also now being adopted by the secular sector. The question to be addressed is how exactly leadership is a spiritual practice no matter where it takes place.

The Hard and Soft Side of Leadership

As we indicated earlier, most of the secular leadership models were developed primarily from observation and research data. As a result, the "softer" or spiritual dimensions of the models were left out. To develop a leadership model in the secular sector, observers would generally focus on the designated leader, consider the skills of those being led, and then measure outcomes in order to find the "best" patterns of behavior or attributes that lead to success. Essentially, the early notions of leadership evolved from a task-driven view of work and so the spiritual side of each person was not taken into account. In light of what we now know about the important connection between tasks (work) and spirit (the whole person), the discipline of leadership would be ignoring a constitutive element of effective leadership models if it continues to ignore this important link. Fortunately, it appears that the current process for developing secular leadership models is awakening to the idea that to account for the human person fully in a model, the dynamics of the spirit must be acknowledged and included:

> Recently, theorists have begun to conceptualize leadership as a broader, mutual influence process independent of any formal role or hierarchical structure and diffused among the members of any given social system... If leadership is not simply prescribed because of one's role in an institutionalized hierarchy, then a fundamental question remains to be answered is how leadership and leader-follower relationships develop in organizations. What are the relational and social processes involved in coming to see oneself, and being seen by others, as a leader or a follower? (Derue & Ashford, 2010, p. 627).

This is a significant turning point in the evolution of the leadership discipline.

Leadership training and development has remained a high priority for almost every organization in North America. No other country in the world is so passionate about preparing leaders formally as a means of ensuring the success of the organization. In an article published in the *Journal of American Academy of Business* (March 2006), Steward Tubbs and Eric Shultz estimate that about $50 billion is spent each year on leadership development. In 2002, Hewitt Associates surveyed CEOs and human resource executives at 240 major U.S.-based, multi-nationals and found that 77% of the companies they surveyed had formal processes and programs to develop their leaders. Given the proven relationship

33

between leadership development and organizational success, this statistic is probably even higher today.

Yet despite these significant efforts to train and prepare better leaders to ensure organizational success, dissatisfaction with current leadership programs is starting to emerge. Questions are being raised over the increasing number of spectacular ethical failures among senior U.S. executives. In light of the substantial resources being applied to providing the best available leadership training, these ethical failures raise a serious question about the efficacy of current leadership-formation programs. The causes of the abysmally poor choices made by these executives seem to not be addressed by current leadership-formation programs. The rash of leadership scandals coming from American corporate boardrooms points to at least one key missing element in leadership development.

To be sure, the "hard" side of leadership (methods, tactics and procedures) is clear to most of the population of trained leaders. Yet there is a blind spot in current training programs that points to a need to re-emphasize the "softer" side of leadership. As a veteran consultant of leadership, Rich McLaughlin puts in words what so many of us have already known anecdotally for some time. In an article published in *Executive Excellence* (2004), he notes:

> Having spent the last 10 years delivering leadership workshops, I am confident that people in leadership positions already have most everything they need in terms of skills and competencies. If anything, what they consistently lack are courage and faith: a lack of courage to confront practices that don't make sense, and a lack of faith in letting the people who do the work self-organize. Issues of faith and courage are choices to be made, not skills to be taught. (McLaughlin, 2004, p.8)

Interestingly, McLaughlin's statement that topics such as "faith" and "courage" are part of good leadership, suggests that something essential is missing in the preparation and behavior of our leaders. Also, a significant underlying assumption in his statement is that leadership is not only about the "hard" topics of techniques and practices, but also about a "soft" side that guides the choices leaders make in performing their duties and responsibilities.

The growing list of leadership scandals among executives of major corporations in the United States would also suggest that learning the techniques and practices of leadership models alone is insufficient to practice effective leadership. Well-known failures of top business leaders in companies such as AIG, Tyco, Qwest, WorldCom, Global Crossing and Adelphia are only a few examples of prominent, well-trained and experienced executives making spectacularly poor choices. How is it that leaders of this caliber, so carefully screened, recruited and trained, make such disastrous decisions?

A Wall Street Journal/NBC poll released during April 2002 assessed public esteem for business leaders and showed that it had declined significantly in recent times (Harwood, 2002). In fact, the survey shows that about 57 percent of the respondents said the standards and values of corporate leaders and executives have dropped in the past 20 years, compared with 38 percent who said standards and values are the same or higher. Four years earlier, the results were considerably more favorable to business leaders, as 53 percent of the respondents noted that business executives' standards were the same or higher.

Yet the failures of leadership in recent times go beyond American corporate boardrooms. Non-profit organizations are certainly not immune from flawed leadership practices. In an article titled "Turnaround needed: How to get started" (*Non-profit World*, Nov/Dec 2004), Gary Snyder quotes a recent survey showing that up to 75% of executives at non-profits have significantly large compensation packages for doing as little as attending a few meetings a year, and that about one-third of them use organizational services for their personal gain. Even in the pastoral sector, how often does the behavior of pastoral leaders suggest that they may be engaged in Church activities more for satisfying unhealthy ego needs than for serving those entrusted to them? And who can forget the Abu-Graib torture and prisoner abuse, or the more than 50 female cadets who have alleged they were sexually assaulted or raped while attending the Air Force Academy, or the Navy's Tailhook scandal? Even more close to home, who can deny the apparently poor choices of Church leadership, both clergy and laity, in dealing with known sexual predators within the Church? If all of these leaders across so many sectors have been well trained in the latest and greatest in leadership practices, what is missing in the development of these examples of failed leadership?

Even after billions of dollars have been invested yearly in leadership training using "proven" training techniques, something essential remains missing from these efforts. The landscape of significant leadership failures confirm for us that, despite well-established training for the "hard" side of leadership, the "soft" side of leadership remains weak, if not underdeveloped.

This "softer" side of leadership is only recently emerging as a crucial missing element from the basic understanding of leadership functions. For example, in his dealings with leadership among multiple cultures, Carlos Rodriguez in "Emergence of a third culture: Shared leadership in international strategic alliances" (*International Marketing Review*, 2005), argues that a leader's *personality* is relevant to effective leadership as well as the *worldview* in which the leader lives, grows and exercises power and influence. In yet another article, Bob Gunn (co-founder of Gunn Partners, a consulting firm) uses the term "the normalization of deviance" to explain how leaders and followers have become complacent with failures in leadership. In analyzing the causes of poor decisions made by executive leaders, he suggests looking at a deeper problem, not related to the training of leadership practices but to the cause of errors in judgment (i.e. making wrong choices). He notes,

Most corporate wrecks are like garden-variety accidents: caused by a small error in judgment that is magnified by a cascading sequence of decisions and actions. They aren't stopped because no one ever questions that first, faulty premise. So how does a leader learn to walk the "razor's edge"? No matter what the circumstance or how great the pressure to do something right now, how do leaders learn to make the right choice? (Gunn, 2005, p. 9).

Again, it seems that scholars, researchers and practitioners are taking a deeper look at leadership's "softer side" by focusing on nontraditional topics such as worldview, values, morality and spirituality. Accordingly, this recent interest in the "softer" side of leadership has prompted a surge of models attempting to correct this shortfall. Many of these innovations have also been influencing the thinking about leadership in pastoral ministry circles. Some of these recent developments include "ethical leadership," "transformational leadership," and models based on personality, forms of intelligence or charisma..

The ethical leadership model is based on an understanding of ethical paradigms and personal codes as the context for the effective practice of leadership (Shapiro & Stefkovich, 2005). Transformational leadership is characterized by developing a macro-vision (worldview) and leading by example toward the fulfillment of this common vision (Bass, B. "From transactional to transformational leadership: Learning to share the vision." *Organizational Dynamics*, 1990: 19-31). Charismatic leadership refers to a model by which leaders can successfully change the needs, values, self-concepts and goals of the followers (*Charismatic leadership and follower effects*, Conger, J.A., Kanungo, R.N., Menon, S.T., 2000). Interestingly enough, some of us have already seen attempts to import these models into Church ministry; sometimes having been set in motion by the clergy.

Yet a more in-depth and nuanced analysis of these "soft" centered leadership models leads to a disconcerting fact: These models are attempting to put back into leadership what has been missing for decades – the spiritual dynamics of leadership – by adding it rather than integrating it fully into the model. For too long the development of leadership ideas has ignored the dimension of the "soul" and the implications of the "soul" and "spirit" in the leader-follower relationship. How can a leader offer suggestions on improving relationships when relationships are at the heart of spirituality, which is never adequately or seriously considered? Margaret Wheatly (in *Leadership and the new science: Discovering order in a chaotic world*, 2006, Berrett-Kohler Publishers) makes an astute observation about the true source of power and influence in leadership practice:

> In organizations, real power and energy is generated through relationships. The patterns of relationships and the capacities to form them are more important than tasks, functions, roles, and positions.

The fact that leadership models are focusing more on the relationships between leader and followers is encouraging, but without a comprehensive spiritual perspective, these models remain underdeveloped and of minimal utility. Spirituality and leadership are about relationships, and relationships without the spiritual are at best superficial, as they ignore the totality of the person.

Although this "lack of soul" may be apparent to many Church leaders, much of secular leadership's theoretical developments have evolved over the last 50 years without this realization. The original simplistic models of leadership that suggested an unconditional response from the followers (attributes models, contingency models), evolved into models that recognized the value of the dynamics between the leader and the followers (participative models) and were primarily propelled into the mainstream of popular interest as a result of the Total Quality movement. The climate of collaboration fostered by these participative models eventually led to the realization that contributions were enhanced when the "softer" concepts (such as culture, vision, values, ideals, aspirations, etc.) became part of the mix.

The influence of spiritless leadership theories that for decades continued molding the workforce to specific organizational cultures and values led to a predictable outcome. Workers began to reflect on the implications of "molding" their lives to an organization's culture and hence to question the impact of these "transformational processes" on their personal development, family relations and worldview outside of the work environment. Employees also began challenging the leader's ability to effectuate these changes in themselves, or to "walk the talk" of what was being said. "Do as I say not as I do" was no longer an acceptable leadership practice. Profound philosophical questions began to emerge from within the ranks of many organizations: Is the organization's culture taking me where I want to go or is it moving me away from where I want to go? Are my personal values consistent with the values that are being suggested by the organization? What are the implications of my values being different than the organization's values? What if my plan for my life goes beyond what the workplace has to offer? To what extent am I going to continue to allow the workplace to determine the path of my growth and development?

These personal and group reflections set the stage for the next iteration of models called value-based leadership constructs (i.e., how values are applied to what we do, how we share values among us and how we incorporate these values into our lives and into the lives of others). A popular example of a values-based leadership model is what we currently recognize as Servant Leadership. The fundamental concept behind the development of the servant leadership model defined and proposed by Robert Greenleaf is the value of "stewardship." However, in its current manifestation, the focus of the model is more individualistic than communal.

Both the emergence of values-based leadership models and the rash of scandals in American corporations are driving the latest interest of practitioners, researchers and academics in the "softer" factors of the leader-follower dynamic. The fact that failures in leadership are also occurring in the military, the nonprofit sector and even within the Church, increases the relevance of this effort for all sectors, perhaps even more so in the pastoral sector. Added to this landscape of an increased interest in developing more holistic models of leadership is the evolving and sometimes controversial phenomenon of "Spirit at Work." This is a movement interested in the study and practice of spirituality in the workplace as a way to extend the depth of the current models. As a result, not only are "values and ethics" being discussed openly in corporate boardrooms, but topics such as "spiritual" leadership and "followership" have become the new areas of interest for those developing the next generation of leadership models. Leadership and spirituality *are* connected, and the current work on the next generation of leadership models are beginning to seriously consider what the pastoral sector has known all along.

In one of the most widely known compendiums of leadership theory entitled "The leader's companion: Insights into leadership through the ages," J. Thomas Wren (1995) argues that the concept of leadership is an essential activity of human endeavor, and that the study of leadership "...should be as all-embracing as the human experience itself." Yet despite the evident appeal of understanding leadership to be an all-embracing activity of human endeavor, it seems persuasive that the extent to which the *spiritual dimension* of leadership remains largely ignored, leadership theory will continue to be under-theorized and under-developed. Put another way, unless and until the "fullness of the human experience" includes the spiritual dimension of the person, leadership theory will remain largely incomplete and marginally helpful in developing effective leaders in the workplace and certainly in the ministry sector.

After conducting more than 90 in-depth interviews with executives and managers, authors Ian Mitroff and Elizabeth Denton in their book "A spiritual audit of corporate America" (1999) characterize the effects of this "soul-less" leadership effort:

> We believe that today's organizations are impoverished spiritually, and that many of their most important problems are due to this impoverishment. In other words, today's organizations are suffering from a deep, spiritual emptiness.

On the other hand, excitement over the promise of leadership models that take into account the whole person should not overwhelm a need for prudence and careful analysis. A willingness to consider these so-called "spiritualized" models of leadership should be accompanied by caution, as the current models typically incorporate notions of spirituality that are inconsistent with mainstream spiritualities already prevalent in the ministry sector. Popular notions of spirituality tend to work against the very qualities of traditional spirituality that contribute significantly to its efficacy.

There are at least three aspects of the current theoretical framework of leadership models that include spirituality that result in these models diverging from acceptable ministry practice. Assessed from a ministry context, the particular areas of concern of these models include: (a) the definitions of spirituality employed, (b) the individualistic nature of the notions about spirituality, and (c) the implicit understanding of leadership" as "position power" or as an essentially hierarchical function.

With regard to the definitional characteristics of spirituality employed by current leadership theory, it is clear that they are constructed in isolation from religion (Mitroff & Denton, *A Corporate Audit of Corporate America*, 1999). Religion is associated with a sense of belonging and the practice of a tradition, whereas most spirituality definitions concentrate on a personal commitment to a holistic inner development separate from religion. This separation of spirituality and religion may be an artificial, academic convenience, but it has started to foster some "spiritualities without religion" as observed by M. Rooney in "Spiritualism at what cost? One campus movement promises self-awareness, but some question its approach" (*The Chronicle of Higher Education, 2003)*. Such a focus will contribute to movements promoting a separation between religious institutions and individuals. As a consequence, leadership models that encourage a spirituality that is independent from religion ignore the richness of the many spiritual traditions that exist in the ministry sector, and also threaten the potential of fostering community and more broadly *communio*. A spirituality separated in this way from its life's blood will inevitably end up on life support and will serve no one particularly well.

Another aspect of current spiritual leadership models is the individualistic character of the spirituality. Catholic theologian Lawrence Cunningham notes: "Much spirituality ... is highly narcissistic and not easily distinguished from old self-improvement schemes" (*Notre Dame Magazine,* Autumn, *2002*). This "me-first" spirituality is already a well-established and controversial issue in colleges and universities as observed by D. Schaper in "Me-first 'spirituality' is a sorry substitute for organized religion on campuses" (*The Chronicle of Higher Education,* 2000). Not only is this newly identified spirituality individualistic in nature, but as E. Lesser notes, it also is characterized as being driven by consensus. As a result, we end up with a spirituality that is fundamentally individualistic and "democratic" in its praxis (Elizabeth Lesser, in *The New American Spirituality: A Seeker's Guide.* Random, 1999). To be sure, a highly individualistic and democratic spirituality may appeal to the American pluralistic society at large, but such a spirituality is fundamentally incongruent with Church ministry. Constructs that are fundamental to ministry such as community, communion, sacrifice, justice, as well as the Church's hierarchical and teaching authority, are clearly at odds with the individualistic and democratic spiritualities implicitly promoted by current leadership models.

A third aspect of current notions of spiritual leadership that diverge from acceptable ministry practice is the perception of the leader as the center of attention and activity. Leadership, and regrettably even spiritual leadership, is commonly understood in relation to "position power" in the organizations rather than as a function among equals. In the case of ministry leadership models, a leader in the Church is assumed to be primarily an extension of the hierarchy, and hence a sharer in positional power. In the article "Investigating organizational fit in a participatory leadership environment," Adrianna Kezar presents this "position power" as an implicit attribute of early leadership theory that is still a common thread in many current leadership models, including the spiritual models (*Journal of Higher Education Policy and Management*, 2001). Yet being a lay leader in the ministry sector is not about "power" nor does it imply that being a ministry leader makes that person part of the Church hierarchy. In fact, the ministry sector recognizes the interdependency of a hierarchical (ordained ministry) and a pastoral leadership (non-ordained ministry or lay apostolate) with a vital connection to single spiritual worldview as articulated in the constructs of communion, and the Body of Christ, among others.

These three characteristics of current spiritual leadership models: the separation of spirituality from religion, individualistic spirituality and the power-based models of spiritual leadership justify a great deal of caution when applying secular models to sectors that already have effective spiritualities, ministry practices and ecclesial model. On the surface, these secular spiritual models present an appealing supplement to ministry leadership models, but further study justifies a healthy dose of caution and reflection before accepting the promises of these seriously flawed models.

To be sure, the fact that spirituality has become an item of interest in the recent evolution of secular leadership models is encouraging, to say the least. It's inspiring to know that formal research in spirituality may lead to new career fields, expanded professional disciplines and a more holistic approach to research with human subjects. It's even more encouraging to see how this trend may promote a wider acceptance of spirituality in the discipline of leadership and in day-to-day organizational activities across the business, non-profit, government and pastoral sectors. At the same time, it is important to bear in mind that the spiritual dimension of secular leadership models is quite limited, and if applied without reflection, may result in less-than-optimal situations for the pastoral sector.

One way to understand why spiritual leadership models are appealing, yet seriously limited when applying them in the ministry setting, is by exploring the processes through which spirituality developed as a topic in leadership theory in light of what we understand about spirituality in the ministry sector. Central to this understanding is the fact that the secular leadership models were developed outside of and without serious contact with the ministry sector. It is only recently that spirituality was identified as a missing component of leadership practice in the secular models. On the other hand, the ministry sector has at one level or another always understood that leadership involved spirituality; it just struggled to develop the "hard" topics of leadership on its own. Unhappily, as it adopted and reaped some of the benefits of secular leadership models, the ministry sector misplaced the spiritual component by not fully adapting these models to their needs. Perhaps the presumption was that secular organizations have nothing to offer the ministry sector about spirituality. Nevertheless, it seems that the ministry sector in adopting secular ministry models overlooked the fact that putting a solid rocket booster and inertial guidance systems on a car doesn't make the car a spaceship. It's still a car. Likewise, simply adding prayer, reflection, and faith sharing to a secular leadership model does not turn the model into an appropriate ministry leadership model. It's still a secular leadership model.

So the current challenge of the pastoral sector is to bridge the gap between the emerging types of spiritualities in secular leadership models with the traditional spiritualities already present in the ministry sector. An additional challenge is for the ministry sector to remain aware of and sensitive to the fundamental need to adapt any borrowed leadership model so it is consistent with the philosophy and theology of ministry. Bridging the gap between the developing secular spiritualities and the spiritual traditions of the Church represents the next big challenge in pastoral leadership research, training and practice. There is still much work to do to reconcile secular leadership theory with the spiritual traditions of the ministry sector.

One thing is certain, the pastoral sector is starting to claim its place as a distinctive field of study requiring perspectives of leadership practice unique to its mission and goals. There are encouraging signs that the pastoral sector is starting to react to the "leadership of spirituality" models and is becoming increasingly aware of its ability to present the "spirituality of leadership" as an alternative response and contribution to the development of leadership theory.

In summary, it seems that the "hard" side of leadership is well understood by the population of trained leaders. Also, because of the many secular leadership failures, a recent tendency to explore the "softer" aspects of leadership has begun to emerge. This recent interest in the "softer" side of leadership has created a sudden increase of models attempting to correct a shortfall in leadership development and training, notably the lack of a meaningful dynamic of spirituality. Bridging the gap between these new developing secular spiritualities and the spiritual traditions of the Church represents the next big challenge for lay and clergy leadership and also for those responsible for their formation. Here is perhaps one of the greatest challenges facing the lay ecclesial ministers and the permanent diaconate as well, the two fastest-growing elements of leadership in the U.S. Catholic Church.

The "Best" Leadership Model?

So what is the best leadership model for ministry? What can we do to overcome potential biases when applying secular leadership models to ministry? How far can we safely go with these models? How can we introduce a more complete spirituality by using the leadership models available? Is it better to modify secular models or should we consider developing our own? These are essential areas of interest and research for the pastoral sector in the United States, since to our knowledge, very

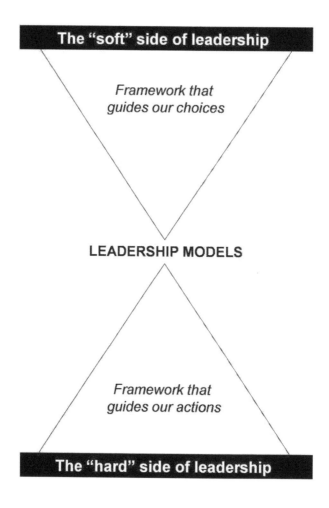

Figure 1, The hourglass model

few formation programs in the pastoral sector are offering focused courses or workshops on the fundamentals of pastoral leadership as a spiritual practice.

One approach to resolving this shortcoming could be to consider an entirely different paradigm of leadership for the pastoral sector, akin to reversing the observation viewpoint. In other words, instead of trying to view spirituality from the *leadership* perspective, why not reverse the point of view and look at leadership from the *spiritual* perspective? Instead of looking at the possibilities of spirituality within leadership, would it not be more productive for us to understand leadership as a spiritual practice? In this way, leadership is seen as another opportunity to help others grow spiritually, rather than as merely a "hard" disciple onto which one grafts the "soft" aspects of the discipline as needed.

One implication of this reversed approach is that leadership now becomes a construct that is framed by spiritual practice and not the other way around. In other words, spirituality as the bigger view, a worldview, influences our understanding of leadership, despite the specifics of the leadership model chosen. This way of thinking offers a very practical approach to any leadership model. With this perspective, spirituality moderates leadership, not the other way around.

The reversal of view satisfies the need in the pastoral sector, but also in the secular world. Consider again the comments of Rich McLaughlin's quote stated in the previous chapter:

> Having spent the last 10 years delivering leadership work-shops, I am confident that people in leadership positions already have most everything they need in terms of skills and competencies. If anything, what they consistently lack are courage and faith: a lack of courage to confront practices that don't make sense, and a lack of faith in letting the people who do the work self-organize. Issues of faith and courage are choices to be made, not skills to be taught. (McLaughlin, 2004, p. 8)

47

This statement illustrates a significant shift in the way one views the leadership construct. Namely, leadership is not only about the "hard" topics of techniques and practices that guide actions, but it is just as much about a "soft" side that influences the choices leaders make in performing their duties. And, of course, the choices we make are a result of our spiritual formation and growth.

If this interpretation is used as a basic framework, then leadership models have a both a "hard" and "soft" side to their anatomy (see Figure 1). Both sides are essential to effective leadership. Each side dynamically nurtures the other, one providing the mechanics of appropriate and effective technique, while the other contributes an internal navigational component. In this way, leadership becomes a discipline for influencing others and events, originating from both a personal and collective view.

An analysis of a few recent definitions of leadership from the scholarly literature should help illustrate the distinction between the hard and soft sides of leadership, how they are related and why this approach is a better fit for ministry. In the book "Making common sense: Leadership as meaning making in a community of practice" (1994), Drath and Palus define leadership as "... the process of making sense of what people are doing together so that people will understand and be committed" (p 4.). In this definition, "meaning making" represents the "soft" side whereas process represents the hard side of leadership.

In another definition of leadership, Richards and Engle (In J.D. Adams Ed., *Transforming leadership*, 1986) state, "Leadership is about articulating visions, embodying values and creating an environment within which things can be accomplished" (p. 206). Clearly, the means used to accomplish things represent the hard aspects of leadership practice, while terms such as "values" and "creating an environment" suggest the "soft" aspects of leadership practice.

For Jacobs and Jacques (In Clark & Clark Eds., *Measures of leadership*, 1990), leadership "...is a process of giving purpose (meaningful direction) to collective effort, and causing willing effort to be expended to achieve purpose" (p. 281). The words "giving purpose" and "causing willing effort" represent the "soft" side of leadership. Ideas such as organizing "collective efforts" and focusing the group so as to "achieve purpose" are phrases typical of the "hard" side of leadership.

In E. Schein (Organizational culture and leadership, Jossey-Bass, 1992), leadership is "… the ability to step outside the culture… to start evolutionary change processes that are more adaptive" (p. 2). Words such "values," "vision," "culture" and "environment" typify the "softer" side of leadership, whereas "changing processes" reflects the "hard" side of the discipline.

Even the rigorous and many times emotionless discipline of military leadership models taught at the service academies such as the United States Military Academy at West Point are tempered with a softer side with concepts such as "duty, honor, country." Interestingly, some leadership models are defined precisely by their "softer" side. Recently developed leadership models such as ethical leadership, values-based leadership and the spiritual leadership models use a "softer" approach (ethics, values, spirit) to define their unique contribution to the leadership discipline.

As a way of demonstrating the relevance of the softer side of leadership, we share a technique we have used in numerous pastoral leadership workshops. During the training session, the participants are asked to map out their professional life on a piece of paper. Invariably, participants end up with a comprehensive diagram that illustrates their professional growth since high school, from their first employment all the way up to their most recent professional achievements. We then ask them to turn the sheet of paper over and render a diagram of their spiritual life. After a few awkward moments and considerable additional clarifications of the assignment, most of the participants (some even reluctantly) draw the picture of their spiritual life. Invariably, the rendering of their professional life is considerably more elaborate and detailed than the picture of their spiritual life.

A discussion usually follows as to *why* the professional life is easier to draw than the spiritual life. After a few minutes spent on philosophical justifications and a few jokes about artistic skills (or the lack of skills) the participants come to realize the extent to which spirituality as a "softer" side of life is often overpowered by the "hard" and more visible dimensions of a professional life. Once this realization sinks in, we ask them to identify "the connections" between both sides of the paper, or the relationships between the professional life and the spiritual life.

In our research to date, no one has articulated this combination of the "hard" and "soft" sides of leadership better than Stephen Covey. Well known for the "7 Habits of Highly effective People" (1989), Covey has provided a clear and practical template for effectiveness that has become second nature to many managers, leaders and organizational cultures, even in the ministry sector. To this day, we hear pastoral teams note that attending a Covey workshop or reading and studying Covey's books will help them become more effective pastoral leaders.

Interestingly, Stephen Covey (2004) has published "The 8th Habit," apparently not so much to remedy the omission of an important habit, as many seem to believe, but out of an insight that he felt compelled to articulate. Covey states:

> The 8th Habit, then, is not about adding one more habit to the 7—one than somehow got forgotten. It's about seeing and harnessing the power of a third dimension to the 7 Habits... The 8th Habit represents the pathway to the enormously promising side of today's reality... It's the voice of the human spirit... (p. 4-5).

This insight regarding the "hard" and "soft" sides of leadership merits a more in-depth explanation since it is fundamental for understanding leadership as a spiritual practice.

Again, the "hard" side of leadership can be defined as the framework that addresses *external actions*. It addresses the set of arrangements that channels actions in a team, an organization or a community. The "hard" side of leadership can be described by words already present in many definitions of leadership. Words like "goals," "processes," "working together," "getting things done" and "exercising influence and power" are among the most prevalent. Conversely, the "soft" side focuses on frameworks that guide choices. Terms such as ethics, values and spirit are typical of the "soft" side of the leadership discipline. It is here, in the realm of the softer side of leadership, where there is an opportunity to engage in leadership as spiritual practice. Here is the "open door" to establish a strong and permanent relationship between spirituality and leadership for ministry.

In formulating that ministry leadership is about (a) frameworks that guide our choices (soft aspect of the discipline) and (b) those that guide our actions (hard aspects of the discipline), we can establish that the preeminent framework to *guide our choices* in based on spirituality. In doing so, we allow leadership to become spiritual practice *regardless* of the leadership model used and the spiritual tradition selected.

As a synthesis of what we have presented so far, consider the following image: The interdependency of leadership's "hard" and "soft" sides operate much like an hourglass (Figure 2). This insight allows a broader interpretation of the leadership function, one where the soft side is complementary to the hard side and vice versa. In fact, visualizing these two sides of leadership as an "hourglass" captures the dynamics of the interrelationship between these two aspects of leadership. The top side of the hourglass represents the framework that guides our choices (the soft side of leadership) and the bottom of the hourglass symbolizes the hard side, or the actions of leadership. The leader is then at the convergence point where the soft and hard sides intersect, and the sand moving back and forth illustrates the dynamics between them. Unlike a hourglass, however, the dynamics of leadership cause the sands to shift in greater and lesser proportions constantly.

This back-and-forth motion is akin to the act of breathing. One cannot survive by exhaling alone, just as a leader cannot survive by actions alone. A combination of inhaling and exhaling converges into a

51

single concept we call "breathing." Similarly, the dynamics between the soft and hard sides converge into a concept we refer to as "leadership."

When reflecting on this image, we see the possibility of deeper layers of both the hard and the soft dimensions of leadership. Since there are already many theories and models explaining the topics of goals, processes, getting things done and exercising power and influence, it seems appropriate to emphasize the softer side and explain it with terminology and concepts more directly related to spirituality and spiritual practice. Nevertheless, the "hard" aspects of the leadership discipline continue to be important and necessary for an effective leadership model in the ministry sector.

The adage "Vox tempori, Vox Dei" *(The voice of the times, the voice of God)* comes to mind as a valuable rule to identify some key areas of attention in pastoral leadership. With the help of many of the pastoral leadership teams for which we have consulted in the past, through conversations with faculty and students of various ministry leadership schools, a variety of other non-profit institutions, seminary faculty, and through formal research, we have found some practices that provide an effective basis for composing a spiritual framework for ministry leadership as spiritual practice.

By using the pastoral leader's calling or vocation as a starting point of the softer side of leadership as spiritual influence, and moving progressively from a personal dimension to a team or small group dimension, and then to a wider macro vision of Church or an ecclesiological dimension, we offer the following spiritual practices as "pillars" or guiding principles for pastoral leadership and hence for the models that guide the discipline in the ministry sector:

(a) One's ***personal calling*** or vocation is the dimension of pastoral leadership that addresses the origin and fulfillment of one's life plan. This dimension connects the exercise of the leadership function to one's fundamental identity.

52

(b) Building *character* is also related to personal identity. However, it also relates to self-regulation, resilience and maturity. This dimension is associated with "interior conversion" and provides some measure of protection against corruption and making poor choices by engaging in unethical behaviors in exercising the leadership function.

(c) The ***primacy of relationships*** is the dimension that emphasizes the value of connections among individuals, which are many times more important than tasks. Spirituality is fundamentally relational, and therefore this dimension allows for a natural flow of values such as love and forgiveness, while honoring the relationship with the dynamics of the supernatural (e.g., Divine Providence) in performing the leadership functions.

(d) Exercising leadership can create and nurture ***spiritual communities*** rather than just organizational development. Rather than focusing mainly on team or group performance, the optional objective is to recognize and nurture a sense of *communio*.

(e) The dimension of ***envisioning or worldview*** allows the pastoral leader to work, make decisions and interact with others from a framework that includes the best articulation of what it means to be Church. In this way, responsible stewardship and an enduring evangelization is maintained.

(f) ***Discernment*** provides a form of "contemplative wisdom" that integrates, moderate, and harmonizes the use of spiritual influences as a form of leadership.

Each of these six influences that characterize the essential elements of leadership as spiritual practice are enacted within the scope of

Figure 2, Pastoral Leadership model

any leadership model and is not limited to just one form of spirituality (see Figure 2). This means that most models of leadership, including secular models, can be appropriately adapted to the needs of the pastoral, and that the spiritual influences can be enacted from a variety of spirituality schools and forms. Which model is selected is not as important as the focus on leadership as a spiritual discipline. What matters most from the pastoral perspective is that leadership be exercised as a spiritual practice that provides for the adoption of practices and worldviews regardless of the many schools of spirituality in the Church.

Of course, the five pillars of leadership as spiritual practice is by no means an exhaustive list, but it does represent a reasonable and comprehensive starting point for ministry leadership development.

Each one of these influences will be discussed in greater detail in the chapters that follow. As a way of introducing the significance and value of each of the five pillars of leadership as a spiritual discipline, we provide an overview of the value of each.

Personal Calling

Although it seems basic to recognize the value of leadership as an element of one's *personal calling* or vocation and to be sensitive to the influence of personal calling on leadership, the scholarly literature on secular leadership models is essentially silent on this topic. "Personal calling" as used here means recognizing and remaining true to one's unique and personal gifts, talents and resources. It also refers to the person's response to the life's mission (or purpose in life, soul-role) that emerges from discerning one's unique skills and tendencies that are at the core of an individual's identity. A fundamental assumption in including one's calling or vocation as one of pillars of ministry leadership as spiritual discipline is that one's gifts, talents and resources are the fundamental tools we employ as we exercise leadership. Leadership is not just a job, a title or a position of power but an opportunity to harness and employ spiritual strengths in support of one's unique calling to the service of others. The uniqueness of this dimension is that it blends who the person is with the functions of leadership and fully incorporates the adult growth processes that affect and are affected by the leadership functions. The role of leader changes the person, and the changes in turn influence how the role is carried out. What is essential is that the changes be positive ones, directed to growth and directed to the benefit of others.

Character Building

The second principle of engaging in leadership as spiritual practice is *character building*. Over the past half century, character building has taken a back seat to personality developmental. There is a lot of talk about fixing the "personality" but very little discussion and action on sustaining strength of character and will. A focus on personality alone generally results in an ego-centric perspective of issues, and largely ignores the communal dimension of the problems. A focus on character, on the other hand, maintains a dual focus – on the growth of the individual as well as on how the person's actions are affecting others.

The tendency to prefer personality over character development has recently become a significant concern, particularly as it relates to the behavior of youth. A rise in drug, alcohol and tobacco usage, pregnancies, violence and other problematic behaviors in schools over the past decades is prompting educators to refocus efforts on character building over the value-neutral personality approach. Considering the increase in the number of corporate executives, politicians, pastoral leaders and even some clergy who have engaged in patterns of unethical behavior, a focus on character building rather than personality development seems more appropriate. The great potential for misusing and abusing influence and power in a leader presents an opportunity to test character and apply spiritual wisdom. Power and influence may tend to have a corrupting effect, yet for any leader the use of power and influence also represents an opportunity to exercise *character building* as spiritual practice. The value of this dimension is that character building involves and presupposes the continuous maturation of identity and the exercise of self-regulation. Both of these growth activities are directly relevant to the practice of leadership and both are well recognized and fundamental spiritual growth processes.

Primacy of Relationships

The third pillar of leadership as a spiritual practice is the *primacy of relationships*. Leadership involves the exercise of power and influence, but it is also about relationships (Glaser, 2006). So is spirituality. The extent to which current leadership models ignore the dynamics of relationships, and the importance of relationships to social and psychological maturation is remarkable. This significant blind spot in current leadership models makes it impractical for their adopters to harness the fruits of the spiritual depth that bind, direct and mobilize. Relationships, particularly those framed in the business domain, are too frequently reduced to "transactional exchanges." As a result, such relationships lack meaningful depth and fail to develop the transformational and "transfigurational" potential of relationships. The transactional mindset typical of the interpersonal relations in the business sector excludes God when plans and decisions are made. On the other hand, an essential dimension of Church ministry is the nurturing of relationships that are transformational in character. A key value of leadership in the pastoral sector lies in the ability for relationships to harness and develop spiritual strengths in support of one's unique calling to serve others. In this respect, pastoral leadership is *service-oriented*, rather than self-serving.

Spiritual Community

The fourth dimension of pastoral leadership is the recognition that, in accepting the primacy of relationships, the leader is also sustaining and nurturing *spiritual community*. The current emphasis on the notion of "building community" has failed to address the relevant interactions among leadership, spirituality and Church. It is common to hear about "building community" in a parish setting, yet the results are difficult to find. The notion of "building community" is ambiguous and seems to lean too much toward the harder side of leadership practice, often at the expense of the softer side of sound leadership practice. As a result, a key strategy for our parish consultations is to define and assess the state of the community dimension. Any secular consultant can initiate organizational development interventions in a parish staff, yet very few can help the parish staff— and the parish—grow with the primary focus of becoming a spiritual community (*vivencias* of *communio*). In this way, we avoid the problem of creating good parish "organizations," at the expense of building a community. We believe the terms "spirit in community" or "animation of communities" to be a more complete models for pastoral leadership.

One example that illustrates this point is an encounter we had during a consultation for a parish in the Archdiocese of Chicago under Project INSPIRE. The entire pastoral staff in this parish had an open discussion about teamwork issues (goals, objectives, collaboration, cooperation, projects for the upcoming liturgical year, getting things done) and after a few hours of venting and reflecting they concluded that in fact they were not only a good pastoral team, but a *great* team. The question we posed the pastoral staff was, *"Is team the ultimate model of Church community?"*

This initiated an animated discussion that led to a significant realization: The *spiritual* sharing and nurturing among them was deficient. The "feeling at home," the moving presence of God among them, the attending to emotional needs, the opportunities for celebration, the yearning for a climate of informality, and the emphasis on the important things in life had been excluded from their working relationships as a small community. They had achieved the status of a great team by any corporate standard, but they were not yet a spiritual community. Once they realized that they had mastered corporate techniques, but not community building in the spiritual and pastoral senses of the term, they were able to address their blind spot. In forming and sustaining *spiritual community,* that is where pastoral leadership becomes spiritual practice.

Envisioning as Influence (Worldview)

The final dimension of leadership as spiritual practice comes from the power of living in a different paradigm, or worldview. Some secular leadership models already speak to the significance of "worldview" as an important aspect of leadership practice. In fact, transformational leadership is fundamentally about finding a "vision," and sharing and inspiring growth along that vision. Yet in analyzing these corporate worldviews, the "vision" is restricted to life as defined by the organization and to its financial security, whereas from a spirituality perspective, a worldview encompasses all aspects of life both at work and away from work.

Understanding *ecclesiology as worldview* and applying it to leadership models is probably the easiest and most effective way to preserve leadership as spiritual practice. A worldview is basically an overall perspective from which one understands and interprets events; it is an ideological standpoint from which one derives meaning and from which one makes choices. Spirituality seeks to align a broad perspective on how life should be lived with the day-to-day choices made in living that life. Bridging the gap between knowing what should be done and what we do may be viewed as a process of conversion. This process of conversion allows leadership to be much more than a matter of simply "getting things done." Additionally, worldview provides drive, intensity and meaning when facing paradoxical situations. Dealing appropriately with paradox allows also allows space for "faith." A worldview also allows for a sense of resilience in the face of adversity, gives meaning to the difficulties we face and serves as a faithful monitor of potentially harmful cultural influences.

Worldview encompasses the entire framework of the "soft" side of leadership practice by providing a coherent ideology within the larger vision of a spiritual perspective. An ecclesiology as spiritual *worldview* provides the lens from which we view the choices we make as leaders. This is a worldview rooted in Church, in *communio*. In our case, an ecclesiology provides the worldview of pastoral leadership. It is this worldview that prompts pastoral leaders to eschew power and position and to become good stewards in the care, guidance and sanctification of others. Prayer, discernment, sacraments, Scripture, Church teachings and all the dimensions of formation (human, pastoral, spiritual and intellectual) *naturally* enter the leadership landscape.

The continuity, richness and interplay of these five spiritual influences as "soft" factors of leadership have significant implications for spiritual practice. Each pillar, when conducted with a spiritual intent, has the possibility of being a contributor to spiritual growth.

Yet the most significant skill set we found that preserves the integrity of leadership as spiritual practice and promotes a sense of harmony between the soft and hard sides of leadership is *discernment*.

Discernment as spiritual influence

All the spiritual influences we have discussed so far require choices, and decision-making is the quintessential leadership task. Accordingly, decisions that emerge from the *envisioning* influence require decision-making, and in continuing the main theme of leadership is a spiritual practice it's only natural that we would chose discernment as the preferred method to make decisions.

Although we recognize the multiple possibilities of defining discernment, for our purposes *discernment* is the process of assembling and sorting out knowledge with respect to the way toward God. It tests the ends and the means and creates a critical center. *Discernment* also ties together all of the spiritual influences we have mentioned in this book, since all spiritual practices demand day-to-day choices within a broad "vision" or worldview. Then it is through *discernment* that a leader and the group (team, community) are able to enhance knowledge, critical thinking and receptivity to God's will and ways (Grothe, 2008; Valk, 2009). In this sense, *discernment* provides a "contemplative wisdom" that looks at a person's and community's life journey and *envisions* its perfection through the divine (Waaijman, 2002). Therefore we consider *discernment* as an influence of spiritual decision making for the pastoral leader.

Well-honed discernment skills sustain the connection between the natural and supernatural as a single reality in the exercise of the discipline of leadership. The synergy of a person's identity, gifts and abilities with *Vox Dei* is a unique attribute of pastoral leadership, something that secular models, to date, have been unable to recognize. The ability to discern is the unifying skill that sustains the integrity of pastoral leadership as spiritual practice. Without the continuous and wise exercise of discernment, we fall back to the secular leadership models, in which decisions are made without regard to the *Vox Dei*.

As a summary of this chapter, leadership is fundamentally a *relational* influence and therefore also a spiritual endeavor. Attempting to develop leadership theories and form leaders while ignoring the "softer" (and spiritual) side of human endeavor is to accept an incomplete view of the human reality. The fullness of leadership requires engaging the fullness of human nature in body, heart and soul.

Pastoral leadership is best conducted by viewing leadership as the "stewardship of others." Rather than focusing on organizational performance in order to create effective parish "organizations," the primary objective of ministry leadership needs to focus on the notions of "animating" communities, "spirit in community" or "stewards of *communio*" in our parishes. In this way, pastoral leadership is not just a "job" or a "function," but an opportunity to harness and employ spiritual strengths in support of one's unique calling at the service of others, and engage the souls of those entrusted with the mission of the parish.

In the next chapters of this book, we will explain in more detail the implications of the five pillars for pastoral leadership and the breadth of opportunities for spiritual growth that they engender. After addressing each of these pillars in more detail, a chapter entitled "Putting it All Together," describes the relevance of discernment skills to pastoral leadership and provides a few fundamentals of discernment for those who may need assistance in getting started. Those who have the requisite discernment skills will benefit from the chapter in that they will be able to explore how discernment applies to pastoral leadership. As a capstone chapter, we present the results of a series of interviews we conducted with prominent pastoral leaders in various sectors of the Catholic Church as a way of sharing with the reader their experiences of dealing with the different dimensions of pastoral leadership. By sharing these stories, we hope to provide the reader with actual cases of inspiring and successful modeling of pastoral leadership.

Case Study

The parish of St. Alphonsus Ligouri, canonically established in 1973, is one of the largest and most successful parishes in the diocese of a major U.S. city. With over 4,000 families, about 15,000 members, and a budget of over $3 million, the parish is a major contributor to the diocese from both a financial and pastoral perspective. Financially, the parish is a role model of total stewardship, with 89 percent active family participation, representing the largest single source of diocesan revenues. From the pastoral perspective, the parish manages over 80 active ministries, many considered as benchmarks or role models for other parishes in the surrounding states. The pastor of St. Alphonsus, Father Jay Felins, has a staff of 18 full members, and has been with the parish for 12 years. He publicly recognizes that the success of the parish resides in the talents and dedication of the ministry leaders and the ministries they represent.

Last week, one of the deans from a Catholic university within the diocese emailed Father Jay and asked for a special favor. A petition of the dean's graduate school noted that there are too few studies on Catholic ministry leadership. So in order to get a line of research started, the dean asked Father Jay if he could survey a few of the ministry leaders and request that they define the leadership attributes that have contributed most to the success of the parish. Father Jay obliged and had his secretary contact Patti Jensen, the chair of the Parish Council and vice president of a successful financial institution. His secretary also contacted Mark Newfield, the parish coordinator for lay leadership development and Director of Catholic Charities in the diocese.

Father Jay felt that these two people were ideal candidates to meet the dean's request. However, when the meeting took place a few days later, Father Jay was surprised that he could not get them to agree on the leadership attributes that contributed most to the success of St. Alphonsus. Patti's argument was that a strong knowledge of business leadership principles and their effective use is the most significant contributor to parish success. Mark strongly disagreed, claiming that the success of the parish resided in the ability of most ministry leaders to collaborate and satisfying the specific spiritual needs of their respective members. Patti agreed with Mark's statement, but asked, "How can you satisfy their needs without being able to apply good leadership skills?" Mark responded with the question, "How do you measure success in ministry? By just assessing the impeccability of an agenda and minutes of a meeting? They can get that training elsewhere. Success is measured by spiritual growth, not by administrative processes." Patti then took her case further: "I know that, Mark, but what good is spiritual growth if we all remain isolated in our little ministry groups? How do we keep the parish family together without leadership principles?" Mark replied, "The parish will maintain its unity, just as the Church has for over 2,000 years."

During the discussion, Father Jay was silent but very attentive, reflecting on the pros and cons of each argument. After almost two hours of discussion without reaching a consensus, Father Jay asked Patti and Mark for closing arguments. He also let them know that, in his opinion, both arguments were both right and wrong. Father Jay concluded the meeting by thanking both for their thoughts, and asked if they would meet again after asking other ministry leaders for their opinions. Both Patti and Mark agreed.

A week later, Father Jay traveled to your hometown to visit his classmate, your current pastor. While there, your pastor mentions to Father Jay that your parish is having a retreat on parish ministry leadership, and asked if he would like to attend and collect some ideas for his project.

Based on the case presented above, consider the following statements and questions for discussion.

1. Patti's argument is that a strong knowledge of secular leadership principles and their effective use is the most significant contributor to parish success. What part of Patti's argument do you think is correct? Give specific examples within your experiences in ministry leadership to demonstrate your points.

2. Mark strongly disagrees with Patti, arguing that the success of the parish resides in ministry leasers' ability to collaborate and satisfy specific spiritual needs of their respective members. What makes Mark's answer also appropriate in describing ministry leadership?

3. How would the criteria of "ecclesiology" apply to the discussion between Patti and Mark?

4. What hard side and soft side of leadership are at work in this case, and which seem to be missing?

64

5. What are some of the dangers and pitfalls a pastoral leader must face and overcome when using secular leadership models?

6. How would the five pillars or principles that characterize the essential elements of leadership as spiritual (see Figure 2) apply in this case?

Workshop Activities

1. Search for and describe the different sources of "power" that are available to a leader. Which sources of power seem to fit or not fit in the pastoral setting? What are some fundamental problems with the "power" approach to leadership in ministry?

2. Are team or group sources of power different than sources of power available to individuals? How so? How do the sources of power relate to the harder side and softer side of leadership?

3. Search for and discuss 3-4 contingency models of leadership. What is the definition of "contingency leadership models?" Can *spiritual leadership* also be considered a contingency model?

4. As a group, compose a list of "best practices" of pastoral leadership. What practices seem to be addressed in the contingency models? What effective practices seem missing?

Personal Reflective

1. Search for and compose a definition of "spirituality." Reflect on how this definition relates to the leadership functions you currently perform

or would aspire to perform in the future. Is your current spiritual life robust enough to sustain leadership as a spiritual practice?

2. Are you naturally inclined to the "harder" side of leadership or to the "softer" side? Why is that relevant to your understanding of leadership as a spiritual practice?

3. We mentioned the term "spiritless leadership." Have you experienced forms of "spiritless leadership?" What are the consequences of using "spiritless leadership" in the pastoral setting?

4. Which of the five pillars or principles that characterize the essential elements of leadership as spiritual (see Figure 2) seem easiest for you? What ones would require you to dedicate more time to understand and practice?

5. Reflect on an experience in which you may have failed as a leader. What learning can you derive from this experience as you analyze the failure within the context of the five pillars or principles that characterize the essential elements of leadership as spiritual in nature?

Chapter References

Bass, B.M. (1990). From transactional to transformational leadership: learning to share the vision. *Organizational Dynamics, 18* (3), 19-31.

Blanchard, K. (2002). *Whale done.* New York: Free Press.
Conger, J. A., Kanungo, R. N. and Menon, S. T. (2000), Charismatic leadership and follower effects. Journal of Organizational Behavior, 21: 747–767. doi: 10.1002/1099-1379(200011) 21:7<747::AID-JOB46>3.0.CO;2-J

Covey, S.R. (2004). *The 8th habit: From effectiveness to greatness.* New York, NY: Free Press.

Cunningham, L. (Autumn, 2002). Stairways to heaven. *Notre Dame Magazine*, pp. 25-29.

DeRue, D.S., & Ashford, S.J. (2010). Who will lead and who will follow? A social process of leadership identity construction in organizations. *Academy of Management Review, 35*(4), 627-647.

Drath, W.H., & Palus, C.J. (1999). *Making common sense: Leadership as meaning making in a community of practice.* Greensborough, NC: Centre for Creative Leadership.

Glaser, J. (2006). Power and influence: Decipher the language of leadership. *Leadership Excellence, 23*(3), 16.

Grothe, R. (2008, July). Editorial. *Clergy Journal.* p. 2.

Gunn, B (May, 2005). The normalization of deviance. *Strategic Finance,* 85(11), 8-10.

Harwood, L. (2002, April 11). Public's esteem for business falls in wake of Enron's scandal. *Wall Street Journal*, D5.

Jacobs, T. O., & Jaques, E. (1990). Military executive leadership. In K. E. Clark & M. B. Clark (Eds.), *Measures of Leadership* (pp. 281-295). West Orange, NJ: Leadership Library of America.

Kezar, A. (2001). Investigating organizational fit in a participatory leadership environment. *Journal of Higher Education Policy and Management, 23* (1), 85-101.

The Challenges of Pastoral Leadership

Lesser, E. (1999). *The American spirituality*. New York: Random House.

McLaughlin, R. (2004). Empowering leaders: Leadership breaks down in two places. *Executive Excellence, 2*(5),8

Mitroff, I.I. (1999). A study of spirituality in the workplace. *Sloan Management Review, 40*, 83-92.

Richards, D., & Engle, S. (1986). After the vision: Suggestions to corporate visionaries and vision champions. In J.D. Adams (Ed.) Transforming Leadership. Alexandria, VA: Miles River Press, pp. 199-214.

Rodriguez, CM. (2005). Emergence of a third culture: shared leadership in international strategic alliances. *International Marketing Review, 22*(1), 67-95.

Rooney, M. (1/10/2003). Spiritualism at what cost? *The Chronicle of Higher Education, 49*(18), p. A31.

Schaper, D. (August, 18, 2000). Me-First 'Spirituality' is a sorry substitute for organized Religion on campuses. *The Chronicle of Higher Education*, p. A56

Schein, E. H. (1992). *Organizational culture and leadership.* (2nd ed.). San Francisco: Jossey-Bass.

Shapiro, J. & Stefkovich, J.A. (2005). *Ethical leadership and decision making in education: Applying theoretical perspectives to complex dilemmas (2nd ed.).* Mahwah, NJ: Lawrence Erlbaum Associates,

Snyder, G. (Nov/Dec, 2004). Turnaround needed! How to get started. *Nonprofit World, 21*(5).

Tubbs, S., & Shultz, E. (2006). Exploring a taxonomy of global leadership competencies and meta-competencies. *Journal of American Academy of Business 8*(2): 29-34.

Valk, J. (2009). Knowing Self and Others: Worldview Study at Renaissance College. *Journal Of Adult Theological Education, 6*(1), 69-80. doi:10.1558/jate2009v6i1.69

Waaijman, K. (2002). *Spirituality: Forms, foundations, methods.* Leuven: Peters

Wheatley, M.J. (2006). *Leadership and the new science: Discovering order in a chaotic world.* San Francisco, CA: Berrett-Kohler Publishers.

Wren, J. T. (1995). *The leader's companion: Insights on leadership through the ages.* New York: Free Press.

The "soft" side of leadership

Discernment
Envisioning (Worldview)
Spiritual community
Primacy of relationships
Building Character
Your Calling

PASTORAL LEADERSHIP

Goals
Processes
Working together
Getting things done
Exercising influence & power

Framework that guides our actions

The "hard" side of leadership

"Every calling is great when greatly pursued"
Oliver Wendell Holmes

70

CHAPTER 3

The Influence of *Personal Calling*

The *personal calling* is one of the five dimensions of pastoral leadership. It addresses the origin and fulfillment of one's life plan as it relates to the leadership function. This dimension connects the exercise of leadership to one's deepest resources and purpose in life, which are topics that traditionally are associated with personal identity. Here, the dimension of *personal calling* provides a framework for relating the inner world of the person's identity to the outer world of leadership practice. It is a place where person meets practice, each of which is influenced by the other.

Historical Background and Recent Trends

Historically, leadership modeling has been directly associated with the personality and natural charisms of the leader. In fact, the first models of leadership were based primarily on personality attributes. Even before leadership became a discipline of study and practice, leaders were admired and emulated by their followers for the strength of their personalities. Among the first models of leadership was the Great Man Theory. This theory led to an anecdotal and non-scientific set of models that emerged largely from observations of popular leaders performing exceptional feats during times of great crisis. Although the name of this theory reflects the gender biases of the period before the mid-twentieth century, the personalities to which it refers have been widely known and admired. Individuals such as Winston Churchill, Theodore Roosevelt, and later Mohandas Gandhi, Martin Luther King, Jr., Nelson Mandela, Pope John Paul II, Lech Walesa, John F. Kennedy, Mikhail Gorbachev and Ronald Reagan, are generally admired as the great leaders of our century. Great women, such as Eleanor Roosevelt, Margaret Thatcher and Mother Teresa have also been recognized as role models under the Great Man Theory of leadership.

However, the rise of behavioral sciences beginning in the 1950s began to influence leadership theory, and new approaches began to emerge. Instead of emphasizing the values that made great leaders, leadership modeling began looking at quantitative and empirically based models from which behavioral theories, contingency theories and leadership competency models later emerged. These scientifically based models made it possible to systematically study the results of their application. On the other hand, the very characteristic that made these models easier to study, also limited their application. In order to apply these models of leadership effectively, one had to precisely follow their norms, which more often than not ignored the dynamics of the leader's identity. An unintended consequence of these models is that the practice of leadership became much more of a "role playing" function than an activity related to identity and personal growth. Adopting the persona of a leader became more important than building on who the leader was and who the person was becoming.

As a result, we have and continue to experience serious ethical failures of many CEOs and high-level leaders. Catastrophes such as Enron, Tyco, WorldCom, ImClone, HealthSouth, Adelphia, Global Crossing and Quest, not to mention the near collapse of the world economy, are painful examples of what can occur when role trumps identity. An analysis by corporate psychologists and management experts of these and similar failures pointed to inner weaknesses and incompatibilities in the executives including poor self-image, a false sense of worth, unchecked fantasies, loneliness and boredom (Bruce Horovitz, USA Today, 2002, p.2B). The individuals at the center of these corporate collapses seem to have been capable actors in the role of leadership, but lacked the internal compass to keep the role congruent with the person. Power and influence trumped who these leaders were or could have been as a person. The soul of the person was lost to the role.

These troubling scandals by ostensibly well-trained leaders may explain why more recent leadership theories have moved away from the role of leadership and focused more on the inner realities of the leader as a person.

> The scientific method does not lend itself to the study of phenomena such as Being (Desroches, 2003). Connor and Mackenzie-Smith (2003) observe that the primary focus of leadership research has been the doing of leadership, with little attention to the Being [e.g., existence and essence]. (Campbell, 2007, p. 137).

By attempting to measure leadership on a strictly empirical basis, scientifically based models are restricted to measuring observable phenomena. As a result, they ignore the essence of the identity of the person who is the leader. Under these conditions, the identity or essence of the person-leader is considered to be irrelevant.

The emphasis of leadership as a role and its consequences to personal identity are not limited to business executives. Leadership as a primarily role is apparent at all levels, in all types of organizations. Every time someone adopts a model of leadership without considering the full implications to the person's identity and calling, there is a significant risk of subverting who one is as a person as well as one's potential.

73

The cognitive dissonance that results from holding multiple, conflicting realities at once seems to resolve itself in favor of the person adopting a role, rather than remaining open to growth. It seems reasonable to argue that in many ways the notion of leadership as primarily a role has the potential to become a significant barrier to meaningful internal transformation. In fact, this is currently one of the main objections raised to the transformational leadership model. What is not specified by the model is the nature of the transformation and its end-product.

"Playing leader" or leadership as a role, in which one adopts techniques or models contrary to one's identity or personal calling, unfortunately occurs also in ministry. Slick and catchy names of leadership models such as "transformational leadership," "charismatic leadership," and "spiritual leadership" may sound attractive, but the reality is less so. These models, which have been derived strictly from empirical research, do not incorporate the Catholic understanding of transformation, charisms and spirituality. Words don't always mean what they seem. For example, Brazilian grass does not come from Brazil, nor does it even grow in Brazil, and it isn't even a grass at all; eggplants have nothing to do with eggs; hamburgers do not contain ham. In similar fashion, just because a leadership model has the words "transformational," "charisms," or even "spirituality" doesn't automatically mean it was developed for or is appropriate to the pastoral setting.

Perhaps one of the best examples of leadership models that risks derailing a proper sense of calling in the Catholic Church is the model called servant leadership. In its original state, servant leadership was described as a model in which the desire to serve and to empower followers was the optimal way to achieve organizational goals (Greenleaf, 1977). Christians began using servant leadership primarily because it was "mandated" by Christ (Refer to Matthew 20:25-28; 23:11-12), not because of a desire to achieve organizational goals.

Yet there are increasing levels of concern with the servant leadership model within Protestant denominations as well as in the Catholic Church. In Protestant denominations there have been cases studied in which Christian leaders abuse the use of "influence and power" as servant-leaders rather than truly serve their followers (Enroth, 1992; Farnsworth, 1998; Johnson & VanVonderen, 1991). Along these same lines of inquiry, Wong and Page (2003) from Trinity Western University found that servant-leadership behaviors led to justifications for "ambitious, self-seeking leaders to lord over people in God's name," a phenomenon not foreign to some Catholic leaders.

In the Catholic Church, the controversies with servant leadership have proven more dramatically related to personal calling. The servant-leader model, as it has been applied in the Catholic Church, has demonstrated a propensity for overemphasizing function over identity. "Doing" becomes more relevant than "being," which creates a barrier against inner growth and spiritual development. Especially in the ministry sector, "doing" depends on "being" and when "being" is sacrificed to the "doing," eventually the "doing" becomes the undoing of the minister. More to the point, the functionalistic drive intrinsic to servant leadership has been identified as a cause for priestly resignations:

> We have additional data from research on men who have already left the priesthood. Both in the 1970 and in 2000, the men who had resigned from the priesthood told investigators that they held to a more servant-leader, participatory model of the priesthood than the priests who have remained in service. [...] Our data does not tell us why – both in the 1970 and again in the 2000— the servant leader type priest had lower morale and more thoughts of resigning. Our best guess is that possibly they felt a less distinctive priestly identity, providing them with less self-affirmation and esteem (Hoge, Shileds, Griffin & Wengerr, 1995, 125-126).

In the specific case of the servant leadership behaviors applied to the priesthood, Father David Toups notes, "The functional role has been stressed in recent years to the detriment of the sacral role" (Toups, 2004, p. 90). Here, functional trumps identity, to the detriment of both the ministry and the person. One can only imagine the impact of servant-functionalism in the broader circles of the Church among the laity. Basically, the servant-leadership model appeals to our American functionalistic values and can dominate the way we express our faith. To the extent that occurs, it is at the expense of discerning and developing our vocation as Catholics. Never has a leadership model seemed so appealing yet turned out to be so controversial as servant leadership in the ministry sector.

Personal Calling is a Discovery Process

We have offered these examples to illustrate how leadership as a role creates the real risk of becoming a significant, opposing force to one's personal calling. Of course we recognize that there are exceptions to this condition, in which the leader is able to take advantage of the leadership function as a way to apply and discover more about his or her personal calling. Our point is that the norm for Catholic leaders would be to integrate the practice of leadership with a person's calling, which flows from who the person is. That is why *personal calling* is a dimension of pastoral leadership.

One's calling speaks to "why we are here" (and more fundamentally to "who we are"), while the practice of leadership speaks to "where we want to go." One's calling defines purpose in life, the vision and intentionality of living and leading. As the person grows in purpose, the leader grows. Leadership is a way of living one's calling; one's identity in relation to others. But leadership starts with leading oneself:

> As a way of life, leadership means *find yourself, be yourself, show yourself*. Because people regard leaders as special, leadership has become a framework for coming to terms with one's special capacities—one's identity—and then living accordingly. Leadership is not centered on life at the top; it's centered simply on life. The moment we recognize this fact, we are in a position to see that leadership begins as that solitary step

76

wherein we first assume responsibility for leading ourselves. (Ackerman, 2000, p.6)

How are we able to be leaders in ministry if we are unable to lead ourselves? And isn't the activity of finding how to lead oneself a spiritual endeavor related to one's calling?

Leaders who are able to align the personal calling with their use of power and influence are more energetic, resilient, effective, and better interpersonally connected (Cashman, 2008). Leaders who exhibit difficulty reconciling their calling to their work are more prone to satisfy the lower level needs of money, power and prestige but have difficulty fulfilling higher spiritual needs. Leading "within the calling" energizes the person, builds convictions and unifies, whereas leading "outside the calling" becomes a burden, an "energy drainer," and an objectionable job that leads to burn-out. A person leads based upon who she or he is:

> Leaders lead by virtue of who they are. As they learn to master their growth as a person, they will be on the path to mastery of Leadership from the Inside Out. Leadership from the Inside Out is about their journey to discover and develop their purposeful inner capabilities to make a more positive contribution. (Cashman, 2008, p.1)

Essentially, effective pastoral leadership starts with a clear understanding of one's personal calling.

The idea of "calling" is expressed in different ways. Some authors refer to calling as a "central life task" (Bogart, 1994), or as a "personal ideal" (Reed, 2000). Reed bases her definition of discovery of self on Plato's concept of "diaonia," and refers to personal calling as the "wholeness of being realized when one uses rightly the highest moral ideal or vision within one" (Reed, 2000, p.10). A different interpretation is offered by Jung , who noted that...

> True personality always has vocation, which acts like the Law of God from which there is no escape. Who has vocation hears the voice of the inner man; he is called. The greatness and the liberating effect of all genuine personality consists of this, it subjects itself of free choice to its vocation. (Jung, 1934, pp.175-176)

We understand the term "vocation" used in the quote above as a unique calling, a personal journey, which may or may not coincide with a selected occupation or profession. In this context, the term "vocation" refers to more than just a job through which wages are earned. Other authors refer to it as "a central facet of the narrative that a person constructs to make sense of his or her personal history," (Bogart, 1994, p.10) or "a single directive principle unifying one's inward and outward life" (Progoff, 1986, p. 78).

Theological support for the concept of vocation or calling is illustrated in Psalm 139 and is also interpreted as the ontological meaning of the "given name" (Kentenich, 1991). The Catechism of the Catholic Church explains how the "ontological given name" of a person relates to the calling:

> A name expresses a person's essence and identity and the meaning of this person's life. God has a name; he is not an anonymous force. To disclose one's name is to make oneself known to others; in a way it is to hand oneself over by becoming accessible, capable of being known more intimately and addressed personally. (CCC, 203)

In this sense, the "ontological name" is the meaning and calling of one's life or the point where mission and identity converge:

> First of all, there is biblical evidence to suggest that a new identity is given to people when they are given a mission, or given some preeminent mission. The paradigmatic cases cited by Balthasar are those in which men's names are changed:

Abram-Abraham, Jacob-Israel, Simon-Peter. Identity is thus given along with the mission. (Badcock, 1998, p.62)

Although not all name changes may be theologically significant, throughout Holy Scripture one can see how God reveals the "ontological name" as the icon of the person, the essence and calling of life. Such is the case of the name change of Abram to Abraham (Gen 17, 5), Sarai to Sarah (Gen 17, 15), Jacob to Israel (Gen 35,10), Hosea's son and daughter (Hosea 2: 1-23), the prompting of Zacharias and the given name for his son (Luke 1, 13), as well as the name change from Simon to Peter (Mt 16, 18), and Saul to Paul (Acts 9:1-4; Acts 13:9). One of the most surprising and intriguing name changes in Holy Scripture occurs in Exodus 6, 2-3 in when and how God reveals His own name:

> God said to Moses, "I am the Lord. As God the Almighty I appeared to Abraham, Isaac, and Jacob, but my name, Lord, I did not make known to them.

More specifically, the Catechism of the Catholic Church provides an explanation of the significance of what we call the "ontological name" and of God's own revealed name:

> God revealed himself to his people Israel by making his name known to them. A name expresses a person's essence and identity and the meaning of this person's life. God has a name; he is not an anonymous force. To disclose one's name is to make oneself known to others; in a way it is to hand oneself over by becoming accessible, capable of being known more intimately and addressed personally.
>
> In revealing his mysterious name, YHWH ("I AM HE WHO IS", "I AM HOW I AM" or "I AM WHAT I AM") God says who he is and by what name he is to be called. This divine name is mysterious just as God is mystery. It is at once a name revealed and something like a refusal of a name, and hence it better expresses God as what he is—infinitely above everything we can understand or say: he is the "hidden God", his

79

> name is ineffable, and he is the God who makes himself close to men.
>
> God, who reveals his name as "I AM" reveals himself as the God who is always there, present to his people in order t save them (CCC 203, 206, 207)

Although not everyone may have the immediate "grace of clarity" in seeing their "ontological name" like the cases from Holy Scripture stated above, each of us has an "ontological name:"

> God calls each one by name.[87] Everyone's name is sacred. The name is the icon of the person. It demands respect as a sign of the dignity of the one who bears it. (CCC, 2158)

This "ontological name" is the unique and unrepeatable truth of what it is to be a person, the "self" as envisioned by God even before one existed in the flesh. It is the "original idea" of every person already thought by God from all eternity, which provides an original and decisive "blueprint" for each person's "being" and action:

> You formed my inmost being; you knit me in my mother's womb. I praise you, so wonderfully you made me; wonderful are your works! My very self you knew; my bones were not hidden from you, When I was being made in secret, fashioned as in the depths of the earth. Your eyes foresaw my actions; in your book all are written down; my days were shaped, before one came to be. How precious to me are your designs, O God; how vast the sum of them! (Psalm 139, 13-17)

Each person is a unique and irreplaceable "love-thought" of God, so to speak, that has always existed in God's heart yet awaits for the "right time" in history to become flesh. Each person is "…his or her own end and is never used as an instrumental means" or as a specimen, a generic object" (Crosby, 1996). Although cultural biases, social sins and our own selfish and unhealthy desires try to pull each one of us away from the "ontological name" and unique calling, the anchor for the discovery of our own selves will always remain contained within the uniqueness that God gave each of us:

> In our human statistics, human categories, human political, economic and social systems and mere human possibilities fail to ensure that man can be born, live and act as one who is unique and unrepeatable, then all this is ensured by God. For God and before God, the human being is always unique and unrepeatable, somebody thought of and chosen from eternity, some called and identified by his own name (John Paul II, *Urbi et Orbi* message, Christmas 1978).

Many traditional schools of spirituality within the Catholic Church already address the relevance of what we call here the "ontological name." In fact, these traditional schools of spirituality as well as other forms of spirituality and the formal research from the social sciences prefer using the term "discovery of self" for this lifetime search of a personal, axial life-principle. One such research, for example, analyzes 27 definitions of spirituality in the social sciences and finds that this "discovery of self" process—albeit with some degree of definitional variance—is a prevalent topic (Rojas, 2005). What we stress here is the value of a healthy discovery of self, preferably framed around the "ontological name."

As an aid to the reader, we offer some additional perspectives to facilitate one's reflection on the importance of attending to one's calling and, by implication, one's identity or "ontological name" in the pursuit of a viable leadership practice in ministry.

First of all, the importance of engaging in the life-long project of identifying and honoring one's calling and identity—although more commonly applied to the clergy and religious—applies as well to every lay person in the Church. In the Apostolic Exhortation on the vocation and mission of the lay faithful in the Church and in the world (*Christi-fideles Laici*), John Paul II remarks:

> The fundamental objective of the formation of the lay faithful is an ever-clearer discovery of one's vocation and the ever-greater willingness to live it so as to fulfill one's mission...In fact, from eternity God has thought of us and has loved us as unique individuals. Every one of us he called by name, as the Good Shepherd "calls his sheep by name" (*Jn* 10:3). However, only in the unfolding of the history of our lives and its events is the eternal plan of God revealed to each of us. Therefore, it is a gradual process; in a certain sense, one that happens day by day. To be able to discover the actual will of the Lord in our lives always involves the following: a receptive listening to the Word of God and the Church, fervent and constant prayer, recourse to a wise and loving spiritual guide, and a faithful discernment of the gifts and talents given by God, as well as the diverse social and historic situations in which one lives. (n. 58).

Here again we see the discovery of the "ontological name" as the *sine qua non* of Catholic formation and fulfillment of one's calling. We discover our "ontological name" through the day-to-day events of our personal history. And having identified our "ontological name" we can develop the basic tools to assist us in our Christian formation, through which we discern our talents, gifts and calling.

A simple analogy that we have used in the past to illustrate Pope John Paul II's process for discovering one's "ontological name" lies in the heuristics used to put a jigsaw puzzle together.

When we reflect on the basic skills and techniques we use to compose a very large jigsaw puzzle, we recognize that we do not usually select the first piece at random and then select the other pieces of the puzzle one by one to see if we can find the second piece that fits the first piece. That would certainly be a solution, but it would require an eternity to complete the puzzle that way.

Instead, when solving complex problems such as a jigsaw puzzle, we use a combination of heuristics. Heuristics are mental models that provide shortcuts to solve complex problems. In the case of the jigsaw puzzle, common heuristics would include grouping pieces by color or pattern, working with the frame or end pieces first, or using the picture on the box as a guide to how we assemble subsets of the main picture that eventually are fit into the larger and complete picture. Putting together a jigsaw puzzle is an exercise of heuristics skills that is more than just a desperate search for the "right" piece (although this, of course, also happens).

In similar fashion, one could view the identification of the "ontological name" as an attempt to fit multiple aspects of one's life into a coherent jigsaw puzzle picture. Many of the heuristics are similar. The frame and corner—we can say—are the outlines of one's personal history. A personal journal or diary can be instrumental in developing one's personal history, which is the foundation for discovering one's "ontological name." By grouping different life events, one begins to compose a picture. Questions to assist in the grouping include: What is the significance of where I was born and events of my youth? What significant religious experiences guided me in the early parts of my life? What discoveries can I make about my upbringing? What resonated deep in my heart during preparation for the Sacraments?

In a second phase of the heuristic, one can add a list of gifts and talents. Questions to ponder in this effort include: What are my unique talents and gifts? What are my preferences and what do they reveal? What are my strengths and struggles and what are their contributions to clarifying the overall picture? What religious images, symbols, liturgies or artifacts seem to "echo" a deeper reality of myself that begs to be discovered?

Finally, one would consider how these major representative groups of one's uniqueness and calling come together into a more unified, coherent theme. Here, one may want to consider discoveries one has made about oneself during retreats, days of reflection or conversations with friends, family, one's spouse or co-workers. Particular attention would be focused on those moments when phrases such as "That is so 'you'..." have been used.

To be sure, composing this picture may require help from more experienced external sources, such as a spiritual guide, a retreat master, a spiritual director, a confessor or a formator. There may be parts of the puzzle that seem missing or misplaced. Other pieces may have been forced into place. One may even have acquired pieces that don't belong. This maturing picture does not have to be completely composed in order for one to be able to intuit one's "ontological name," just as one can develop a good idea of the overall picture of a jigsaw puzzle simply by standing back and looking at the major pieces already in place. Once the framework of the puzzle and some major groupings are in place, you can usually perceive with more certainty the "ontological name." It is a long, enduring journey however, because only God has the complete picture on the puzzle box.

The "Ontological Name" and Leadership

Although other analogies to explain the variety of processes and techniques to construct the picture of one's deepest identity and vocation are possible, the jigsaw puzzle offers a simple way to understand how the discovery of self and the "soul role" or "ontological name" is such an integral part of the choices we make in our day-to-day life, and to our relationship with others, and to our relationship with God. Yet the value of the "ontological name" in relation to others, to God and to one's uniqueness are not lost when applying them to the Pastoral Leadership model.

As we said earlier, the term "ontological name" is used to underscore the relationship with God, with the Church and with the Church's traditional schools of spirituality as expressed not only in Sacred Scripture and Church history, but also in Church documents. Although this may not be the right place to provide a more structured theological substantiation, we suggest that in discerning our own "ontological name" as an ongoing spiritual process, we each discover our calling, and in doing so, we find a central facet that provides meaning to our personal history, a firm principle unifying one's inward and outward lives.

Also, our intent is to prevent one of the possible perils of "discovery of self" processes – that of performing an interior analysis of self in isolation from God, or with fragmented reference to God. With our preference for the term "ontological name" we intend to stress the relevance of each person's uniqueness directly in relation to God and in relation to others:

> The differences among persons belong to God's plan, which wills that we should need one another. These differences should encourage charity (CCC, 1946).

This represents a valuable opportunity to overcome in ourselves some of the individualistic tendencies in our American society and the dangers to our growth and relationships of those tendencies:

> Our relations are usually structured from within ourselves as their center. The reverse side of our relational life is a spiritual opportunity: "There is more to the other than our internalized image. We see the other as an independent person, with a distinct individual history and with his or her own injuries from the past that may have been transmuted into harmful conduct. From this recognition and insight flows the grace of forgiveness and new reconciliation with 'enemies'" (Waaijman, 2002, p.40).

85

This continuous discovery of the "ontological name" places God in the center of the discovery process, has the Church as the source of inquiry for this discovery process, and directs the discoveries of one's uniqueness to one's unique calling to the service of others. This calling is considered more of an invitation than a mandate, a framework for intimate dialogue not a mandate that would infringe upon an individual's freedom—which seems to be one of the main objections of this perspective. Using another analogy, one could say that God as the architect has the design of what one was built for, but each one of us as the "contractor" for the project is responsible for managing the day-to-day activities of growth.

In this sense, the "ontological name" becomes a continuous encounter with God through dialogue and prayer, and a main theme in the lifelong search of a personal, axial life-principle, a theme that finds expression in and is nurtured by the leadership function:

> The encounter with God touches the heart, awakens in it hidden capacities, opens it up, draws it out of itself, recollects it, heals its brokenness, reveals hidden sides, challenges one to grow, teaches one how to live through pain, leads one into a new life. (Waaijman, 2000, p. 885)

What is central throughout this discussion is that leadership *is in fact* predominantly a spiritual practice, and as a spiritual practice it is inextricably related to one's calling, to the discernment and fulfillment of one's "ontological name." Leadership is a discipline in which one applies the evolving interpretation of one's personal calling. But it is also where one makes "breakthrough discoveries" about one's personal calling. This fundamental dynamic of discovering self and applying one's talents with a providential conviction that is respectful of one's freedom is what makes "calling" one of the dimensions of the Pastoral Leadership model.

As one reflects on those moments in one's history in which one was faced with making an important decision, it is instructive to consider how one approached the problem as a way of discerning the extent to which we have allowed who we are to determine what we do. Did we reflect on the possible alternatives to adopt within the context of our personal calling? To what extent did our course of action resonate with our deepest self?

Our conviction is that every leadership opportunity should reflect one's personal calling as a series of "actions from within." Moreover, every leadership opportunity should contribute to one's calling as one discerns the consequences and implications of our actions to one's calling, and to the calling of those entrusted to us—even, and perhaps, especially, in moments of failure.

So far in this chapter we have shown how "playing leader" or leadership as primarily role, results in using techniques that are often at odds with one's identity or personal calling. Within the Pastoral Leadership model we present here, the leader is expected to take advantage of the leadership function as a way to apply the calling and discover more about his or her personal calling, since leaders lead best when they are able to "lead themselves." This idea of "calling" is a central life task, for which leadership is both an expression and a vehicle to further the discovery process. At the core of this "calling" is what we have identified as the "ontological name" which places God in the center of the discovery process. The Church provides resources for discovering this name. The name is an integral component of our relationship with God and is oriented to discovering our uniqueness so that we can serve God and others. The *personal calling* is identified first as a dimension of pastoral leadership because it addresses the origin and fulfillment of one's life plan, which is fundamental to carrying out the leadership function.

Case Study

Father Brendan Larkin, from St. Augustine parish, is having a discussion dinner with various leaders of the parish. This discussion dinner is an opportunity to gather pastoral leaders from the parish and from the three missions associated with the parish.

This year, Father Brendan would like the discussion to focus on character strengths, flaws and on ways to build and sustain better parish leadership. He is convinced this topic will be of interest to the participants at the dinner, and at the same time, the discussion will serve as a milestone to start a new focus on maintaining character strength as an attribute of parish leaders and as a component of spiritual growth.

Father Brendan's approach is to have a respected lay leader within the parish start the discussion with a brief presentation. You have been selected as the presenter and facilitator of this parish event.

Questions for Discussion:

1. How would you structure your presentation and guide the discussion?

2. How would you insert the value of personal vocation (soul role, ontological name) into the presentation?

3. If someone in the group asked how to search for their "soul-role," how would you respond?

4. Can you think of Saints or Popes who seemed they were driven by their "soul-role?"

5. What advantages to personal growth to you see possible when there is a picture of the "soul-role" (ontological name)?

Workshop Activities

Discovering the *personal vocation* (ontological name) is a "reverse-engineering" exercise, which means constructing an abstract concept from a compilation of observations. So for this module we handed out parts of a toy (one at a time) and ask each group to figure out what the toy "IS" based on the parts. Parts are given to each group one at a time. The group conclusions were then compared with a picture of the toy (fully assembled) and an analysis of the process follows. What are some advantages of the inductive process to find the personal vocation? What are some flaws of this process?

Personal Reflective

What is your personal vocation (soul role)? What are major elements that convince you of your perceived soul-role? What "per name" do you think God has for you? What religious image is so appealing to you that you believe it encompasses your ontological name? Remember to collect and sort out these and other thoughts using a journaling process, because this discovery process may take a long time.

Chapter References

Ackerman, P. L. (2000). Domain-specific knowledge as the "dark matter" of adult intelligence: gf/gc, personality and interest correlates. *Journal of Gerontology: Psychological Sciences, 55B*(2), 69-84.

Babcock, G.D. (1998). *The way of life*. Grand Rapids, MI: Wm. B. Eerdmans Publishing.ISBN:0802844901

Bogart, G. (1994). Finding a life's calling. Journal of Humanistic Psychology. *34*(4), 6-37. doi: 10.1177/00221678940344002

Campbell, C.R.(2007) On the journey toward wholeness in leader theories. *Leadership & Organization Development Journal, 28* (2), 137 – 153.

Catechism of the Catholic Church (1994). New York, NY: Doubleday.

Chasman, R. (2008). Storytelling on the Northern Irish border. Indiana University Press, ISBN: 978-0-253-35252-1

Crosby, J.F. (1996). The selfhood of the human person. Washington, DC: Catholic University of America Press.

Enroth, R.M. (1992). Churches that abuse. Grand Rapids, MI: Zondervan.

Farnsworth, K. E. (1998). *Wounded workers: Recovering from heartache in the workplace and the church.* Mukilteo, WA: WinePress Publishing.

Greenleaf, R.K. (1977). *Servant Leadership: A journey into the nature of legitimate power and greatness*. Mahwah, NJ: Paulist Press.

Hoge, R., Shields, J.J., Griffin, D.L. Wenger (1995). Changing commitments and attitudes of Catholic priests, 1970-2001," Sociology of Religion (1995) 56 (2): 195-213. doi: 10.2307/3711763

Horovitz, B. (2008, October 11). Scandals grow out of CEOs' warped mind-set, *USA TODAY*, p. 2B.

John Paul II (1978, December 25). Urbi et orbi.
http://www.vatican.va/holy_father/john_paul_ii/
messages/urbi/documents/hf_jp-ii_mes_19781225_urbi_en.html

John Paul II (1988, December 30). Chirstifidelis Laici.
http://www.vatican.va/holy_father/john_paul_ii/apost_exhortations/
documents/hf_jp-ii_exh_30121988_christifideles-laici_en.html

Johnson, D., & VanVonderen, J. (1991). <u>The subtle power of spiritual abuse</u>. Minneapolis: Bethany House.

Jung, C.G. (1934). *The development of personality. Collected works (Vol. 17)*. Princeton, NJ: Bolligen.

Kentenich, J. (1991). *Pedagogia schoenstattiana para la juventud* (S. D. Acosta, Trans.). Buenos Aires, Argentina: Editorial Patris. (Original work published in 1931).

Progoff, I. (1986). *The dynamics of hope*. New York, NY: Dialogue House Library.

Reed, M.A. (2000). Composing dialogues to express self-differentiation and Burke's rhetoric: A way to comprehend multilevel inner growth. *Roeper Review*, 23, 10-17.

Rojas, R.R (2005). *Spirituality in Management and Leadership*. Bloomington, IN: Authorhouse.

Toups, D. L. (2004). *The sacerdotal character as foundational to priestly life. Dissertatio ad laurem in facultates theologia*. Adpud Pontificam Universitatem S. Thoma in Urbe. Romae.

Waaijman, K. (2002). *Spirituality: Forms, foundations, methods*. Leuven: Peters

Wong, P. T. P., & Page, D. (2003). Servant leadership: An opponent-process model and the Revised Servant Leadership Profile. Paper presented at the Servant Leadership conference.

Framework that guides our choices

Discernment
Envisioning (Worldview)
Spiritual community
Primacy of relationships
Building Character
Your Calling

PASTORAL LEADERSHIP

Goals
Processes
Working together
Getting things done
Exercising influence & power

Framework that guides our actions

"It is absurd that a man should rule others,
who cannot rule himself.
(Absurdum est ut alios regat, qui seipsum regere nescit.)
Latin Proverb

CHAPTER 4

Influencing through *Character*

A second dimension of pastoral leadership is *character.* As noted in the previous chapter, knowing one's *calling* is an important endeavor, but to fulfill one's calling in life requires strength of character. "Becoming a leader is synonymous with becoming yourself. It is precisely that simple, and it is also that difficult," notes Dr. Warren Bennis, professor of business at the University of Southern California.

Those of us who have been studying leadership theory and models from a pastoral perspective over the years have been astonished at how little attention has been given to the topic of *character.* Yet the large number of ethical lapses of CEOs in recent years, and particularly in American business, have reaffirmed the importance of *character* in leadership development.

> Recent news brings us to a steady flow of reports on character failures of leaders and influential personalities in corporations, sports, the entertainment industry, politics and nonprofit organizations. Of course, all humans are flawed by varying degrees of weakness and shortcomings, and character lapse is

nothing new in leaders. What is disturbing, however, is the current frequency of failures, the range and depth of their impact, and their span across virtually every type of business and occupation. (Klann, 2007, p.vii)

Leadership models may guide our ideas, but how are the leaders' choices being guided? Said another way, power, wealth and influence can be a toxic combination if placed upon weak shoulders. Leadership inescapably requires that the leader be sufficiently grounded to avoid the spectacular character failures that have been the source of dismay to so many.

Whether in secular leadership or in the pastoral leadership setting, strength of character can no longer remain merely an assumption. The irony is that character strength is a natural subject matter for the pastoral setting, in both theory and practice, yet it receives little direct attention in our leadership models. After all, aren't formation, conversion and spiritual development the very processes that eventually lead to building strength of character?

In this chapter, we will present *character building* as a crucial element of pastoral leadership. To help the reader develop a coherent perspective of this dimension of leadership, we will present a brief history of character development in leadership models in United States, followed by a discussion of the relevance of character building in relation to leadership development. We will then discuss the process of "rebuilding character" as an integral competency of pastoral leadership. "Rebuilding character" means formulating a scheme to assess character weaknesses (fissures) and identifying specific actions designed to help strengthen and sustain healthy, maturing character as an integral part of leadership as spiritual practice. Finally, we will offer specific recommendations for rebuilding character in the form of a character rebuilding plan for pastoral leadership development.

Evolution of Character Formation

The issue of *character development* remained a primary focus of education for the first 150 years of history in the United States (Clowney, 2001). It is only in the last half century that education in character formation has been replaced by an emphasis on "neutral" values and on the construct of *personality* (Ries, 1999). Consequently, a separation of "character" and "personality" became a dominant trend in academic literature in those later years. The term "building character" was initially associated with family values. As schools began absorbing the responsibility of values formation as a result of social and economic changes, they adopted a focus on personality partly as a means of facilitating assessing and addressing the growing needs of their students. The construct of *character* became associated with "moral philosophy" and "volition," and the concept of personality with "individuality" (Sperry 1999), was something schools were already focusing on effectively. At the time, educators seem to assume they were well positioned to educate and build character. Yet toward the second half of the last century, the implicit under-estimation of character and an over-emphasis on personality began affecting the fields of counseling, education and religion (Warren, 1998).

Inevitably, this preference for personality development over character development led to significant problems, particularly as it related to children's behavior. An emphasis on self-actualization, self-discovery and self-confidence, at the expense of developing strength of character, seems to have contributed to an increase in serious behavioral and character issues in our society. An increase in the use of drugs, alcohol and tobacco, the number of teen pregnancies, and the amount of violence and other pathological behaviors in schools prompted educators to refocus efforts on *character building* over the "neutral" values of personality alone (Gobeau, 1998; Ries, 1999). A few authors even believe that the increase in the number and degree of anti-social behaviors are signs of a broader crisis of character (Hayes & Hagedorn, 2000; Sankar, 2003).

So what of all those youth from decades ago who grew up without a strong character foundation and who have become the adults and leaders of today? Interestingly enough, the formal research and scholarly literature remain relatively silent as to the outcomes of the generation that did not receive sufficient character development training during the '60s, '70s and perhaps beyond.

Even though there seems to be an increased awareness of the significance of character formation in adult development and maturity, character formation remains for the most part, poorly addressed in the classroom setting. One study, based on approximately five hundred teenagers from twenty different high-school classes, reveals that most are lacking contemporary models of strong and healthy character (Steen, Kachorek, & Peterson, 2003). Another study notes that although competency and character are both linked to success in adulthood, its discourse remains scarce in literature (Colby, James, & Hart, 1998).

If character is considered the conduit through which an individual's past and present flow into the future (Walton, 1988), and a gap in character development exists because of an emphasis on personality, one has to wonder what risks this gap presents to the adult population of the United States. One can only surmise that the rise in scandals among business leaders (Gray & Clark, 2002), political figures (Strong, 1999), athletes (Milton-Smith, 2002), and recently among the clergy (Sheler & Peterson, 2003) may be representative of an underlying need to institute programs for character rebuilding.

There are three more reasons to suggest that observable fissures in character development may warrant considering a character rebuilding agenda for young adults and adults within the Church in the United States. Each of these reasons is related to assumptions that no longer hold true. One assumption has to do with endurance or stability of character. Here the assumption was that strength of character is an enduring and stable attribute, something that current research disputes. The second assumption concerns the failures resulting from an over-reliance on and uncritical application of traditional personality assessments. Just because someone has passed a personality screening test for a leadership position does not mean the person has the appropriate character strength for leadership. The third reason is related to an incorrect assumption about religion and character. Again, just because someone appears to be religious does not guarantee a stable character. Plenty of recent evidence of this exists.

Regarding the assumption about the stability of character, although it is generally considered an enduring and stable attribute of a mature and successful adulthood (Colby, James & Hart, 1998; Sperry, 1999), some data suggest otherwise. For instance, the actual strength of character measured in 4,817 respondents after the September 11 attacks showed dramatic variance before and after the attacks. Levels of character strength measured 10 months after the terrorist attacks were lower, but remained slightly above the percentages observed before the incident. This may suggest that character is circumstantial and subject to significant change. Contrary to expectations (Peterson & Seligman, 2003), character does not seem as stable as depicted in the academic literature. In broader terms, adults are subject to complex patterns of change, yet their effects on character have not been properly studied (MacDermid, Franz, & DeReus, 1998). Of course, significant life events are in themselves moments of character building (Kaplan). If character is in fact an enduring and stable attribute in adults as purported, why is it that a significant variance in strength exists in this considerably large sample of adults?

The second false assumption has to do with the over-reliance on and uncritical application of traditional personality assessments, especially in job applications for leadership positions. For decades, personality assessments have been used by employers to search for the optimal job applicant (Black, 1994). Yet recently, some concerns have emerged about the possibility of "faking" personality assessments to mask true character (Mueller-Hanson, Heggestad, & Thornton, 2003). This concern has emerged from a review of the post-employment performance of candidates who were selected for executive positions by personality assessments. In conducting a study of these assessments, Hogan & Sinclair (1997) found that close to 50 percent of the executives selected using personality assessments had derailed as leaders. This supports an argument against personality assessment alone and for character assessment as a crucial selection criterion (Sperry, 1999). As character assessments become widespread for leadership and management positions, the questions about character strength, character fissures and character rebuilding are likely to increase. Even in the case of selection for pastoral leaders, personality tests are still used.

The third false assumption in support of character rebuilding is the presumption that if a person is religious, that the person also has a strong character. In other words, the assumption is that religiosity implies strength of character. Yet there are emerging studies that dispute this assumption. For instance, studies attempting to correlate religiosity and ethical behaviors are inconclusive (Clark & Dawson, 1996; Weaver & Agle, 2002). In fact, religiosity as a construct has been studied as a factor in compliance with the law (Grasmick, Kinsey, & Cochran, 1991), as a potential deterrent for drug usage (Khavari & Harmon, 1982), in relationship to delinquency avoidance (Jenson & Erickson, 1979), and as a modifier of ethical judgments (Clark & Dawson, 1996). The studies note that despite the common assumption to the contrary, being religious offers no guarantee of strength of character. Clearly, the data and experience suggest that, along with a rigorous religious education for the pastoral ministry leaders, emphasis in rebuilding character is equally relevant as a core competency.

As noted earlier, the character building of children more often than not falls on the shoulders of educators (Sharp, 2002). But it is not clear in the literature how character is maintained, developed and if necessary, rebuilt throughout adulthood, as circumstances change and fissures are uncovered. The evident gaps in character development research, the variability in character strength observed in large adult samples, the lack of emphasis on character as a component of personality assessments, and the abundant and spectacular failures of leaders across many disciplines suggest a large number of "fissures" in character strength that need attention.

There is an important point here for the leadership formation efforts within the Church. For the welcome focus on leadership formation in the many diocese and archdiocese of the United States to be effective in the long term, it will require a comparable focus on the processes of building, maintaining, and when necessary, rebuilding character strength. Otherwise, the risks of developing pastoral leaders with fragile characters to the lives of those who are called to serve are already apparent. As a matter of fact, can any organization that touches one or more aspects of people's lives in significant ways afford to have leaders with seriously flawed character?

Character and Leadership

In leadership theory, abuse of power and corruption are frequently studied along with issues of character strength (Lloyd, 1996). In the more recently developed models, such as charismatic leadership, the darker side of charisms is very much controlled through a leader's character (Sankar, 2003). It does not take a lot of imaging to clearly see how much damage a charismatic but sociopathic leader can inflict. Character strength also protects the servant leader from the darker side of the servant leadership model. One of the problems of the servant leadership model is that the notion of "service to others" can be distorted to the extent that it becomes a self-serving activity. If character strength is lacking in spiritual leadership, all that is left are soothing words and empty rhetoric. Even the simple adage "lead by example" is affected by character, since character forms the structure of one's actions.

The leader's character is considered foundational in achieving success as a leader (Clowney, 2001; Fertman & Van Linden, 1999; Hartman, 2001; Sankar, 2003). The leader is not only a passive role model of character, but also is expected to possess the skills and courage to correct indications of corruption in the organization (Barnett, 2002). Leaders without character are not truly leaders at all (Klann, 2007). Simply yet profoundly stated, Bennis (1998) defines leadership as "character in action."

There are studies that suggest that a leader's character strength is valued even more than the proficiency of leadership skills or ability to inspire with new ideas. In a seven-year survey of leadership expectations from thousands of respondents, honesty was rated as the highest expectation (87 percent), whereas competency was rated as the second-most important attribute (74 percent) (Best Practices, 1999). In a more recent study by Barlow and Jordan (2003), a character measurement scale was developed to assess character levels among front-line, middle and executive leadership positions. The results of this study of approximately 1,000 participants were used to refine formal and informal leadership-development programs within the entire organization. The authors observed that different degrees of character strength are required at the front-line, middle, and executive levels of leadership. Arguably, both of these studies demonstrate that knowledge of leadership models and even a proficient leadership skill set are secondary to the value of character in the perceived effectiveness of leadership.

Based on these observations, the topic of character formation in pastoral leadership is one that requires more focus and continued attention. Questions such as, "Are there common character fissures that may affect pastoral leadership?" "Is there a relationship between character strength and collaboration?" and "What kind of influences and power do pastoral leaders have over those entrusted to them, and what levels of character strength are appropriate to mitigate the negative influences?" are relevant to the effort to develop pastoral leaders who are effective beyond the numbers and dollars sense of the term.

In conducting workshops for parish staffs, we usually ask the attendees to define "character" and to illustrate character with one or two behaviors or attributes, and how they may affect leadership performance. Invariably this ends up being a very awkward and slightly embarrassing activity, since it seems we end up with as many definitions as we do participants. So before we explore additional important perspectives about strength of character, it seems appropriate to first present the fundamentals of character and character building.

Understanding More about "Character"

Although there are many definitions of the term "character," the preference here is to seek a practical definition of character that incorporates the common themes we emphasize in this book, namely, the so-called "softer" side of factors that influence leadership formation.

In researching the literature for a practical definition of *character*, the works of Len Sperry are helpful. In a lecture for the 1999 Annual Convention of the American Psychological Association (APA), he stated the following:

> My view is that character is that dimension of personality that describes how individuals conduct themselves in interpersonal and organizational situations and is shaped through the simultaneous development of self-identity and self-regulation. (Sperry, 1999, p.213)

From this definition, Sperry (1999) identifies two major pillars of *character* formation that also point to key aspects of pastoral leadership, that of self-identity and self-regulation.

Self-identity, as foundational to character formation and leadership, is a dynamic interaction among: (a) self as personal identity, (b) the self-in-relation to others in one-on-one relationships (dyads) and (c) self-within-community (small groups) and community of communities (or-

101

ganizations). What we know about ourselves as individuals affects our one-on-one relationships, small groups and communities, especially of those in leadership positions. But it's also true that the influences of one-on-one relationships influences a leader's relationships in groups, and also affects relationships within organizations. These interactions are very organic, so they tend to influence each other in complex ways.

Even in the secular world, these organic dimensions of self are recognized and form the basis of many leadership models. The identity of self as a leadership model is best illustrated by the "Great Man Theory" (also known as the "trait theories" of leadership). This theory defines leadership based on the study of the traits of great leaders, men and women, who projected the light of their inner strengths in many of the darkest moments of their times. The one-on-one relationships as a model of leadership dynamics came to the forefront of leadership theory primarily thanks to Fiedler's Leader-Member Exchange model (LMX). Many of the contingency leadership models address the dynamics of influence and power, of common interests, common values and common aspirations within the context of a small group.

New to the leadership discipline is the emphasis on the impact of group identity to the organization as a whole. These models, such as transformational leadership and servant leadership, emphasize vision, culture, values, etc. In this case, Wech, et al. (1998) make the following observations regarding the inevitable consequences of identity in small groups in larger organizations:

> After all, it is in the organizational context that group members are able to actualize their agency beliefs through involvement and participation. It should not be surprising, then, that in cohesive work groups, positive feelings members get from exercising their agency may spill over to the organization (p.474).

Throughout all these leadership models, the mutually nurturing dimensions of self-as-person, self-in-dyads and self-in-community (small and large groups) are illustrated as a one of the pillars sustaining character formation.

A dramatic and timely way to illustrate the value of the inter-relationships of these three dimensions of identity and how they relate to character strength and pastoral leadership is using the example of leaders in a parish that is being merged with other parishes as a result of the shortage of priests that is occurring in many dioceses. In merging parishes, the most immediate dimension of identity affected is that of the parish as community. For many years and even generations of families, the parish has been the center of Church identity. Baptisms, First Communions, Confirmations, Marriages, funerals, retreats, ministry work, friendships and the succession of pastors and associates form the experiences that give a parish its identity. Because identity at group (in the different parish ministries) and organization dimension (the parish) are at the forefront of a parish merger, there is considerable confusion, hurt and discontent. Losing any form of identity is never painless, nor should it be taken lightly. And since all three dimensions are so intimately linked to each other, personal identity is also affected in a parish merger. Leading this type of event not only takes strength of character in the self-discipline sense of the word, but more importantly, requires character strength in the form of identity.

In looking at secular leadership models for guidance on how to manage organizational mergers, there is much to learn about the mechanics and the tasks ("harder" side) of leadership. But what these secular models lack more often than not is a deeper understanding of the softer side of leadership, and in particular, the spiritual component of leadership. Here, the pastoral model has a lot more to offer, especially along the lines of character strength and the dynamics of identity.

In taking the pastoral leadership approach, we have already affirmed that leadership is a spiritual practice, and therefore, the leading of merging parishes must also be viewed as a spiritual event, a way to grow individually and collectively. If we attribute a spiritual quality to the dynamics of personal calling, to our vocation as coming from God, can we ignore the fact that collective callings and identities are also from God and are also dynamic? Here is where the pastoral leader exercises character strength in recognizing the past, the present and the future as a continuous identity journey that has God's fingerprints all over it. In this sense, merging parishes is not only about economy of scale, but also about the evolving identities within the same spiritual journey. The pastoral leader exercises influence in convincing the followers that the past speaks to the future, that what has been invested in the previous identity schemes is not lost or discarded, but used as a foundation for the emerging identity within the local Church. Under this view, merging parishioners are no longer just victims of economics or a personnel shortage, but active participants in building the new identities of the local Church in the diocese and in the United States. Yes, there must be some healing, but more importantly, the pastoral leader is charged with identity-forming, and identity-forming is part of character strength.

In a broader sense, the universal Church has also undergone significant changes that seem related to the evolving understanding of her identity and serves as guidance for pastoral leaders. For example, think about the reaction to the first non-Italian Pope, or consider the more nuanced and complete sense of Church that resulted from the prayerful thinking that occurred at the Second Vatican Council. How did these events affect our understanding of Church? Consider also the restoration of the diaconate as a permanent rank after the Church sustained the diaconate as a temporary rank for over half of her life. These are not changes that are cut off from the past, but changes that emerged from who the Church is and has been. In that way, they help us understand more about the Church and God's plans. In this same way but on a difference scale, the local Church also undergoes significant changes that are related to her identity, and the pastoral leader, clergy or laity uses the strength of character in the form of experiences in dealing with identity as a way to influence and lead the People of God.

Having presented *identity* in its three dimensions as one of the pillars of character formation, what follows is a discussion of the second pillar and more commonly associated attribute of character strength, that of *self-control*.

What we regard popularly as "self-control" is actually described in self-determination theory as a spectrum with "self-determination" at one end and "self-control" at the opposite end (Deci & Ryan, 1987). Self-determined behaviors "...are characterized by autonomous initiation and regulation," which means that a leader is capable of making decisions with minimal external compulsion. To be self-determining means to experience a sense of choice in initiating and regulating one's own actions. On the other end of the spectrum, "self-control" refers to behaviors that determine when to stop or override a powerful influence. To be self-controlled means to experience a sense of "will power" in the face of situations greater in might, influence or force.

Self-determination is being true to oneself in the face of external pressures, whereas self-control is recognizing when to say "enough" or "this needs to stop now" and make it so. Self-determination is the strength to decide *what is right over what is easy*, whereas self-control is the *strength to stop* when enough is enough. For example, the liturgist of a multi-cultural parish recognizes that each culture has its own forms of prayer and that seldom are there opportunities to conduct liturgies that express "One Body, One Church." As a pastoral leader, the liturgist can decide what is easy—that is, to continue facilitating liturgies for each cultural preference in the parish, or what is right—which is to foster opportunities to recognize the unity in the diversity. In this example, the pastoral leader shows strength of character by deciding what is right over what is easy.

In another example, the director of religious education and the business manager have difficulties tolerating one another. The director of religious education thinks the business manager has no understanding of Church, and the business manager believes the religious education director has no sense of responsible management practices. When all the staff meets with the pastor as the pastoral leadership team of the parish, the tension between these two is obvious to everyone. Finally, both are

105

approached by the pastor and told in clear language that their feud is not serving the parish well and hence needs to end. The pastor's intervention is a "wake-up" call for the business manager and the director of religious education. In recognizing that "enough is enough" and in finding ways to relieve the tensions between them, both these pastoral leaders would be exercising self-control over their perceived differences and participating actively (instead of passive-aggressively) in building cooperation among the parish staff.

In a third example, a head usher has access to the collection each Sunday, and as a result sees opportunities to take money that is not yet accounted for. Yet this pastoral minister has the strength of character to resist taking any money while at the same time advising the business manager of this risk and helping to mitigate those risks. This leader has demonstrated self-determination in bringing this situation to the attention of the business manager, and shows self-control in refraining from taking any monies. These examples illustrate how self-determination and self-control are both related to character strength, and how character strength is related to the leadership function.

Note that so far we make no distinction between applying character strength to secular leadership models or to the pastoral leadership model. As expected of the "softer" dimension of leadership, character strength applies to both classes of models. What is truly different is the process by which one builds character strength (self-determination and self-control) under secular leadership models in contrast with the possibilities afforded by an appropriate pastoral leadership model. In secular models, the process to build and sustain character is rarely explicitly identified, as it is assumed. On the other hand, for the pastoral leadership model, as noted earlier, leadership is defined as a spiritual practice and as such, character formation and continued formation are integral to a spiritual practice; as such they are both the focus of a sustained and serious effort to develop and maintain them.

For years, the formal research has demonstrated the value of religious and spiritual practices to character formation and transformation

(Redman, 2008). As children, teachers in both public and Catholic schools have seen how religion and spiritual practices have the ability to build character (Revell, 2008). In cases in which students transfer between schools, grade-school teachers have a rare opportunity to experience the differences between schools that focus on character formation and those which do not. After childhood and moving into adulthood, Catholics who continue benefiting from the sacraments and continue working seriously on their spiritual development are also able to benefit from character strengthening (Bloomberg, 2006). In fact, continued spiritual formation is directly related to the unfolding and reaffirmation of identity, character and ethical behaviors (Spohn, 1997). In cases in which adults fall victim to addiction in its many forms, the 12-step recovery programs used to restore and heal the person are essentially structured spiritual practices that refocus efforts on identity (Kellogg, 1993) and on defects in character (Grant, et.al., 2004).

From a practical, day-to-day point of view for most Catholics, the notions of identity (in its multiple dimensions) and character formation (self-determination and self-control) are integral parts of their religious beliefs and spiritual practices. The Lenten disciplines of self-denial (from giving up dessert, to not eating meat on Friday) were intended to build self-control, and in that way, build character. Similarly, the early discipline we learned as children to attend Mass regularly and to pay attention to the liturgy, the New Year's resolutions we strive to keep as adults, the attention and discipline required to learn the Lord's Prayer and Hail Mary as children, and the struggles we might experience as adults to the Sacrament of Penance (Reconciliation), are spiritual practices that help build up strength of character.

So why is it so seemingly difficult to see leadership as another spiritual practice, where identity and character are continually tested and formed? Why is the important connection between leadership and spiritual practices usually missing, or at best tenuous? The unnatural separation of spirituality from leadership is particularly difficult for the pastors of parishes who often see the demands of leadership pulling them away from their vocations. Yet leadership, properly construed and exercised, is a spiritual practice that can strengthen character and affirm the priestly vocation. Here lies one of the most powerful potentials and presumptions of the pastoral leadership model.

Indirectly, the spiritual practices that foster and nurture identity, self-determination and self-control are strengthening character, and in strengthening character these spiritual practices are also providing better leaders. Even though spiritual practices are much more available and easier to understand under the pastoral leadership model, the truth of the matter, supported by studies, is that spiritual practices that build character also benefit leadership in all industry sectors, because character strength is foundational to any form of leadership. For individuals in pastoral leadership, however, the connection between leadership practice and spiritual practice should be a direct one. Spiritual practices help build character, and since leadership is (or should be) a spiritual practice, leadership from a pastoral perspective becomes simply another opportunity to continue building character and identity.

This is an example in which pastoral leadership may lead the way by making a contribution to secular leadership models so that they recognize the value of character and find effective ways to develop it. In this sense, pastoral leadership models can help restore the important connection between leadership and spiritual practice.

So far we have made a case for character formation as a dimension of the "soft side" of leadership in general, and for pastoral leadership in particular. We also defined character in terms of two sustaining pillars, namely, identity and self-control. To review, the *identity influence* in the pastoral leadership model, consists of three dimensions that are constantly interacting and helping each other unfold. These are the dimensions of personal identity, identity in relation (dyads), and identity in community (small groups and organizations). When discussing what is normally referred to as *self-control*, we recognized that we are really talking about a continuum or a spectrum bound by *self-determination* and *self-control*. To be self-determining means to experience a sense of choice in initiating and regulating one's own actions; to be self-controlled means to experience a sense of "will power" in the face of situations greater in might influence, or force.

What remains to be discussed are some practical points for character formation within the pastoral leadership model. Naturally, many of the recommendations suggested are related to spiritual practices since our form of leadership is inherently a spiritual practice. This is the intent of the next and last section of this chapter.

Practices to Sustain Character Development

As we have indicated so far, power and influence, albeit in different degrees, are inherent to any leadership function. We assert that sustaining character development is crucial to the proper use of power and influence. For leaders who have been given much influence and power, character strength is a significant pillar that moderates and controls the proper use of this power and influence. But this is also true of any leader. When power and influence exceed character strength, or when there are expanding fissures and cracks in the leader's character, the pillar may not be able to effectively carry the weight of the responsibilities. Here is where unethical leadership behaviors start to emerge.

It's fascinating to see the significant number of leadership training programs, especially in the U.S. business sectors, that provide skills development and leadership models based on the assumption that participating leaders have the appropriate levels of character formation. In fact, many of the ethical programs in the U.S. business sectors have largely emerged to address the failures of well-trained leaders who used their power and influence inappropriately. In other words, these programs are generally remedial in nature, and are usually nothing more than over-simplified, yet earnest, attempts to fix a deeper flaw. The usual response to serious leadership failures is to require most of the senior management of the organization to undergo periodic ethics training, as if

109

they had simply failed a course in algebra or physics. Additional study and some serious time in the classroom will certainly not fix the problems of leadership. Most of these programs, it seems, are intended as organizational safeguards, designed to eliminate bad press and to mitigate the damage of lawsuits. None seem to address the fundamental problems in the characters of the leaders. According to a 2007 European Corporate Integrity Survey, flaws in these safeguards are expected to trigger the next generation of corporate scandals (NP, 2007).

Character formation is a complex process that takes time and energy to develop, and even more to sustain. Character formation deals with the issues of identity, self-control and self-determination, topics that go beyond the reach of most corporate ethics training programs. Even programs offered by the better business schools are limited in that they tend to be helpful mostly to those who already possess the character traits needed to behave ethically, even under difficult circumstances. With regard to strength of character, "preaching to the choir" does not address character formation, it merely provides a false sense of security. Yet, as we look at the pastoral leadership model, we see a more natural fit between character development and leadership. This is not to imply that pastoral leaders will possess flawless character. Events have demonstrated clearly that not to be the case. However, our major contention here is that leadership is a spiritual practice, and with that premise, leadership is also related to formation, to conversion and to a fundamental calling to be holy (not holier than thou). In promoting character building as part of spiritual growth, leaders and followers benefit. In performing the leadership function, evolving areas of identity, self-control and self-determination for the leaders and followers are discovered and possibly strengthened. In the pastoral leadership model, the dynamics of leadership and spiritual growth are woven into each other as a seamless fabric. So when a leadership failure occurs in this setting, the response can be a holistic one, which addresses the whole person as well as the whole failure. A leadership model that has as its premise that leadership is a spiritual practice will not only foster the development of character as an integral part of the person, but it will also be more likely to address all of the aspects of a leadership failure when it occurs.

There are many practical opportunities to consider with this perspective of how character building, spirituality and leadership are interrelated. We offer some suggestions both to illustrate the relationships, and to offer practical applications for integrating them into an ongoing leadership formation process.

Character Building is a Lifelong Endeavor

Character is related to values, and spirituality is the way we live those values with the aid of the Spirit. This is why definitions of spirituality always contain the notion of personal growth, of moving away from what is artificial and self-deceptive, from the inauthentic to the authentic. This is why so many times spirituality and psychology overlap (Kinerk, 1981). In promoting values and authenticity through spiritual formation, character is also being addressed. Just as the spiritual journey is a lifelong endeavor, so is character formation.

One suggestion for sustaining character strength is to perform periodic character checkups. Typical questions that could be posed in such a checkup include: "What values and strengths of the Spirit in my life (spirituality) are being used to support my leadership responsibilities?" "What new discoveries am I making about myself as I perform the leadership function?" "What weaknesses or fissures have I noted, and what are the risks of working on these fissures while performing the leadership functions?" "Are there any important functions or responsibilities I have as a pastoral leader that may be seriously affected by these weaknesses, or that would aggravate the fissures?"

A periodic checkup on character strength can take many forms, including theological reflection, journaling, examination of conscience, professional character assessment tools and Christian psychological counseling. What is relevant to the pastoral leadership model is the need to periodically conduct these check-ups, to feel more confident in how the strengths of character are being applied to the leadership function, and to take advantage of being a leader to discover more about the artificialities and self-deceptions we may be allowing ourselves. This way leadership is not only a task, but is another window to help move from the inauthentic to the authentic. That, after all, is also spiritual growth.

Identity Gives Purpose and Perspective

Leadership, especially in turbulent times, is most related to identity because identity provides a sense of purpose and perspective when dealing with an uncertain future. In the language of organizational development, the identity of the organization is expressed in its mission and its vision. Leaders who are able to harness the power of identity provide their groups or organizations with cohesiveness, resolve, resilience and a feeling of security. When we speak here of groups and organizations, we are also referring to ministry groups and parishes. Many ministry groups and parishes have mission and vision statements that may seem like a management technique borrowed from the business sector, but in fact have the value of being able to crystallize identity and provide purpose and perspective. As consultants to parish pastoral teams, we many times find ourselves conducting "envisioning" exercises, leadership team retreats and coaching sessions with pastoral staff to help foster a sense of identity for the parish or ministry. Whether in a ministry, in the parish, in a non-profit institution, in government or in the business sector, leaders are also managers of identity.

For better or worse, spirituality as a discipline has been primarily associated with individual growth, and therefore much more with individual or personal identity. Emphasis on self-in-relation (identity in relation to dyads) and self-in-groups and organizations, is not emphasized enough in our Western individualistic culture. Although sometimes helpful in completing a project, work teams are often more a matter of individuals working under a rubric of a collective than they are a group of individuals working as a community. For example, generally, few members of a work team are able to subordinate their egos to the needs of the project. Union gets confused with unity. Tying two cats together by their tails and throwing them over a clothesline does not yield unity; it yields union at the expense of unity.

Unity, after all, is more than just sharing the same clothesline. It requires a suspension of our presumptions, preferences and biases for the sake of a greater good. Leadership as a spiritual discipline requires that we subordinate our needs to a greater good. Perhaps business, government and non-profit organizations need the equivalent of a spiritual director to help these organizations develop a meaningful and authentic sense of the other. In that way, the strength of character of the organization may be increased and the service to their constituencies will be improved.

In this context, by addressing the sense of identity in its multiple dimensions (self, dyads, groups, organizations, even movements) the pastoral leadership model highlights a major cultural weakness and offers opportunities for significant improvements in purpose and perspective beyond what we can learn from the business sector. Within pastoral leadership, what we know about effective "work teams" remains relevant, but with a spiritual component there is an opportunity to build spiritual community, a spiritual identity that nurtures all other dimensions of identity. Now dyads can also work as "spiritual partnerships" and larger organizations can actually envision the power of purpose and perspective that "One Bread, One Body" offers an a parish or diocese.

Identity gives purpose and perspective, so we can always benefit from secular models up to a point. But what they can teach us about living as a *communio,* as Church, is quite limited. The pastoral leadership model offers the opportunity to foster spiritual identity processes in dyads, groups and parishes in a way secular leadership models can't even dream about. In fostering spiritual identities, we also energize our ministries and parishes with purpose and perspective, even in turbulent times. At the same time, we might be able to influence, for the better, the evolution of leadership models in other sectors.

Self-control and the Other Cheek

This is probably the most commonly known spiritual practice affecting leadership. Spiritual formation thrives to achieve discipline and self-control (Zell & Baumeister, 2005). It's well known that spirituality and religion set standards for what is right and what is not, for establishing behaviors that are acceptable and unacceptable, for promoting a search for meaning over surrender to selfish passions, for offering ways to deal with inappropriate desires, for controlling raw emotions, and for administering a fair dose of guilt if self-control fails (Bland, 2008).

What is less known is the relationship between self-control and leadership practice. J. Clifton Williams explains how self-control is directly related to effective leadership:

> If our character and emotional control remain intact only when we are treated fairly and with kindness, they fail us when we need them most. And, if they fail us when put to the test, we should not expect to maintain a strong influence. To be effective leaders we must consistently live by our values and maintain emotional control when under fire. (Williams, 1997, p.9)

For a pastoral leader, the best example of self-control is having the left cheek available when struck by a follower on the right cheek (Mt 5: 38-42), even if just figuratively. It's going to hurt, be embarrassing, and make the blood boil. But there is a clear distinction between reacting emotionally to the incident and acting as a leader-in-control. This may represent a new form of self-control for some, but nevertheless, it's a discovery that may need to be addressed and managed under spiritual formation.

Self-determination is Being Able to Lead Yourself

In a study of unsuccessful leaders, George and McLean (2007) made an interesting discovery that leaders who had failed seemed inca-

114

pable of leading themselves. This makes intuitive sense in that someone who is unable to manage his or her life effectively is unlikely to be able to lead others very well.

We have noted that, as a pillar of character formation, self-determination is essentially the ability to lead oneself. Having a keen sense of where one is going and being able to take oneself in that direction is an essential element of character and of leadership:

> Highly effective leaders have a well-developed "self-structure." That is, they know who they are and where they are going. They know because they have made decisions about themselves. They are internals. While acknowledging that they are not always in control of their environments, they nevertheless do not feel controlled by others. They assume full responsibility for their actions and emotions regardless of what others do or say. (Williams. 1997. P.9)

A spiritual journey typically involves learning to "lead oneself" out of dry spells, failures, hostilities, urges and passions, fears and distractions, among other challenges. The spiritual journey provides a sense of direction, and most directions have plenty of obstacles. Part of spiritual formation involves developing a better understanding of these obstacles and finding ways, with the Spirit, to move forward. This is the meaning of "leading oneself," of self-determination; and this is also an attribute that affects the performance of any leader.

Discernment Skills are Integral to Leadership

Another less-obvious connection to character that secular leadership models overlook, probably because of its spiritual content, is the need for well-developed discernment skills. Not every leadership decision requires extensive reflection and prayer, yet leadership at any level tends to involve decisions that can result in life-defining moments, and life-defining moments should not be addressed casually. In fact, in his article "The discipline of building character," J.L. Badaracco observes that the three most prevalent types of defining moments for managers and leaders are related to identity of self, identity in groups and identity in organizations (Badaracco, 1998). If leadership involves dealing with defining moments, and if defining moments are about identity, it stands to reason that discernment should also be a natural competency for leadership, given that our identities are defined and formed in the Spirit. We refer to the process of being defined and formed in the Spirit as our spiritual journey.

There are many definitions of discernment according to the multiple spirituality traditions in the Church, but for practical purposes, we distinguish discernment from decision-making skills, or even from critical thinking skills, in the following way:

> Discernment is a time-honored spiritual discipline that helps us engage our intuition and spiritual senses as well as our rationality. Its purpose is to explore the relations between our longings, souls, knowledge, power, purpose, life, the divine, and love. (English, Fenwick, & Parsons, 2003, p. 24)

For a leader to reflect on (and even sometimes agonize) over a big decision is part of what it means to be a leader. Some of the best leaders, whether secular or religious, will take time to reflect, think through the implications of each decision, dig deeply into their minds and souls for insights, consult with others, and sometimes... even pray. What we suggest is that pastoral leadership can go beyond these practices and freely benefit and contribute to discernment processes. In other words, we propose that discernment competency, in the spiritual and traditional sense of the phrase, is also an integral part of leadership as a spiritual practice. Leadership provides many opportunities to exercise and develop discernment competencies. To better understand the implications and practice of discernment skills within the pastoral leadership model, we have only to look at the great founders of movements and spiritual traditions in the Church. Many of them had to make life-

116

changing decisions, and their biographies (and autobiographies) illustrate how serious they were about their leadership role and the discernment process. We each have, perhaps to lesser degrees, comparable opportunities to integrate discernment into the leadership function.

Effective pastoral leadership as a spiritual practice is not only about prayer, meditation and contemplation; it's also about discernment *competency*. Pastoral leaders are not only "good" at discerning, they are expected to be exceptional at discernment.

In this chapter we focused on the second attribute of the "softer" side of pastoral leadership, that of character formation. We have explored the history of character formation in the United States and seen that, although character has always been part of traditional education, during the middle of the previous century the emphasis shifted to personality. Consequently, character development took second place, and generations of children, many now adults, were deprived of opportunities to build strong character. Now, many of these fissures are showing up in the form of leaders who can't lead themselves, especially in the American business sector. Yet in looking at the defining elements of character formation and understanding how both leadership and character formation are related to spiritual processes, we were able to offer practical suggestions on rebuilding and sustaining the formation of character.

Just as "personal calling" and "vocation were offered as the first attribute of the "softer" side of leadership in introducing this chapter on character formation, we use this chapter to introduce the next chapter on the primacy of relationships as the third dimension of pastoral leadership.

Case Study

A group of participants in a lay ministry development course were asked to canvas their respective parishes and find an unfulfilled need. Each participant was then asked to develop a new ministry program to address this unfulfilled need.

After two months of research, discernment and writing, each student came up with a feasible proposal on how to structure, operate and sustain the new ministry. Each participant gave a ten-minute presentation on how he or she would approach the pastor and the bishop for approvals.

Upon the completion of the last presentation, their instructor and facilitator, Deacon Bob Snyder, remained pensive for a long time. Finally, Deacon Bob rose and communicated his concern. "All of you have done a great job of researching, organizing and systematically presenting your proposals," he stated. "But I have to admit that your professional experiences are showing. Each proposal is a solid business plan, not a ministry implementation plan. Something that is missing in every single proposal is to demonstrate how the new ministry leaders are going to ensure a spiritual component to the new ministry activities." After more discussion, the participants still were not sure how to incorporate spiritual enabling in their plans.

Questions for Discussion:

1. Based on your personal experiences, discuss ways that ministry leaders can become "enablers" of spirituality in ministry activities.

2. Certain ministries are more oriented toward a specific relational mode. For instance, Eucharistic Adoration, as a ministerial activity, is oriented to the suprapersonal relational modes. Ushers, as a ministry, are oriented to the interpersonal modes. In groups, create a list of ministries and by consensus, establish their relational mode orientation.

3. Pick a ministry for which most group members have a basic working knowledge. Discuss which relational modes seem lacking, and what enabling activities could be instituted to ensure a broader base of relational modes.

Workshop Activities

As a group exercise, we ask each group to come up with three character flaws they have seen in other leaders (at work, or elsewhere) and discuss the potential impact of those flaws had they been present in a pastoral leader. The exercise is intended to create awareness of how character strengths and weaknesses affect the leadership functions, and can help reinforce what has been said in this Chapter about character and leadership.

Personal Reflective

1. As an individual exercise, take the *VIA Inventory of Strengths* from the VIA Institute on Character (see http://viacharacter.org). This website offers free and in-depth (fee) validated assessments of character along 24 character strengths. The assessment takes 30-40 minutes to complete and prioritizes all 24 strengths.

2. Take a look at each of the top three strengths (1-3) and journal on how you believe these character strengths are an advantage to you as a pastoral leader.

3. Now take a look at each of the bottom three strengths (22-23-24) and journal on how you believe these character traits may affect your functions as a leader and how you would compensate for them.

Chapter References

Badarraco, J.L. (1998). The discipline of building *character. Harvard Business review*, 76(2), 115-124.

Barlow, C.B., Jordan, M., & Hendrix, W.H. (2003). Character assessment: An examination of leadership levels. *Journal of Business and Psychology*, 17, 563-584.

Barnett, R. (2002). Character leadership. *Executive Excellence*, 19(10), 20.

Bennis, W. (1998). The character of leadership. In M. Josephson & W. Hanson (Eds.). *The power of character. Prominent Americans talk about life, family, work, values and more.* San Francisco: Jossey-Bass.

Best Practices. (1999) Establishing the credibility factor. In A.H. Bell & D.M. Smith. *Learning Team Skills.* (p.14). Upper Saddle River: Prentice Hall.

Black, K.R. (1994). *Personality screening in employment. American Business Law Journal, 32,* 69-124.

Bland, E. (2008). An appraisal of psychological & religious perspectives of self-control. *Journal of Religion and Health, 47*(1), 4-16.

Blomberg, D. (2006). The Formation of Character: Spirituality Seeking Justice. *Journal of Education & Christian Belief, 10*(2), 91-110.

Clark, J.W., & Dawson, L.E. (1996). Personal religiousness and ethical judgments: An empirical analysis. *Journal of Business Ethics, 15,* 359-372.

Clowney, K. (2001). New definition of leadership. *Executive Excellence, 18(3),* 8.

Colby, A., James, J.B., Hart, D. (Eds.). *Competence and character through life.* Chicago: University of Chicago Press.

Deci, E.L., & Ryan, R.M. (1987). The support of autonomy and the control of behavior. *Journal of Personality and Social Psychology, 53,* 1024-1037.

English, L.M., Fenwick, T.J., & Parsons, J. (2003). *Spirituality of adult education and training.* Malabair, FL: Krieger.

Fertman, C.I., & Van Linden, J.A. (1999). Character education: An essential ingredient for youth leadership development. *NASSP Bulletin, 83(609),* 9-15.

George, B. & McLean, A. (2007). Why leaders lose their way. Strategy & Leadership, 35(3), 4-11.

Gobeau, D. (1998). Building character in sports a winning brand of ministry. *National Catholic Reporter, 34*(12), 21-22.

Grant, B.F., Stinson, F.S., Dawson, D., Chou, S.P., Ruan, W.J., Pickering, R.P. (2004). Co-occurrence of 12 month alcohol and drug use disorders and personality disorders in the United States. *Archives of General Psychiatry*, 61(4), 361-368.

Grasmick, H.G., Kinsey, K., & Cochran, J.K. (1991). Denomination, religiosity and compliance with the law: A study of adults. *Journal for the Scientific Study of Religion, 30,* 99-107.

Gray, K.R., & Clark, G.W. (2002). Addressing corporate scandals through business education. *International Journal on World Peace, 19*, 43-62.

Hartman, E.M. (2001). Character and leadership. Business & *Professional Ethics Journal, 20(2),* 3-21.

Hayes, B.G., & Hagedorn, W.B. (2000). A case for character education. *Journal of Humanistic Counseling, Education & Development, 39,* 2-3.

Hogan, R., & Sinclair, R.R. (1997). For love or money? Character dynamics in consultation. Consulting Psychology Journal: Practice and Research, 44, 256-267.

Jenson, G.F., & Erickson, M.L. (1979). The religious factor and delinquency: Another look at the hellfire hypothesis. In R. Wuthnow (Ed.). *The religious dimension: New directions in quantitative research* (pp. 157-177). New York: Academic Press.

Kaplan, R. (1993). The person behind the leader: The value of personal development. *Executive Development, 6,* 24-25.

Kellogg, S. (1993). Identity and recovery. *Psychotherapy: Theory, practice and training*, 30(2) 235-244.

Khavari, K.A., & Harmon, T.M. (1982). The relationship between the degree of professed religious belief and use of drugs. *International Journal of the Addictions, 17,* 847-857.

Kinerk, E. (1981).Toward a method for the study of spirituality. *Review for Religious*, 40, 3-19.

Klann, G. (2007). *Building character: Strengthening the heart of leadership.* San Francisco, CA: Jossey-Baas

Lloyd, B. (1996). The paradox of power. *Futurist, 30*, 60.

MacDermid, S., Franz, C.E., & DeReus, L.A. (1998). Adult character: Agency, communion, insight and the expression of generativity in mid-life adults. In A. Colby, J. James and D. Hart (Eds). *Competence and character through life.* Chicago: University of Chicago Press.

Milton-Smith, J. (2002). Ethics, the Olympics and the search for global values. *Journal of Business Ethics, 35*, 131-142.

Mueller-Hanson, R., Heggestad, E.D., & Thornton, G.C. (2003). Faking and selection: Considering the use of personality from select-in and select-out perspectives. *Journal of Applied Psychology, 88*, 348-355.

N.P. (2007, May). Prepare for another Enron. *International Financial Law Review, 26*(5), 9-9.

Peterson, C., & Seligman, M.E.P. (2003). Character strength before and after September 11. *Psychological Science, 14*, 381-384.

Redman, D. (2008). Stressful Life Experiences and the Roles of Spirituality among People with a History of Substance Abuse and Incarceration. *Journal of Religion & Spirituality in Social Work, 27*(1/2), 47-67.

Reis, E. (1999). A question of character. *Techniques: Making Education & Career Connections, 74(5),* 26-29.

Revell, L. (2008). Spiritual Development in Public and Religious Schools: A Case Study. *Religious Education, 103*(1), 102-118.

Sankar, Y. (2003). Character not charisma is the critical measure of leadership excellence. *Journal of Leadership & Organizational Studies, 9(4)*, 45-55.

Sharp, K. (2002). Building character: Discovering and developing character traits. *Journal of School Health, 72,* 303-304.

Sheler, J.L., & Peterson, T. (2003). A stubborn scandal. U.S._*News & World Report, 134(21),* 30-32.

Sperry, L. (1999). Character assessment in the executive selection process. *Consulting Psychology Journal: Practice and Research, 51,* 211-217.

Spohn, W. (1997). Spirituality and ethics: Exploring the connections. *Theological Studies, 58*(1), 109-123.

Steen, T.A., Kachorek, & L.V., Peterson, C. (2003). Character strengths among youth. *Journal of Youth and Adolescence, 32,* 5-16.

Strong, R.A. (1999). Pondering the post-scandal election dynamic. *Christian Science Monitor, 91(75),* 11.

Walton, C.C. (1988). The ethic of character: The personal dimension. In C.C. Walton (Ed.). *The moral manager.* Cambridge: Ballinger.

Warren, H.A. (1998). The shift from character to personality in mainline Protestant thought, 1935-1945. *Church History, 67,* 537-555.

Weaver, G.R., & Agle, B.R. (2002). Religiosity and ethical behavior in organizations: A symbolic interactionist perspective. *Academy of Management Review, 27*(1), 77-97.

Wech, B.A., Mossholder, H.N., Steel, R.P., & Bennett, N. (1998). Does work group cohesiveness affect individuals' performance and organizational commitment? *Small Group Research*, 29, 472-494.

Williams, J. (Fall, 1997). Self-control. *Baylor Business Review, 15*(2), 9.

Zell, A., & Baumeister, R. (2005). Religion, morality, and self-control: values, virtues, and vices. *Handbook of the psychology of religion and spirituality* (pp. 412-432). New York: Guilford Press

The "soft" side of leadership

Framework that guides our choices

Discernment
Envisioning (Worldview)
Spiritual community
Primacy of relationships
Building Character
Your Calling

PASTORAL LEADERSHIP

Goals
Processes
Working together
Getting things done
Exercising influence & power

Framework that guides our actions

The "hard" side of leadership

*"Leadership is always dependent on the context,
but the context is established by the relationships we value."*
Margaret Wheatley

CHAPTER 5

Relationships as Influence

What we are about to discuss in this chapter represents the most significant underlying dynamic that makes leadership, and more specifically, pastoral leadership, a spiritual practice that is unique to the leadership discipline. At the core of the principle of *leadership as a spiritual practice* is a more profound understanding of the meaning, purpose and capabilities of interpersonal relationships. In other words, it is within the domain of interpersonal relationships, where spirituality and leadership converge, to generate what we are defining as the pastoral leadership model. Just as relationships are an essential component of spirituality (relationship with God, relationships with others, relationship with self), the practice of leadership is also about relationships. In the pastoral leadership model, these same relationships (God, others and self) are dominant.

As we said earlier in the book, leadership is about interpersonal influences; about the "softer" dimension of the leadership function. Similarly, what is spirituality without being able to establish a relationship with God, and self? Or for that matter, what is leadership without being able to establish relationships with others? And why can't leadership also be about relationships with God and with self? Yet as we are about to see, the popular understanding of interpersonal relationships in Western society is heavily transactional in nature, making it much more difficult to appreciate the more profound potential of leadership as a spiritual discipline.

We have argued in the previous chapters that spirituality is about interpersonal relationships -- those between individuals and those inclusive of the divine. In fact, spirituality is a function of the *quality* of relationships with others much more than anything else (Hall, et al., 1998). Said in a different way, creating spiritual awareness or working spiritual projects individually becomes more effective when there are a healthy set of interpersonal relationships to work with. In this sense, it's easy to see how a strong relational maturity has a high correlation with a strong spiritual maturity (Tenelshof, 2000). Even from an empirical point of view, there are studies that suggest a link between improved levels of interpersonal relationships and spirituality (Hall & Brokaw, 1995; Hall, Brokaw, Edwards, & Pike, 1998). As one of the most referenced studies on spirituality, Waaijman (2002) notes, "Our reflections lead to the conclusion that the object of the study of spirituality can be defined as: *the divine-human relational process* considered from the viewpoint of transformation" (p. 6). Then, central to spirituality is the relationship with the divine, the relationship with self and the relationship with others, all with a transformational objective.

If spirituality is fundamentally a relational phenomenon, so is leadership. Leadership may be about power, but leadership is also about relationships.

> During a parish leadership retreat, the pastor was trying to emphasize the need to avoid stovepipes between ministries and the need to foster interconnections that are essential to parish life. Previous to the retreat, the pastor had reflected on how well structured the organization of the parish is, but how little influence the structure had on parish life. At the beginning of the retreat and in front of all ministry leaders he placed 50 loose beads on top of the table and said "This is a rosary." The

126

leaders were perplexed and told the pastor that 50 loose beads hardly make a rosary and that the connections to the beads were missing. To that the pastor replied, "So just because we have 50 ministries in our parish, it does not mean we have a healthy and progressing parish life. We also need to look at the connections."

In the book "Leadership for the Twenty-first century," author Joseph C. Rost performs a rare and much-needed analysis of the definitions of leadership since the beginning of the discipline, and then composes a detailed landscape of where leadership theory was, where it is, and where it is headed. He looks at original definitions of leadership from 1900 to 1979, discusses evolving trends that emerged in the 1980s, and connects much of the corporate America scandals and ethical problems observed in the 1990s as a source for the evolution of some of the newer models of leadership. Yet after such a comprehensive analysis, his conclusion about leadership is simple: *leadership is about relationships*. The author Ed Weymes, in "Relationships not leadership sustain successful organizations" (*Journal of Change Management*, 4, 319-331) emphasizes, "The terms leadership and relationship are connected, since one cannot occur without the other" (p.319).

Of course, leadership is about power and influence, about traits and attributes, about circumstances and contingencies, about charisms and transformational efforts to get things done. But deep down, leadership is also about relationships. Notably, the definition of leadership that best satisfies Rost's comprehensive search is *"leadership is an influence relationship among leaders and followers who intend real changes that reflects their mutual purposes."* Curiously, if you add to Rost's definition of leadership the connections with the spiritual domain (God's intentions as well as our mutual purposes), you end up with a working definition of *spirituality*. Leadership is a phenomenon that occurs within a web of interrelationships, and in the case of pastoral leadership, relationships that also include the spiritual domain.

As we have said many times, the overlapping of spirituality and leadership is uncanny. Although the origins of leadership theory were based on the figure and personality of the leader (Great Man Theory), much of the recent thinking on leadership theory points toward a more in-depth understanding of the interpersonal relationships between leaders and followers. The beginnings of modern theories of leadership are attributed to Thomas Carlyle (1841), a Scottish philosopher who postulated that the chronicles of history are fundamentally the narratives of great personalities that gathered and guided the masses. What makes Carlyle's proposal interesting and relevant to pastoral leadership models is his statement that a leader is above all *a spiritual person*, which seems to have become lost in the contingency modeling of leadership proposed by behavioral scientists and the leadership theories that followed. Leadership was about a person at the service of history, but more importantly, that person was a spiritual leader.

Is this not what we expect from our parish pastors? We believe there are too many instances in which pastors and priests are forced into a weak position, a position for which they are not trained, for which they do not have expertise, and for which they have no interest at all because it is foreign to their priestly vocation. Too many times we have seen priests who are forced to take executive coaching classes, 360° feedback sessions, and sometimes even MBA classes to make them better executives in a parish. Yet the effects of these training sessions, primarily secular in nature, create a spiritual divide for which they struggle to find answers. Although these executive training sessions have value, should we not provide training sessions and techniques that place our pastors and priests into a stronger position, a position for which they have been trained and formed most of their adult lives?

Here is where leadership as a spiritual practice has value to pastors and associates, as well as to deacons, religious women and ministry leaders because it is a form of leadership that can be enacted from a spiritual foundation. In fact, for the pastoral leadership model, relationships—both among ourselves and with the divine— are the antecedents to action.

One of the most significant challenges for understanding pastoral leadership as a model is not necessarily a lack of understanding of leadership principles or a lack of understanding spiritual processes. The truth is that most experienced ministry leaders have a good understanding of both. What seems the most challenging in fully understanding what we suggest as the Pastoral Leadership model is the *interdependency* of these two endeavors—leadership and spirituality— by means of relational dynamics.

In attempting to understand the deeper possibilities of interpersonal relationships and the implications for leadership and spirituality, we have to recognize some serious challenges. Some of these challenges are discussed in the paragraphs that follow.

Challenges of Interpersonal Relationships

Although having a deeper practical understanding of interpersonal relationships is essential to both spirituality and leadership, we also have to recognize there are serious challenges that can undermine the understanding, development and maturity of interpersonal activity. Some of these challenges include: the perception that leadership in our society is mostly enacted as an instrumental function (as task-oriented) rather than as a relational orientation; that we live in a worldview that values transactional (instrumental) relationships more than formational relationships (relationships that contribute to the growth of an individual); that family dysfunctions seriously limit our ability to achieve relational maturity; that we lack a language to fully express what occurs as interpersonal relationships mature; and that the current cultural bias is to view relationships as a value irrelevant to leadership rather than as a fundamental human value. Recognizing the limiting effects these challenges pose in exploring, understanding and sustaining deeper levels of formational relations, including relationships with the divine, is a major step toward internalizing the fundamentals of pastoral leadership.

Because being able to understand and overcome many of these misconceptions is essential to understanding leadership as a spiritual practice, we take the time to present each one with some detail, and at the same time explain the implications they have on leadership as a spiritual practice.

Instrumental Emphasis of Leadership

It should not come as a surprise that in the general discipline of leadership the most common understanding of leadership is associated with "doing," with "getting things done" and with "mobilizing followers" to fulfill specific objectives. Earlier in this book we described this task-oriented emphasis (instrumental or pragmatic approach) as the "harder" side of leadership. What we intend to illustrate in this section is that the instrumental preferences dominant in our culture make it easier to define, enact and measure leadership, but at the same time create a significant obstacle to envisioning leadership as a relational principle, and even more difficult in understanding leadership as a spiritual practice.

This emphasis on the "harder" or pragmatic side of leadership as the dominant approach to leadership seems evident in both the practice of leadership and in the theoretical development of models and theories.

One of the ways to show the urgency and relevance of relationships to practical enactment of leadership is to review surveys conducted with top leaders and managers. For example, according to a study conducted by Leadership IQ in 2005—a Washington, D.C.-based leadership and training company—nearly 50% of newly hired employees failed within the first 18 months at their job because of poor interpersonal skills (Expansion Management, Nov 2005, p. 2). Two studies with 265 executives, directors, managers, business owners and consultants were conducted to find out what makes a leader effective. To them, relational skills were crucial to continued growth and development as leaders (Investment News, July 2004). In 2009, Jim Sirbasku, CEO of a company specializing in personnel assessment and human resource management called Profiles International, commented on reasons for managerial and leadership failures. He noted that "one of the findings is that poor interpersonal and communications skills are one of the most prevalent reasons." In a Harvard Business Review article entitled "Ten fatal flaws that derail leaders" by Jack Zenger and Joseph Folkman, poor interpersonal and relational skills were a major cause of leadership failures. In another survey of 350 U.S. organizations conducted by MCA Associates in Philadelphia (Training & Development, March 1997), the No. 1 negative leadership behavior was poor interpersonal skills. Essentially, the tendency of leaders to perceive individuals as just "followers" reduces the leadership function to a transactional relationship mandated by the organization. Although most leaders would recognize relationships as crucial to the enactment of leadership, when actual styles are assessed, most managers and leaders (from a sample of 2,500 managers) exhibited a style in practice that was more task-oriented than relational (Connerly & Penderson, 2005).

The preference for pragmatic or instrumental leadership styles is not only practical, but is also present in theoretical discourse. In surveying the academic literature within this discipline, the two most recognized leadership styles seem to be the *transactional leadership* style and the *transformational leadership* style (Bono & Judge, 2004). These two styles are relevant to leadership because they address two major realities of leadership, that of the "human activity" or the softer side (employee relations, social networking, customer relations) as well as the harder dimensions of leadership (measurable goals, quantifiable objective).

More to the point, transactional leadership styles refer to a more externally oriented emphasis with a strong accent on maintaining strict procedural controls and establishing processes of compliance, many times at the expense of interpersonal sensitivities (Morhart, Herzog, & Tomczak, 2009). Bass (1990) notes that "Much leadership today subscribes to a transactional framework where … managers engage in a transaction with their employees: They explain what is required of them and what compensation they will receive if they fulfill these requirements" (Bass 1990, p. 19–20). Transactional leadership may have greater potential predictive value than transformational style (Vecchio, Justin, & Pearce, 2008) and therefore produce more immediate and tangible results for the small business. Inevitably, there is always some degree of overlap between both of these styles.

So why does this pragmatic or instrumental preference for leadership represent a challenge to understanding the possibilities of deeper relationships and therefore make it harder to accept leadership as a spiritual practice? This pragmatic approach to leadership reflects a strong predisposition toward transactional ways of thinking. We become so predisposed in our thinking by the *leadership-as-action* approach that it affects the way we view and enact possible forms of relationships. Essentially, relational activity is viewed through the prism of transactional activity. In other words, we are stuck in a transactional paradigm and develop a "giving and taking" language to explain relational phenomena.

When executives, for example, are asked if they would implement *Spirituality in the Workplace* as a program within their respective organizational cultures, the first question they tend to ask is "What are we going to get out of this?" Trying to communicate the depth of relational possibilities using transactional language is akin to attempting to explain religion using business language. It is possible to explain religion using business analogies, but much is lost because there are realities in religion that are difficult to explain or even illustrate with a business-oriented vocabulary.

The best way to explain religion is by using the language of theology, not business. Similarly, the way to understand the depth and possibilities of relationships is by recognizing the limits of this transactional predisposition and learning to use relational language.

Transactional-oriented Worldview

The second of multiple challenges that affects the abilities each of us has to explore, understand and sustain deeper levels of formational relations, including relationships with the divine, is the transactional-oriented worldview of mainstream Western society. From a global perspective, the definition of leadership is affected by the history and culture of a people. In this way, different cultures view leadership in different ways. In looking at leadership from a multicultural viewpoint, the strengths and weaknesses of our own cultural lens become more apparent, and it becomes easier to visualize the roles of interpersonal relationship experiences in relation to the enactment of leadership.

> Some of the biggest challenges in relationships come from the fact that most people enter a relationship in order to get something: they're trying to find someone who's going to make them feel good. In reality, the only way a relationship will last is if you see your relationship as a place that you go to give, and not a place that you go to take. (Anthony Robbins, *Awaken the Giant Within).*

A frequently stated perception from other cultures is that Westerners seem persistently more task-oriented and prefer a low-context power relationship (Wong, Wong, & Pi, 2007). In studies involving comparisons of Western and Chinese business leaders, for example, direct, task–oriented methods were rated more effective by Western managers than by Chinese managers, whereas methods involving interpersonal relationships were rated as less effective (Yukl, Fu, & McDonald, 2003). The Western ways seem to heavily favor a transactional way of thinking and acting, whereas Southeast Asian cultures, for example, tend to be more relational in their ways.

When business men and women travel to China, for example, they are exposed to "guanxi" (pronounced *guan-shee*), which literally means "relationships" and refers to an ancient network of informal relationships in various degrees that determine if and how business is conducted in China and some parts of East Asia. In a "guanxi," or relational dominant society, dealings depend on reputations and trust as a way to moderate opportunistic behaviors. In these types of systems, decisions are slow because it takes time to find the right relationship. So the relationship is not simply a courtesy before a business transaction takes place (as would be expected in the Western culture) but is an ongoing process in which individuals, and even the company, are expected to maintain a reliable and steady relationship if they intend to conduct continued business with the Chinese. Other societies and cultures, such as certain African tribes, Egypt, and some Latin American countries, also display similar relational paradigms (Lovett, Simmons, & Kali, 1999).

Since the interpretation of *leadership* in our society seems to carry a noticeable preference for *task* more than *relational* orientation, a natural consequence of this "primacy of action-over-relations" is that ministry leadership and spirituality are inevitably considered more of a task than a relationship. There is nothing right or wrong about this preference. However, it does represent an area of caution for activities in the pastoral work. The emphasis on *action* may lead to a functional view of ministry, religion and spiritual endeavors. In his book titled "Reclaiming our priestly identity," Father David Toups (STD) points to the damage this transactional mentality (which he calls "functionality") is having on the image of the priesthood. He observes,

> The priest who falls into the trap of functionalism loses sight of his true self-identity as a priest of Jesus Christ. Certainly, charity should be the operative key to everything that the priest does, but he must be aware of overly filling his schedule to the point that this charity eventually becomes a disservice to the

people of God and himself. ... The danger is that the priest could reduce his self-understanding to what he does, with no real value or reflection given to who he is. Because a priest's life is so centered on the Eucharist and the dispensation of the other sacraments, at the end of the day the priest can at times look back and ask himself how much he has accomplished. Certainly, he has accomplished a great deal by having celebrated the very mysteries of Christ, but this evaluation entails a theological and philosophical understanding of spiritual reality, that can be forgotten when too busy. Much of being a priest is not quantifiable. The society of today is very utilitarian, if something does not seem or appear useful, then it is thought to be less important. Therefore, if the priest does not understand the inestimable value of who he is as a priest, he may fall into the temptation of discouragement or despair (cf. *PPLP* 29). According to Fr. William Sheridan, "Functionalism pervades our culture. There is a tendency to measure things, ideas, and even people by what they do or produce. Our culture values usefulness over essence and the bottom line over the human person."[i]

In similar fashion, the diaconate is highly susceptible to this *transactional or functional* orientation to ministry because by its very nature, the diaconate work is based on action in the form of *service*. In our American culture, the sense of "work" is considered a dominant factor in establishing identity (Huntley, 1997). Rather than asking, "Tell me about yourself" as a way of learning more about a person, we instead ask, "Tell me what you do and I'll know who you are." Functionalism prevents a deeper understanding of diaconal identity because it assumes that "service" is a word that places function over form. In the popular vernacular, the word "service" or "employment of duties or work for another" implies a doctrine of action to strive for meaningful change (e.g., social service, political service, customer service), yet this way of thinking seldom addresses the nature or essence or vocational calling of "who" performs these actions or duties. For example, "you are an engineer…" communicates the professional "services" expected but hardly speaks to the innate skills that may or may not be related to the vocational identity of the person. The emphasis on "tasks" overtakes any curiosity of "who" is performing the tasks. If "service as function" becomes the principal measure of diaconal effectiveness, then much of what the deacon "is" becomes at risk of being overwhelmed by what the deacon "does." This tendency, although generalized within our culture, can also be inadvertently perpetuated within a parish or diocesan organization by adopting business practices that already carry this bias. For instance, the use of yearly performance appraisals to measure the effectives of diaconal ministry along a series of functional parameters (organizational effectiveness, performance against a job description) may sound like a good idea, but it has the potential to reduce the diaconate to a "job" at the expense of crucial spiritual realities. Diaconal performance is much more than just measuring task performance.

This overemphasis on *action* and functional view of ministry can also be observed in parish ministry. In our management consultations and leadership development workshops for parishes, we have perceived this sense of undervaluing the spiritual in parish forums such as parish staff, parish councils, finance councils and other mainstream ministries of parish life. One particular story with a newly assigned pastor of a midsize parish in Florida helps illustrate how sometimes the perception of ministry can become more task than spirit:

> The parish council had prepared for their first meeting with the new pastor by putting together a thick binder that contained a brief history of the parish, a summary of activities of the main ministries in the parish, Sunday mass attendance reports, and other relevant materials. The agenda for this first meeting was quite intense and covered areas that in many ways would decide the future of the parish.

When the pastor arrived, he greeted every one of the representatives of the parish council and as everyone sat down he provided a brief introduction and then asked that all the binders, agendas, and any other material be removed from the table. Once that was done he told the parish council, "Today we pray. We pray for our ministry, for the strength to carry this responsibility, and we pray for each and every one of our parishioners and their contribution to parish life." This pastor wanted the first parish council meeting to be one of prayer, reflection and spiritual context that would guide the actions that would follow in other meetings.

However, after the meeting was concluded and during an informal conversation in the parking lot, three parish council members were lamenting on how the evening was a waste of time, that not much had been accomplished that evening, and that if this is what the pastor wanted in their meetings they would move to a different ministry.

This simple example illustrates what perhaps all of us have heard too many times in our dealings with parish ministry throughout the years -- that *task* can all too easily trump both the *relational* and the *spiritual* dimensions of ministry.

In summary, the tendency for task orientation represents a strong opposing influence, that if not identified and adequately addressed, can affect the way leadership as relationship is enacted and the possibilities of fostering spiritual growth and depth. Leadership and spirituality are fundamentally about relationships. Applying pastoral leadership models that give more than a passing acknowledgement to the importance of spirituality is therefore going to take a lot of concentration and effort.

Family as a School of Relational Experiences

The overall Western view of leadership as primarily a functional discipline, and the influence this perspective has had on the way leadership in general and leadership in ministry in particular are enacted, may also influence how we learn the value and depth of relationships. If family life is like a nursery or a school where we learn the fundamentals of relationships, and if, like many school systems throughout the United States, we assign a grade to characterize the quality of learning achieved, we may very well find that a significant number of families end up with a low grade. *Newsweek* magazine (3/18/91) compared the statistics of married couples and non-family households in the United States for the years 1970 and 1990, and reported a 15% reduction in married couples and over a 10% increase in non-family households.

The trend is startling and begs the question as to the quality and depth of relational experiences acquired in this "school" when one or more of the "teachers" are missing. Furthermore, if the quality and readiness of relational experiences could be measured by the quality of spousal relationships in the United States, then again we have some concerns. Despite the confusion and disagreements on the exact divorce rate in the United Sates, it's easy to see that any number above 40% can have a devastating effect on relational learning (*New York Times*, 9/29/2007).

The impact of family as a school of relational knowledge and experience cannot be emphasized enough. Having an abusive or absent father makes it much more difficult to visualize and accept God as Father. Living in a good family but a family with minimal spiritual experiences can become a handicap in being able to participate in spiritual communities. Being a child of second or third divorced parents may make it harder to establish long-term spiritual commitments such as being able to live a "covenant" spirituality. These and similar family situations are intended to illustrate that the fundamentals of the relational-spiritual relationship may be largely absent in many modern families.

Of course not all families are severely deficient in this regard. What is relevant is to consider the favorable and unfavorable lessons learned from one's family life and the impact they may or may not have in being able to go beyond a transactional model of relationships. The family dynamic does have an effect on spiritual growth and development; we believe it also affects a person's understanding of leadership. Although we believe this is a relevant factor in being able to enact and understand leadership as relational, we also note the scarce amount of formal research on this topic. Nevertheless, relational lessons from the family also pose a challenge to understanding the possibilities of deeper relationships and therefore make it harder to accept leadership as a spiritual practice.

A Scarce Relational Vocabulary

As if it were not enough of a challenge to see leadership become principally a transaction to get things done, to live in a culture that tends to favor a transactional over relational worldview, and have to recognize the familial difficulties that can limit one's ability to view relationships as more than a transaction, there is yet another challenge to understanding relationships. We seem to lack a language of relationships.

One of the great difficulties in adopting and internalizing a relational activity is the lack of a common language that can fully express the multiple stages of relational predispositions, paths and maturity. As adults, we can intuit the multiple levels of possible interactions and mutual benefits of interrelationships, but we also find it difficult to express that in words.

> We become inarticulate when it comes to addressing how people intermingle with others, how we need others and need them to need us. Love is perhaps the least definable word in our lexicon, and vague, all inclusive terms such as *affiliation*, *communion* and *intimacy* take us only part of the way. The na-

139

> ture of relationship has remained enshrouded partly because we have so few words and agreed upon concepts to indicate ways in which people connect themselves to others... Because our speech in this realm is so restricted, we end up with a cultural mythology of human intercourse that overemphasizes the easily described phenomena of individuality and ignores or distorts interpersonal bonding. When we wish to know people, we are therefore more likely to ask about what they do than about how they love. (Josselson, 1992. P.2)

Professional disciplines such as psychology, sociology and social work have created specific models and language for relational dynamics, but for the most part are hyphenated creations. The "I-You" word combination, for example, describes the separateness of two individuals, but it also pretends to show that which connects them. Yet the hyphenation fails to communicate what may very well be a series of interactions and interconnections. In fact, what truly matters in relational language is the hyphen itself. Here is where naturally relational cultures, such as the African tribes, can help us see the error in hyphenated relational thinking. In the African tribes there is a word that describes a common bond between all humans, that when cultivated, leads to discovering one's own qualities. The word is "Ubuntu." The South African Nobel Laureate Archbishop Desmond Tutu describes the meaning of "Ubuntu" in this way:

> Africans have this thing called UBUNTU . . . the essence of being human. It is part of the gift that Africans will give the world. It embraces hospitality, caring about others, willing to go the extra mile for the sake of others. We believe a person is a person through another person, that my humanity is caught up, bound up and inextricable in yours. When I dehumanize you I inexorably dehumanize myself. The solitary individual is a contradiction in terms and, therefore, you seek to work for the common good because your humanity comes into its own community, in belonging. (Desmond Tutu, *No Future without Forgiveness: A Personal Overview of South Africa's Truth and*

Reconciliation Commission London: Doubleday Publishers, 1999, p. 22)

Other cultures also have specific terms to characterize relational dynamics for which there is no clear or easy translation into the English language. The Ancient Greek culture has four distinct words for the word "love," each describing a distinct form of loving relationship (*agápe*, *éros*, *philía*, and *storgē*). Most Thai words expressing family kinship have no direct translations into the English language. There is no standard English word for the Yiddish "machatunim" or the Spanish "consuegros" or "cuñado." Native Americans use the phrase "our people" not only to describe their nation, but also the fundamental bond that sustains them as one. Other examples of terms for which there is no English translation include the Danish word *hygge*, which intends to express a sense of warmth and companionship; the Czech word *litost* which refers to a condition of anguish created by the sudden sight of one's own misery; or the Finnish word *talkoot,* which means volunteering to work a serious community project. Again, these examples are intended to illustrate the extent to which relational terms are common in other societies but not so much in American society.

Notwithstanding the absence of a relational language, there are two places in Western cultures that showcase the multiple layers of relational life. In fact, because of a lack of common vocabulary to express these deeper movements, most of the expressions that are used to convey relational depth come about in nonverbal form. The two places that showcase how much we treasure relationships are airports and hospitals.

Airports are among the few places where one can see how much we all cherish what relationships mean in our lives. At airports, we are able to see the anguish of departures and the joy of arrivals. On the departures side of the airport, there are scenes such as the heart-rending departure of a young Army soldier as his six-month-pregnant wife clings to him tightly, not saying a word but saying everything. Farther away, a middle-aged woman embraces her terminally ill father, knowing it may very well be the last time they see each other. Before entering a secure side of the airport terminal and despite all the coming and going of passengers, an entire entourage of four children and their father focus on a single person, wishing the woman among them a safe business trip and a quick return home. On the arrival side of the terminal, just downstairs from the scenes described at the departure terminal, sporadic grateful applause erupt as a group of weary soldiers in military fatigues arrive from an 18-month deployment. A few yards away, a wife receives her business-traveler husband with a long kiss, inadvertently communicating to all in baggage claim how much they missed each other. Exiting the baggage claim area are somber-looking parents walking toward a cab with a young girl who has a bandana covering her balding head, a visible effect of her chemotherapy treatment. Yet, in neither departures nor arrivals, is there a scene of hate, selfishness or anger. What abound in each part of the airport are the wordless expressions of relationships at their best.

The other location that also showcases multiple layers of relational life and the desire to express them despite the scarcity of a relational language are hospitals, and in particular, the emergency rooms (ER). When a loved one becomes seriously ill, the pain of one becomes the hurt of all. It is the place where the young mother with a baby who has a dangerously high fever feels helpless, worried and desperate, yet can dare for hope. It is the place where worried parents come to see the teenagers involved in a car accident, not knowing the actual extent of injuries but always imagining the worst and hoping for the best. It is the place where family meets to find out the extent of damage to an elder person who suffered a stroke. It is the place where a sudden illness or an accident jeopardizes the normal flow of relationships and makes one think of life without that person. "Eighty percent of life's satisfaction comes from meaningful relationships," says Brian Tracy, author and motivational speaker. No wonder a major disruption in a relationship carries such a sobering effect.

This *disruption-of-relationship* (for which we also don't have a word) may also explain why airport chapels are normally empty and why hospital chapels are so well attended. But in either place, the airport or the hospital, we are able to experience the true value of relationships in our life. Where are the words to describe the hidden layers of interpersonal movements we intuit are being affected?

Another *disruption-of-relationship* occurs during spiritual retreats, where superficiality is slowly peeled away and we become more aware and appreciative of the relationship with God and with others. Yet how many of us, after a spiritual retreat where the deeper parts of our relationships with God have been stirred, find it almost impossible to articulate the experience to another? On the one hand we remain dissatisfied with the words we have used to explain the experience, and on the other, the other person--even if it's the spouse—reacts with a blank stare that communicates, "I have no idea what you are talking about."

We argue that experiences such as those described above are formative events for which we may not have a clear vocabulary to communicate. Our point here is that a popular language to characterize different levels of relational activities of everyday activities is lacking, and within this limitation, there are implications for leadership as a relational dynamic, and consequently, leadership as a spiritual practice. The implications for leadership and spirituality are very clear. What if *leadership* could be articulated within a spiritual context that harnessed the formational value of these deeper relational movements?

More importantly, what would we find if we searched how leadership is defined in cultures where the relational orientation is stronger than ours? Would it then be possible to capture a deeper meaning of how relational dynamics are an integral component of the leadership function? Would this understanding also help illustrate what we propose as the Pastoral Leadership model?

We believe this insight can be derived from some of the Hispanic communities within the United States. For many of these communities,

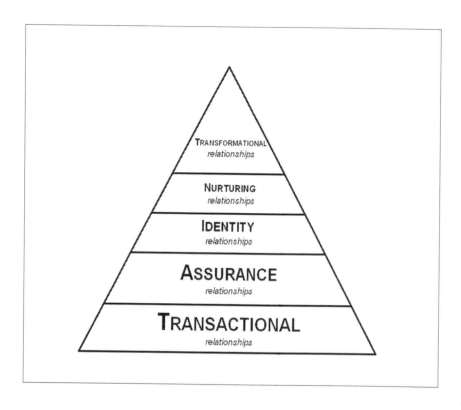

Figure 3, Hierarchy of Relationships

and particularly in Church life, what we call "leader" Hispanics may call "dirigente." Essentially, "el dirigente" is the one who straightens out the path (*enderezar el camino*), who shows the way toward an objective (*lleva rectamente una cosa hacia un término o lugar señalado*), the one who guides others and shows the milestones or mileposts (*guiar, mostrando o dando las señas de un camino*), and the one who counsels, encourages and orchestrates the fulfillment of a project (*orientar, guiar, aconsejar a quien realiza un trabajo*). The "dirigente" doesn't have the illusion of power and control, but the responsibility to get things done by guiding—not directing—others toward the step-by-step fulfillment of an objective. The "dirigente" mobilizes, conducts and organizes (*El dirigente moviliza, conduce y organiza*).

Would this not represent a more rich view of leadership in ministry than using leadership models that are derived from a transactional and relationally limited perspective?

In arguing that both leadership and spirituality are relational phenomena, we have first presented some major challenges that may inhibit a fuller understanding of deeper relational needs and movements. The pragmatic (instrumental or functional) interpretations of leadership, the transactional mentality predominant in Western cultures, the limitations of modern family life to perform as a school of relational learning, and the scarcity of a relational vocabulary all converge in making "relational dealings" a difficult matter. Yet since the pastoral model of leadership is fundamentally relational in nature, we have taken the liberty of composing a model of relational activities and integrated them into a hierarchy of *formational* relationships essential to the leadership function in the ministry setting. In the next paragraphs, we present these levels and relate them to a fuller understanding of the Pastoral Leadership model.

A Relational Framework for Pastoral Leadership

Despite the challenges presented above, we have attempted to develop a language and a model that pulls together a series of *formative relationships* that underscore the dynamics of the pastoral leadership model into what we call the *hierarchy of formational relationships* (see Figure 3). This hierarchy emphasizes the types of relationships that form the person and the group (or ministry) across a variety of possible dimensions (personal, community, pastoral, academic, etc). One of the more important dimensions is, of course, the spiritual dimension. Simply put, we propose that five forms of relationships are essential to engaging leadership as a spiritual practice.

In the next sections, we offer some more specifics to illustrate each of relationships and the dynamics of this hierarchy of relationships within the model of pastoral leadership.

Transactional Relationships

An argument is always about what has been made more important than the relationship. - Hugh Prather

The most fundamental form of relationships across all leadership models are *transactional* relations. Transactional relationships are purely pragmatic or instrumental in nature; the emphasis on the task is greater, and there are minimal considerations for relational activity. "You give me, I give you..."

This form of leading is perhaps the most studied in the business setting because it is measurable, highly predictive and simple to implement. Bass (1990) describes this form of leadership relationship:

146

> Much leadership today subscribes to a transactional framework where … managers engage in a transaction with their employees: They explain what is required of them and what compensation they will receive if they fulfill these requirements" (Bass 1990, p19–20).

This also represents the most pervasive style of leadership within the ministry setting. Such a leadership style is favored even in a setting that calls for a more relational approach, largely because it is a generally accepted form of leadership in the secular environment, it is an integral part of the transactional worldview of Western culture, it does not require an extensive relational vocabulary or nuanced understanding of relationships, and it does not require that leaders be particularly adept at relationships. Essentially, it is a form of leadership that is approachable by those who may be "relationally handicapped" because it requires little engagement in relational matters -- only enough to avoid lawsuits. Despite the apparent appeal for a transactional style of leadership in the ministry setting, such an approach to leadership in the ministry setting proves to be problematic because it tends to ignore the person as a spiritual being in a setting that is fundamentally oriented to spiritual realities.

To be sure, *transactional* relations can become a foundation and gateway to deeper forms of relationships in which leadership is exercised as a spiritual practice. In parish ministry, work needs to get done, so an initial transactional relationship allows things to get started. For example, an Extraordinary Minister of Holy Communion, who is relatively new to a parish, may be required to attend formal training for such ministers in the parish. The experienced minister may not require the formal training to perform in the ministry, but there is a relational imperative that is important to recognize. The minister may very well know what to do, but the community of ministers may not yet know the person very well. In an exercise of *pastoral leadership*, the leader of the ministry would act not so much on the basis of the requirement for formal

147

training, but more so out of a recognition of the importance to both the new minister and the community of ministers to begin to engage the community on a relational level. In the hands of a well-formed pastoral leader, a transactional relationship can become an opportunity to build trust and set the stage for possibilities of deeper relationships.

One risk of transactional relationships is that it tends to isolate individuals from the inevitable realities of relationships. As a result, pastoral leaders (or parish staff) who tend to see their roles primarily as transactional, often avoid the relational dimensions of their jobs because they tend to view such an expansion of their worldview as a messy complication. A case in point: We once witnessed a parish receptionist who was focused on answering the telephone. When a tearful visitor came to the reception area seeking a priest to talk to, the receptionist, without looking up from the telephone, told the visitor that no priests were available. Any role in the parish setting, taken to its transactional extreme, can become the cause of much unnecessary pain and suffering to countless innocent victims.

Assurance Relationships

Remember, we all stumble, every one of us. That's why it's a comfort to go hand in hand. - Emily Kimbrough

The next higher form of relationships that could contribute to exercising leadership as a spiritual practice is *assurance* relationships. This type of relationship provides a sense of psychological or spiritual security, and is very likely to emerge during a crisis. Separation from loved ones, the pressures of day-to-day life or a significant loss are highly stressful situations--more so when they are prolonged--which tend to require all possible emotional and spiritual resources to cope with them. Under such conditions, the need to deal with the crisis and the imminent threat it represents overwhelms interest in relationships for their own sake. The need for the person, group or organization is for strong leadership that provides a sense of hope, stability and assurance.

Assurance relationships are intended to provide emotional and spiritual shelter or protection from intrusive, overwhelming and confusing events. *Assurance* relationships create the "safe space" where the "seeds" of mutuality can grow with minimal interference from the perceived threats. These relational spaces offer the opportunity "to be with…," to "not feel alone," to minimize anxiety, and to be the hands that "hold and not let fall." If *transactional* relationships open doors to build trust, *assurance* relationships define the "playing field" of relationships that are the basis for establishing trust.

One example of pastoral leaders who excel in fostering *assurance* relationships are military chaplains. In the case of the men and women in the military services deployed to a war zone, the relational spaces (assurance relationships) developed at home are under constant threat. The sense of "feeling alone" and of "falling" brought about by the battlefield realities are very real and very damaging to the individual if not properly addressed. These men and women suffer the stresses of separation from their loved ones, a circumstance that removes them from many of their internal "safe spaces." There are also the stresses of extended working hours and battlefield trauma that assault their sense of safety and stability. There are also the stresses of living in field conditions caused by factors such as sleep deprivation, inadequate hygiene and poor nutrition. All these pressures test coping capabilities to the limit and erode the "safe spaces" created by assurance relationships. Yet military chaplains are able to manage these losses of *assurance* relationships by creating new safe spaces that can sustain the men and women in their care and keep them focused on their assigned mission. There is a lot to learn about *assurance* relationships from military chaplains.

If relationships are antecedents of action under the Pastoral Leadership model, then recognizing the function of *assurance* relationships in fostering "safe spaces" is essential to the leadership function. Here, the opportunity for meaningfully articulated prayer, the welcoming of new members in ministry, the recognition of relationally threatening events (e.g., loss of job, illness or death in a family, stresses at home, personal health conditions, etc.) not only affect the ability to perform ministry tasks effectively, but also can become the objective of ministry action. On the other hand, a single-minded focus on getting the job done, which ignores the necessity of *assurance* relationships, can be devastating to a person or to a group. If the work of ministry is to be supported by relationships, then the Pastoral Leaders must find ways to identify, protect and mend the "safe spaces" from where good works can be performed, which sustains both the minister and the ministered.

Identity Relationships

The nature of leadership stems from the leader's personality and soul rather than just from his or her behavior.-
Gilbert W. Fairholm

Because *transactional* relationships open doors to build trust, and *assurance* relationships define the "playing field" of relationships, then finding and fulfilling the identity of this bounded field becomes the next-highest form of relationships of interest to the Pastoral Leader. Now that a "safe space" is defined, why does it exist? What is its purpose?

The form of identity we are most familiar with is the *social identity* of the group. This form of identity defines the functions or tasks of a group within a broader setting, (e.g., a business organization). Social identity is the formal relationships of a group that express the responsibilities assigned to that group and the duties for which they are accountable to higher levels within the organization. This form of identity

150

comes primarily from the "outside;" it's an assigned identity that is repetitive among organizations, and that is normally more at the service of the organization than the group itself. In the language of parish life, there is a similarity to the functional nature of parish councils, parish ministries and parish finance councils. They are identities that refer to the "tasks-from-within" that are the substantially similar from parish to parish.

But another form of identity—less common yet more relevant to Pastoral Leadership—is the *spiritual identity* of a group. Although the functional identity may be the same among groups within similar organizations, the spiritual identity is an inimitability that stems from the relationships among each unique participant, usually independently of the organizational setting. Rather than focusing on tasks, *spiritual identity* addresses the informal relationships that express the internal needs and inner movements of the group with respect to each other and vis-a-vis the divine. This form of identity comes primarily from the "inside," meaning it's a discerned identity as the group is perceived by the "Eyes of God." It is unique even though the social identities could be the same, and is normally at the service of the group (and the individual) more than the organization. If the social identity represents the arms, hands and legs of the group, the spiritual identity expresses the heart and soul of the group. In the language of the parish, a parish council in one parish has characteristics that make it unique as compared to parish councils in other parishes. The *functional identity* is the same, but the *spiritual identity* is unique.

What we argue is distinctive about the pastoral leadership model is the ability to recognize both *social identity* and *spiritual identity* as a single reality within a group. Social identity alone leads to functionalism. Spiritual identity alone leads to inaction. The pastoral leader recognizes the value of both identities as animating the life of the group; this *summative identity* is similar to the act of breathing, which consists of two movements, inhaling and exhaling. Here we recognize a difficult but essential formative objective for all pastoral leaders. Pastoral leaders not only belong to the group but are expected to embody the characteristics that make the group distinct from others. Leaders who separate themselves and who hold very different *summative identities* than the group are less effective than those who can exemplify the group's identity and lead from within rather than from the outside (Reicher, Haslam, & Platow, 2007).

For many reasons, the *summative identity* of parish life has become an urgent relevant topic. Twenty years ago, for example, there was no need to print the parish mission and vision in the bulletin. Today, in light of the threats to healthy parish life that result from competing leadership philosophies and religious ideologies, it seems that parish mission statements have been developed in an attempt to ameliorate the negative effects of these tensions. A second peril to parish identity results from parish closings or mergers, which are driven by financial factors and the shortage of priests. In this case, pastoral leaders exercise leadership in the form of finding and sharing ways to preserve the *spiritual identities* of parishes that are closed or merged. This can take the form of the transfer of concrete symbols of parish life from the closed or merged parish church to the newer consolidated parish. The principle here is to recognize and respect spiritual identities, because they represent the relationships among themselves and the relationship with the divine.

A third illustration of *summative identity* is illustrated by the tensions of multiculturalism within many parishes in the United States. Every parish seeks to cater to each national culture and its devotions, despite limited resources. But the reality is that cultural diversity is on the rise, and parish resources are shrinking. How is one to manage this disparity? In this case, the analysis of social and spiritual identities presented earlier opens doors to new possibilities. National cultures are considered social identities that carry a sense of values and preferences that are spiritual in nature, but fail to address the full spiritual identity of the Catholic family. In other words, there are elements of our spiritual identity as a parish that surpass national identities and bring us to the universal household of a single Father and a single Spirit, and makes us brothers and sisters of Jesus, our brother and Savior. Here resides a *spiritual identity* within each parish that allows a common ground—albeit one that requires intense formation—and a respite from the tensions of increased diversity and diminishing resources. These tensions may continue, but if the spiritual identity remains the weaker element of the summative identity, managing diversity in parishes will remain a seemingly insurmountable challenge.

This may also explain why one parish staff is so different from another, even though they share the same job descriptions, or why there is a perceptible change in dynamics when a parish staff member leaves, or when a new staff member is welcomed. The *functional identity* remains the same but the *spiritual identity* is affected. In the past few years, we have dealt with a few parish staffs that possess a keen awareness of their spiritual identity and used this to their advantage as a way of furthering their understanding of Church and of parish work as ministry. In fact, it seems that this distinction in identities also applies to family life, where in many cases the functional identity is clear but the articulation of a spiritual identity (as domestic church) is lacking or weak. In the case of families with weak spiritual identities, a significant consequence is the inability to discern vocations "from-within," since discernment and vocations are God's callings and by nature, are spiritual activities. This same analogy applies to ministry groups. Should not the leader emerge from within the spiritual domain, rather than primarily as a result of functional abilities?

Through these examples, we suggest that *summative identity* in general and *spiritual identity* in particular, have become "hot topics" that are difficult to address using secular leadership models but are an integral part of pastoral leadership. Pastoral leaders are called to be masters at articulating and promoting action from within the *summative identity* (the integration of social and spiritual identities).

153

Once the *summative identity* of a group or ministry is stable and mature, the group is able to recognize its own needs and desires for deeper relational opportunities. This is the point in which the group becomes more interested in the possibilities of *nurturing relationships*, which is the topic of the next section.

Nurturing Relationships

There is more hunger for love and appreciation in this world than for bread. - Mother Theresa

Now that *transactional* relationships have opened doors for building trust within the group (or ministry), *assurance* relationships have delineated the boundaries of relational possibilities, and the leader is able to articulate and enact action from the *identity* relationships, the next activity associated with leadership as a spiritual practice are *nurturing* relationships.

Although, in general, there is a strong psychological meaning to the word "nurturing," our focus remains on the spiritual dimension of the term. The pastoral leader's role in *nurturing* relationships is in helping "connect the dots," helping make life connections others may not see and interpreting events within the context of spiritual relationships. Here, the pastoral leader carries out a form of critical thinking, which is inclusive of the spiritual perspective. In secular terms, "critical thinking" refers mostly to a rationally structured process of conceptualizing, applying, analyzing and synthesizing with the intent to "see beyond the obvious." Critical thinking is characterized as self-directed, self-disciplined and self-corrective thinking. What we suggest is that when spiritual and faith realities are integrated to the critical thinking process, the pastoral leader is able present alternatives that "go beyond" what is obvious by including a providential component, therefore offering solutions inclusive of a faith and spiritual perspective.

For the pastoral leader, the physical and the spiritual are always interconnected, are equal components of a same reality, are constantly affecting each other and are both taken into consideration when making decisions and guiding the group (or ministry). This means "going deeper" by integrating how discoveries from the spiritual and the physical speak to the decision at hand. The implication is that it's a process that transcends a purely rational analysis. Action is therefore based on the interpretation of "signs and voices" from both the physical and spiritual world; it becomes a "sorting out" of the cacophony of competing "voices."

Remember the example of the bricklayers discussed earlier? Now assume that three bricklayers are working side by side and are interviewed as to what they are doing. When the first is asked about the tasks at hand, he says, "I'm laying bricks." When the second is asked, he says, "I'm building a cathedral." But when a bricklayer who is steeped in the discipline of using nurturing relationships or critical thinking with a spiritual perspective is asked the same question, that bricklayer responds, "Each of us is a *living brick* that makes up this cathedral." The interconnection between the physical and the spiritual seems to be a characteristic of leadership that is lacking in secular leadership models. On the other hand, it is an expectation of pastoral leadership.

In the for-profit setting, half of the decisions made within business organizations actually end up in failure (Nutt, 1999). This is not because of "bad" leaders, but mainly because of actions that are imposed by edicts or bullying, by depending too much on flawed problem-solving techniques, or by caving into time pressures and eliminating potential alternatives too soon. Leadership is inherently full of dangers and pitfalls, and is often affected by frustrations, false expectations and the hopes and fears of the followers. A better way for making decisions exists; both business leaders and pastoral leaders can benefit from discernments skills (Benefiel, 2005).

Naturally, this requires that the pastoral leader acquire a keen ability to visualize the relational connections between the material and the spiritual. Said differently, a key skill in pastoral leadership for *nurturing* relations is discernment--seeing what others may miss, exercising wisdom more than just "being smart," and sustaining within the group a vocabulary of the heart and a climate of discernment. To be sure, the pastoral leader will have opportunities to use decision-making skills and benefit from the many decision-making models that may be available from the secular sector, but framing major decisions within the context of discernment is a *sine qua non* of pastoral leadership against other secular leadership models.

Of course, we also recognize that other meanings of *nurturing* are at play at this level of the hierarchy of relationships for the pastoral leader. As an example, Ruthellen Josselson (1992) recognizes *tending* and *caring* as psychological needs that occur within what we refer to as *nurturing* relationships. *Tending* and *caring* refers to the need and desire to offer ourselves in the service of others. The experience of being nurtured and taken care of—so argues psychological theory—generates the desire to take care of others (Benedek, 1960). Tending and caring means performing many small acts that strengthen the bonds among each other, acts that eventually elicit a sense of gratitude and warmth, and being loved. These may include celebrating birthdays, graduations, job promotions and other life events. But it could also mean sharing in significant parish events, such as welcoming a new staff member or entering into the transition to a new pastor. Some events are quite complicated and require time to "digest" the implications for the group (or the ministry). They will require of the leader coaching and guiding the staff toward "connecting the dots," sorting out the cacophony of voices and "going beyond the obvious."

So far we have indicated how *transactional* relationships are able to open doors for building trust within the group (or ministry), how *as-*

surance relationships have delineated the boundaries of relational possibilities, how the leader is able to articulate and enact action from the *identity* relationships, and how "going beyond" is so essential to *nurturing* relationships in the ministry setting. Yet prolonged exposure to living in a climate of "going beyond" carries a consequence, and that is it offers increased possibilities of transformation. This is the highest form of relational dynamics of relevance to the leadership function and the topic of the next section.

Transformational Relationships

Before you try to change others, remember how hard it is to change yourself. -Bill Bluestein

The more obvious starting point to explain what we mean by *transformational* relationships is to address a difference between what the secular leadership models call "transformational leadership" and what we understand as the *spiritual* meaning of transformation. Although this is a very difficult point to address, largely because the construct has been so widely used in its more limited context, we will address the matter by comparing and contrasting each perspective of transformational relationships as a way of introducing it from the pastoral leadership point of view.

In our research for this section, we found a large number of studies that discuss the transformational qualities of the secular leadership function. As discussed earlier, the two most recognized leadership styles seem to be the *transformational leadership* style and the *transactional leadership* style (Bass, 1998; Bono & Judge, 2004). These two styles are relevant to the secular sector because they address two major areas of organizational dynamics, that of the "human activity" (e.g., employee relations, social networking, customer relations) as well as the operational performance of the group or organization (e.g., measurable goals, quantifiable objectives, completion of tasks). They also represent the bottom and top of what we are calling the *hierarchy of formational relationships.*

In the context of secular modeling, the *transformational* styles of leadership are more directed at establishing a clear organizational vision since, according to many formal studies, employees working for small as well as large organizations expect and are more satisfied when their leaders provide and clearly articulate the intended direction (Papalexandris & Galanki, 2009). Here, the *transformational* leadership styles portrayed in the secular realm are made up of a series of attributes or traits that focus more on the ability to create a vision for the organization while at the same time maintaining high degrees of internal employee motivation, increasing employee job satisfaction and retention, and offering a positive strategy toward the management of a small business (Lin, 2003).

This transformational style of leadership is founded upon a relational psychological contract that results in a strong positive impact on commitment, determination and performance (Atkinson, 2007), and is the type of leadership style that is expected to address values, sustainability and behaviors but is primarily aimed at the organization (Coman, 2008). Transformational leadership models in the secular literature focus on aligning individual desires and expectations with those of the organization (meaning-making) and point to how the member of the organization can be "changed" to agree with a "higher" set of needs set by the organization. Michael Keeley explains in more detail:

> Burns differentiates "lower" needs, such as physical survival and economic security (similar to Herzberg's hygiene factors), from "higher" needs, such as moral purpose and "participation in a collective life larger than one's personal existence" (similar to Herzberg's motivators). The lower needs are addressed by transactional leaders, who may at best defuse conflict by meeting the parochial demands of their different constituents.

> The higher, more "authentic" needs are engaged by transforming leaders who can refocus attention—with much greater effect—on common goals that have transcendent value. (Keeley, 1995, p. 76).

Again, the focus of *transformational leadership* from a secular point of view is to move employees away from "selfish" interests and promote the organizational identity as a "higher form" of needs. Yet there is significant dispute as to how exactly this is accomplished. One of the major objections to the secular forms of transformational leadership is reflected in the question "What are you transforming me into?" This important question is one that the current state of leadership discourse seems unprepared to answer (Yukl, 1999).

Nevertheless, one could argue that the value of aligning one's thinking consistently with the notion of "parish as organization" has a lot of merit and would therefore apply to parish ministry, since our interpretation of "parish as organization" points to the parish identity. As we have indicated earlier, the "parish as identity" is significant to the pastoral leader. Yet what we suggest is distinctive about the pastoral leadership model is the ability to recognize both *social identity* and *spiritual identity* as a single reality within a group. Social identity alone leads to functionalism, which is already a danger within many ecclesial entities, including parishes. The pastoral leader recognizes the value of both identities as the life of the group—or the *summative identity*—in the same way breathing consists of two movements, inhaling and exhaling. So despite this "external" guiding toward aligning individual interest with parish interest, the pastoral leader is also aware of the deeper possibilities of transformation. For example, in persuading parish members to contribute to stewardship by increasing monetary contributions, the leaders in the parish are exercising the secular style of transformational leadership. But by forming the parish to understand the *spiritual* value and imperatives of stewardship, the parish leaders are exercising a pastoral leadership style of transformation.

It's precisely this example of stewardship that highlights the deeper movements of what the Pastoral sector recognizes as *transformation*, a term that exemplifies the intentionality of the divine-human relational process.

> The word transformation is part of a richly varied semantic field: to form, malform, reform, be conformed and transform. Throughout the centuries, spiritual authors have used this semantic filed to bring out the inner logic of the spiritual way. For them, this field—and within it especially the term transformation—refers to the most significant transitions in the divine-human relational process. (Waaijman, 2002, p.455)

As a pastoral leader ascends the pyramidal depiction of formative relationships presented in this chapter, the convergence of spirituality and leadership becomes more apparent.

> To be sure, our spirituality is ultimately the work of God's Spirit at work in us; however, we must cooperate. We must develop a posture of active receptivity, whereby we dispose ourselves to see the gift of God; whereby we are able to discern the movements of God and listen to his promptings. And this involves a true personal asceticism, a true discipline, whereby through prayer we gradually as are able to let go of our false idols, of all that is really our own god and spirit and, in full freedom, be able to perceive and respond to God's Spirit in us. (Caligiuri, 1978, p. 456).

What is particular about transformational relationships for the pastoral leader is that creating the external vision intended to align "individual wants and needs" to organizational priorities, as occurs in secular models, will include a fuller vision that mobilizes internal (spiritual) possibilities, such as receptivity and learning how to "let go," which is more characteristic of ministry models. In other words, the pastoral leader also brings to the group the compelling power of an *internal vision* that complements and interacts with the external vision. Here, the question of "what are you transforming me into?" that seems to haunt secular transformational leadership (Yukly, 1999) has a definitive answer, especially when the internal vision is shared within a common or one of the traditional spiritualities of the Church.

The emphasis on an internal vision of formative relationships based upon a spiritual landscape completes what is lacking from the external vision alone. Again, using the analogy of parish stewardship, the leader who is able to offer a compelling internal vision based on "receptivity" and "letting go" builds the foundation of a "stewardship from within" that complements the external vision of stewardship needs. Other examples of transformational leadership in this context are evident in the vision of the founders of traditional Church spiritualities (e.g., St. Ignatius of Loyola, St. Francis of Assisi, St. Benedict of Nursia, St. Dominic of Osma, St. Bertold, St. Alphonsus Ligouri, and St. Louis-Maire Grignion de Montfort to mention a few), where the external vision of transformation is supported by the internal vision of a well-defined spiritual discipline. Again, if the leader is expected to embody the identity of the group (or ministry) then the leader is also expected to embody the internal spiritual potential of the group, as expressed in its internal vision.

Pastoral Leadership and the Relationships

At the beginning of this chapter we indicated how crucial relationships are to Pastoral leadership and to leadership as a spiritual practice. We noted that the core principle of ecclesial leadership is *leadership is a spiritual practice,* which is based on a more profound understanding of the meaning, purpose and capabilities of interpersonal relationships. Just as relationships are an essential component of spirituality (relationship with God, relationships with others, relationship with self), the practice of Pastoral leadership is also about these same relationships (God, others and self). Therefore, having a deeper practical understanding of interpersonal relationships is essential to both spirituality and leadership. Because leadership in our society is conducted mostly as an instrumental function, and because the transactional worldview of our society, with its implications of undervaluing formational relationships, increasing the risks of family dysfunctions, and ignoring the importance of a relational language, we emphatically insist that leadership, and certainly pastoral leadership, is fundamentally about relational influences.

Relationships tend to occur more as an interconnected web rather than as a neatly presented model. The specific order of formative relationships from transactional to transformational presented in this chapter is not intended to be viewed as a linear process in which one form of relationship must occur before the other. At the same time, our decision to use a pyramidal approach is intended largely as an educational technique to simplify the introduction of the fundamental principle of leadership and spirituality as relational concepts. It's easier to learn fundamentals and then move toward an understanding of the more complex possibilities. A transactional relationship with a stranger can trigger a transformational event, just like it's possible to become transactional while addressing nurturing or identity matters.

Nevertheless, we emphasize the *formative* nature of relationships that underscore the dynamics of the pastoral leadership model into what we call the *hierarchy of formational relationships.* Of course, this hierarchy model addresses only a few of what we consider are the most essential relationships to the Pastoral setting. There are many other forms of relational endeavors, such as the affective and emotional forms, that go beyond the purpose of this book.

What we have highlighted in this chapter is the need to accentuate the value of relationships in both disciplines of leadership and spirituality, and to offer a practical approach using some of the formative

162

types of relational exchanges that have an effect on both disciplines. These formative relationships speak to the interpersonal relationships between the leader and the follower, but they also address group (or ministry) dynamics. In the next chapter we will focus on how these formative relationships affect the group setting, and how the group can grow from being a high-performance team to becoming a spiritual community.

Case Study

Suppose your friend's pastor has asked him to design a weekend leadership workshop for parish ministry leaders. Your friend, a well-respected senior leader in his company, is aware that you are involved in a pastoral leadership workshop and sends you an email outlining his proposal. He asks you to review these recommendations before they are submitted to the pastor. These are his recommendations for the two-day workshop:

- **Conflict Management**--Introduce ways of confining, eliminating, and dealing with ministry conflict. Offer recommendations on how to respond accordingly.

- **Managing Change**--Explore the variables in managing change and how they apply to the Church environment. Discuss how leadership styles affect variables of environmental change.

- **Models of Leadership and Authority**--Explore the five models of leadership and examine participants' own leadership styles of ministry performance.

- **Ministry Performance Appraisals**--Encourage participants to break the employee-employer model. Offer a regular, theologically based appraisal process and guidelines for when and how to conduct such a process.

163

- **Negotiating Skills for Ministry**--Discuss the power of negotiating as applied to ministry. Offer re-commendations and techniques on how to control uncooperative ministries.

- **Empowering Ministries**--Introduce participants to ways to use power in parish ministry: what power is, how it is amassed, and ways of understanding and dealing with it.

- **Redirecting Leadership**--Allows leaders to apply their business skills in the ministry setting. Supported with Gospel examples.

- **Dealing with Church Problems**--Clarify the roles implicit in certain ecclesial job descriptions. Offer methods to correct Church problems.

- **Modern Spiritual Techniques**--Expose leaders to state-of-the-art spiritual techniques to boost spiritual life.

- **Total Quality Strategies for Achieving Personal Balance**--Focus on ways to define and control spiritual processes through deliberate and continuous improvement techniques.

- **Understanding Stress and Burnout in Ministry**--Introduce participants to issues of wellness, stress and burnout. Focus on coping with the "disease of the over-committed" and introduce strategies for self-care.

Case Discussion Questions:

Some of these recommendations are written in such a way that, although they may sound attractive, they suggest practices that may not be appropriate for the pastoral setting. Can you detect which ones? What cautions and suggestions would you make to your friend before he presents this proposal to his pastor?

Workshop Activities

1. Ask each group to come up with their own definition and one example of each form of relationships (transactional, assurance, identity, nurturing and transformational) that can be shared later in plenary session. Then in plenary session discuss how each of these forms of relationship are related to the leadership function.

2. In another exercise, each group of participants is to play dominoes, but with a caveat: Each group must "invent" two new and unique rules. After the groups have played dominoes a few times and have become familiar with the new rules, two players from each group move to another group. Naturally, there will be an explanation of the rules to the "new comers" but it will take a few iterations for the newcomers to adapt to the new rules. Time allowing, implement another rotation of "new comers" (preferable participants who had not rotated yet) and continue making observations. Once the exercise is complete, a plenary session is conducted with a dialogue analyzing the types of interpersonal relationships that were present throughout the exercise.

Personal Reflective

1. Go back and review your character strengths. How do your character strengths affect the types of relationships you have with those who are entrusted to you in ministry?

2. Try to go back and find an example where you—as a leader— enacted each one of the types of interpersonal relationships discussed in this chapter. Which type of relationship was the easiest? Which was the hardest, and why?

3. The academic literature within the discipline of secular leadership discusses only two types of relationships, *transactional* and *transformational*. Why do you think the discussion in the secular sector is limited to only two forms of relationships?

4. What kind of activities can you conduct to better prepare yourself for nurturing and transformational relationships?

5. Visit a hospital or an airport. Observe the interactions between family members and friends and see if you can identify an example of each type of interpersonal relationships.

Chapter References

Benefiel, M. (2005). Soul at work: Spiritual leadership in organizations. New York: Seabury Books.

Bono, J., & Judge, T. (2004). Personality and transformational and transactional leadership: A meta-analysis. Journal of Applied Psychology, 89(5), 901-910. doi:10.1037/0021-9010.89.5.901.

Keeley, M. (1995). The trouble with transformational leadership: Toward a federalist ethic for organizations. Business Ethics Quarterly, 5(1), 67-96.

Papalexandris, N., & Galanaki, E. (2009). Leadership's impact on employee engagement: Differences among entrepreneurs and professional CEOs. Leadership & Organization Development Journal, 30(4), 365-385.

Reicher, S., Haslam, S.A., & I'latow, M. (2007). The new psychology of leadership. Scifmtifii: American Mind. 18[4]. 22-2

Yukl, G. (1999). An evaluation of conceptual weaknesses in transformational and charismatic leadership theories. *Leadership Quarterly, 10*(2), 285.

Yukl, G., Fu, P., & McDonald, R. (2003). Cross–cultural Differences in Perceived Effectiveness of Influence Tactics for Initiating or Resisting Change. Applied Psychology: An International Review, 52(1), 68-82.

Wong, J., Wong, P., & Li, H. (2007). An investigation of leadership styles and relationship cultures of Chinese and expatriate managers in multinational construction companies in Hong Kong. Construction Management & Economics, 25(1), 95-106. doi:10.1080/01446190600632573.

The "soft" side of leadership

Framework that guides our choices

Discernment
Envisioning (Worldview)
Spiritual community
Primacy of relationships
Building Character
Your Calling

PASTORAL LEADERSHIP

Goals
Processes
Working together
Getting things done
Exercising influence & power

Framework that guides our actions

The "hard" side of leadership

"Although (small groups) are intentional organizations, their fundamental reason for existence is quite often to provide deep, intimate interpersonal support... period."

Robert Wuthnow, *Sharing the Journey* (1994)

CHAPTER 6

Spiritual Community

In this chapter, we first explore the secular notions of teams and groups as a foundational framework and then discuss the definitions, values and leadership approaches to communities in the ministry setting. Following that, we will examine the dynamics of spiritual intelligence in the small-group setting, and establish a case for an interpretation of group dynamics that recognizes the spiritual component. Such a community we define as a true community. Next, we identify three dimensions of community potential, namely, the potential as a community of tasks, a community of practice, and the potential for becoming a community with spirit. All of these dynamics are derived from the hierarchy of relationships. Although we believe any group, team or small community, whether in the secular or ministry sector, can achieve these dimensions, we consider the choice and the harmonizing of these dimensions to be most appropriate for the pastoral setting. Finally, we offer practical applications to pastoral leaders on how to inspire teams and small-group communities to become communities with spirit.

A Primer of Group Theory and Leadership

Working in small groups or teams is as natural for parish life as it is for any large organization. Parish ministries offer their services through teams, committees or small groups. Parish staff, parish councils and finance councils perform their functions as a team. Parishes also have liturgy committees, welcoming committees, capital campaign committees, vocations committees and many more. Yet in the same way, many leaders find it difficult to recognize the subtle differences between pastoral leadership and secular leadership models. Many also underestimate the softer side of group dynamics in the ministry setting. The harder side of ministry, that is the side that focuses primarily on accomplishing tasks, although necessary, should never overshadow the softer side of group activities in ministry.

In academic jargon, a group is "a set of two or more people who interact with each other to achieve certain goals or to meet certain needs (George & Jones, 2007). The more common definition of groups is a *set of people who achieve goals*. So the academic definition is a reminder that *interactions* are an essential element of the group definition, an attribute sometimes missed in the popular definitions. The fact that interactions are essential to forming and maintaining a group also allows for different types or levels of interaction, a definitive doorway for the hierarchy of relationships presented in Chapter 5. This same definition also points to the possibility of addressing "needs" that could be external or internal, again allowing the opportunity to discuss the harder and softer sides of ministry. Finally, this academic definition of group presumes that a majority of participants agree on a set of goals or needs, a confirmation that there are often differences of opinion and opposing forces at play.

One of the most difficult situations for understanding group theory in the pastoral setting is the constant interchangeability of the terms "group" and "team." An understanding of these terms that glosses over their differences complicates any discussion of group theory. It's not uncommon to see ministry "groups" going through "team-building" exercises, or ministry "teams" (such as hospitality, altar server or readers) concerned about their "group dynamics." To add to the confusion, there are other terms used in the pastoral setting that promote interchangeability of team and group, such as the "council" or "staff." Is the parish council a team or a group? Likewise, is the parish staff a team or a group? In practice this is a difficult situation to tackle, yet for purposes of this chapter there needs to be some way to reduce the ambiguity between the two terms and provide guidelines that would heighten the sensitivity to what is appropriate and what may be unfitting for parish life.

Again, the academic interpretations of groups and teams are used as a way to distinguish one from the other. In organizational behavior textbooks, there is a clear distinction between formal groups (goals and needs are established by the organization) and informal groups (goals and needs are defined internally). Types of formal groups include the task force, the team, cross-functional teams, the self-managed work team and what we know as committees, councils and boards. The informal types of groups include friendship groups and interest groups (such as prayer groups). A cursory examination of the formal and informal types of groups is established by the main approach, be it predominantly task or relationally oriented. So for purposes of clarifying the differences between "group" and "team," group refers to the broader notion of interaction with each other to achieve certain goals or to meet certain needs to include the formal and the informal, whereas "team" is considered as a subset of formal groups. Granted, the so-called "high-performance teams" refers to teams that also have a high level of interaction, but the relational activity in this case is primarily determined by the tasks at hand. In other words, a team is a subset of a formal group (George & Jones, 2007). Of course there are other considerations such as group size, group composition, group function (contribution), group status (relevance) but what matters to pastoral leadership is the distinction between "group" and "team" since the distinctions reveal different purposes and identities that make up the crucial framework for a group-leader fit.

According to many academics, as well as practitioners, a *team* is a group of individuals who have some form of hierarchical structure but among themselves are interdependent persons responsible for completing assigned tasks and reaching specified goals (McDermott, 1998; Williams, Parker, & Turner, 2010; Zarraga-Oberty & Saa-Perez, 2006). The members of the *team* work together to determine how the specified task or goal will be accomplished among the *team* members, how the work is measured, and what the dependencies are as well has how they will be managed within the team environment (Williams, et al., 2010). The *team* generally has someone responsible for general oversight, a manager or team leader (McDermott, 1998). According to Huusko (2007), he also sees that *teams* abide by two fundamental elements: (a) ensure the work is arranged as to ensure the accomplishment of the specified goal and (b) there must be an identified rank or hierarchy that fits within the scope of the organization.

Again, the definition of "team" tends more toward a task orientation, and although relationships are an integral part of team dynamics, the value resides principally in relation to goal fulfillment. In contrast to what has been noted about teams, a group is less task oriented and more "community" centered, where community is defined both in the context of tasks and as "a group of individuals who have a sense of obligation toward one another" (Hill, 2000, p. 139). It seems, therefore, that a team has a natural emphasis toward completing tasks, although it is open to some depth in relationships provided they are clearly contributing to the successful achievement of the stated goals. Groups, on the other hand, have very specific goals but are seemingly more open to relationships even though some of these relationships may not directly contribute toward the fulfillment of a goal.

Having offered some definitional clarity to the meaning and significance of the terms *team, group* and *community*, the next consideration is a discussion of what would or would not be appropriate for ministry work. Earlier in the book we presented a similar comparison when analyzing the impact of secular leadership models in the Church setting. Just as we indicate that there are secular leadership models that play down some faith values and spiritual dynamics, it is also possible to identify potential limitations of secular "group" modeling.

Here is a brief discussion of our reasoning behind this appeal to sensitivity. Mental models have a significant influence in the way leaders establish priorities, address internal and external forces, and assess effectiveness of alternative courses of action (Zaccaro, Rittman, & Marks, 2001). Although using mental models in ministry is inevitable, there is a substantial risk that some desirable faith values will not be included into the group dynamics because either the desired values are incongruent with the mental model or the mental model is blind to or discourages certain values. Of course, a discussion of mental model management is beyond the scope of this work, but having a basic understanding of the capabilities and limitations of mental models is vital to analyzing what approaches would work or not work in the ministry setting.

For example, a ministry leader whose main value is maintaining order may not be inclined to consider discernment as a valuable dynamic to group decision making. On the other hand, the Church is not a democratic republic, and so an excessive preference for vote counting could also lead to a distorted view of the process of discernment. Or, a leader who is accustomed to managing by objectives may tend to focus largely on task performance and may not know how to effectively define and manage efforts oriented to softer goals, such as formation, spiritual growth and a sense of contribution to parish life. Mental models are tools. Just because you can use a knife as a screwdriver does not mean it is the best way to deal with a screw. Needless to say, it is therefore important to develop sensitivity to the mental models we adopt in the pastoral setting, without ignoring the need to focus on effectiveness.

To further illustrate, here are two additional examples. Two models in broad use in the parish setting are Tuckman's five stage model of group development, and the Spiritual Intelligence model. These models, although extensively evident in the parish setting, have limitations that may require some modification by parish leadership to better align them to pastoral life and community life as understood by the Church.

Tuckman's (1965) five stage model of group development identifies five stages: *Forming* (establishing a common understanding), *Storming* (emerging conflicts and disagreements), *Norming* (developing friendships), *Performing* (achieving goals) and *Adjourning* (disbanding or mourning). Although this model is used quite often as a leadership tool in ministry, the keen observer will note it is too single-dimensional to serve parish life well for long. The focus of this model is primarily the temporal task or goal at hand and gives the impression of a strictly linear progression through each stage. Yet experience indicates something quite to the contrary. Some stages are omitted or occur at the same time, or in a different order. To be sure, the model has value for the pastoral setting in terms of the human dynamics it identifies, but it does not speak to the softer side of group dynamics, such as the spiritual growth possibilities of the group or the potential for developing a "community with spirit." With this model, the implications of *Communio* are largely overlooked. In our opinion, this is a serious flaw because the focus of developing and maintaining a Christian community is the central focus of ministry and parish life. In many ministry groups there is a certain "continuity of tasks" in which the group members may change, but the activities remain fairly constant. For example, a pastor may change the relational setting or priorities of ministries within a parish, but the continuity of tasks continues within the context of the life of the parish life. To suggest that all ministries reach the "Adjourn" stage of development as the Tucker model does, is too categorical an approach and does not fit with what should be the best practices of leadership in the Church.

Another example of a model that may sound appealing yet should be handled with care in the ministry setting is the concept of *spiritual intelligence*. This recent perspective of organizational development has emerged as researchers continue to probe deeper into the complexi-

174

ties of leadership and organizations and seek better ways to manage and lead people in the current complex business environment. In many ways, the characteristics of *spiritual intelligence* complement the dynamics of small communities in a team setting as well as the efforts of the ecclesial leadership function in promoting a more complete sense of community. For instance, McMullen (2003) made an interesting point about the differences in the intelligences that are related to leadership. He explained that if *rational intelligence* is about thinking and *emotional intelligence* is about feeling, then *spiritual intelligence* is essentially about being. Yet *spiritual intelligence* is inherently more difficult to define and seems to be more about questions than answers. It includes understanding the limits of collective knowledge and the seeking of wisdom as a collective value. *Spiritual intelligence* enables the group to reassess their work situation so they can better express their collective identity. These characteristics help members in small groups to make contributions that are more effective to the group than if the group were functioning as a typical team. McMullen (2003) also suggests *spiritual intelligence* as a provider of a more holistic view of life, where mind, body and spirit are interconnected in various degrees within the group setting.

In addition, George (2006) found that in today's business environment, leaders face the difficult challenge of promoting creative and meaningful work with a clear purpose in the workplace. He claims that spiritual intelligence is built on the three deep motivators of *creativity*, *meaning* and *purpose*. Spiritual intelligence thus leads to an awakening of a deeper understanding of oneself as a non-materialistic being.

For leaders, spiritual intelligence can make a positive impact on the way they lead and manage people in the workplace. This is particularly important in the formation of small communities, not only in the workplace but also in Church ministries. For instance, long-term relationships could be built upon an inter-personal understanding, resulting in increased productivity. In addition, implementing and managing change becomes less difficult; overcoming obstacles in the workplace or in ministry could be met with enthusiasm, rather with fear and suspicion.

Essentially, we argue that when reflecting on the mental models of teams or groups, the pastoral leader must assess the ability of the model to develop "community competency" instead of focusing primarily on tasks, with secondary interest in relationships. The primacy of relationships discussed in the previous chapter now becomes the standard for developing "community competency" in all groups within the parish.

A discussion on "community competency" in ministry groups begins with an analysis of some biases within our culture that affect the way community is interpreted and operationalized, both in the secular and religious settings. Three cultural attributes of North American society are identified as hostile toward attempts to develop a broader sense of "community" and thus warrant a focus from the pastoral leader in order to maintain a primacy of relationships. These major cultural biases converge on a rational construction of "self," that by definition, places an emphasis on rational at the expense of relational ways of developing knowledge and action. Only after the effects of these cultural influences are understood, and the concept of self is reframed in relational terms expressed in the previous chapter, can a broader perspective of community be operationalized within the parish setting.

Hostility Toward Community Competencies

It is evident that the conceptual understanding of terminology is influenced by the dominant cultural attributes of a society (Cooper & Denner, 1998). For instance, the understanding of leadership in many Western cultures contains in its common operationalization a notable male-over-female gender bias that is quite difficult to correct (Eagly & Karau, 2002). Just think of the "Great Man Theory" of leadership. Does it imply that there were no "Great Women" leaders? There are and have been great men leaders in Church, but there are also great women leaders, and in fact, some of them are Doctors of the Church. Yet because of this male-over-female cultural bias, the formulations of constructs, definitions and theoretical modeling must be accepted as having limitations or constraints, and where possible, need to be addressed and properly sized (Cook & Campbell, 1979). Under these conditions, it can be assumed that the definition and operationalization of the word "community," as it is known in Western civilization and particularly in North America, may also contain cultural influences that, if left unchecked, may lead to both theoretical constraints and limitations in their application (Zane & Yeh, 2002).

Specifically, three cultural influences dominant in North American society not only impact a fuller understanding of the word "community" but have also been identified as detrimental to the building of community competency. These impediments are (a) individualism, (b) competition and (c) the excessive use of rational ways of knowing.

The cultural framework to which the laity (and, of course, the clergy as well) is exposed in North America is characterized as deeply *individualistic* (Ditomaso, Parks-Yancy, Post, 2003), and consequently, *relationally deficient* (Hay, 2000). Various authors have even gone further and identified some specific negative effects of individualism in the American Catholic Church (Gillis, 1999; Garvey, 1993). Notably, there are cases in which this individualistic influence unintentionally affects some of the definitions of "community" used to characterize Church. For instance, McCarthy makes the following statement: "It's not the Church but I, as Church, who must assume responsibility for creating and manifesting community" (McCarthy, 2000). This definition of Church places emphasis in the "I" and tends to undermine the understanding of the Church community as a "we."

Consequently, it can be reasonably assumed that the laity embodies, albeit in varying degrees, substantially the same attributes of the culture in which it exists. If North American society is identified as basically individualistic, then the laity should be alerted to the need to understand how this cultural factor is biasing the meaning of "community." Said differently, attempts by the laity to form a community made up of

177

members who possess unyielding individualistic orientations may be viewed as impractical. Only when individualism is softened can community emerge: "The kind of individualism that acknowledges our 'interdependence' is the kind of individualism that makes real community possible" (England, 1992, p. 9).

The second cultural attribute detrimental to "community competency" is the "competitive mindset." Competition is recognized as the No. 1 American business value (Stewart-Allen, 2003) since the origins of the American culture (Lee & Peterson, 2000), and is recognized as a barrier to many forms of collaborative efforts (Thompson, Socolar, Brown & Haggerty, 2002). On the other hand, research demonstrates that the most significant indicator of successful "community competency" is a "willingness to work together" (Johnson, Zorn, Yung Tan, Lamontage & Johnson, 2003). Since "working together" rather than "competing against each other," is also a "community competency," individuals with habitual competitive behaviors may find it difficult to adapt and implement certain community values (i.e., selfless giving, forgiveness, empathy, trust). Lawler makes the following observation: "Raised on a coarse diet of individualism, Americans can bring to marriage and family an unhealthy competitive spirit" (Lawler, 1995). Americans can also bring this same unhealthy competitive spirit into Church communities and ministry.

The third cultural bias in our Western Society that hinders a fuller understanding of the "community" construct is the dominance of *rational* "ways of knowing" over *relational* ways of knowing. In a critique of how rational ways become a hindrance to understanding "community," Chickering notes:

> Objective, analytic, experimental. Very quickly this seemingly bloodless epistemology becomes an ethic. It is an ethic of competitive individualism, in the midst of a world fragmented and made exploitable by that very mode of knowing. The

mode of knowing itself breeds intellectual habits, indeed spiritual instincts, that destroy community. We make objects of each other, and the world to be manipulated for our own private ends (Chickering, 2003, p. 41).

Said differently, the rational way of knowing is characterized by a constructivist research method that emphasizes rationality and ignores other forms of knowing (Heron & Reason, 1997). In this sense, the rationalization of "community" may be adequate for the objectivity required in a business setting, but by excluding relational, experiential and practical forms of knowledge, this same understanding of community remains deficient for other sectors, particularly in the ministry setting. The "rational community" is characterized as excessively structured, linear in its activities, selective in its members, objective in its outcomes and exclusive of spiritual matters. Even intuitively, it seems unlikely that the fullness of community can be grasped through only one form of knowing. A receptivity to other forms of knowing, especially spiritual knowing and relational knowing, are integral to the effort to develop "community competency."

The privatized interpretation of self (autonomous, exclusivist and pragmatic) that seems so predominant in American culture and embodied quite well in the business setting (Hewett, 2002) is here considered an impediment to a fuller appreciation of healthy community practices and behaviors. In challenging this rational concept of self and the detrimental effects it has on interpersonal relations, various scholars suggest offering the alternative of more *relational* definitions of self (Anderson & Chen, 2002; Russell, 1999). In other words, redefining the self as more *relational* and less privatized is imperative in overcoming cultural biases that limit the understanding and operationalization of a fuller understanding of community. This "relational self" argues that knowledge about self is not only intellectual, but is also linked to and discovered in others (Andersen & Chen, 2002). Accordingly, this "relational reframing" of self is seen as more apt to nurture and develop relationships

179

as a way to broaden the understanding of self beyond what cultural biases tend to offer (Cross & Morris, 2003).

What we are saying here is that individualism, competition and rationalization are dominant attributes of the North American culture that form a barrier or "shell" that opposes the ability to form "community competency." The detrimental effects of these three cultural biases are evident even in parish life, notably in areas of individualistic traditions as compared to Catholic social teaching (Cima & Schubeck, 2001), in the fierce competition among American religious communities (Kaufman, 2002), and in the way these biases affect the growth of Catholic families as basic forms of community in the United States (D'Antonio, 1985). Although attempts to penetrate this shell have merit, a more robust effect can be achieved by addressing their point of convergence. But what is that common denominator—that if addressed—can make a significant transformation from the "I" as "me" to the "I" as "we"?

In analyzing the apparent contradictions of autonomy and interdependence models in Western cultures, Killen & Wainryb (2000) note a point of convergence, a common root of these two opposite social orientations, which is the "individual."

More to the point, Hewitt (2002) is able to demonstrate that what is labeled as the individualistic, compartmentalized and rational-pragmatic character of American culture is directly related to the interpretation of the self. It follows that if the convergence of individualism, competition and rationalization occur at the interpretation of the "self," then a fuller understanding of "community competency" occurs through the reframing and re-forming of "self" along more open and collective interpretations. Formation processes that provide continuous awareness and methods to visualize the "self," with the community as a contributor of defining the "self," becomes an essential task for the pastoral leader.

Here, the diverse cultures within the Church that possess a more community-oriented definition of "self" provide the pastoral leader with a valuable resource in seeking the possibilities of forming better "community competency" by healing the individualistic interpretations of "self." Instead of primarily looking for things to do, less "privatized" small communities would be more open to "finding themselves through others." Hence the formation of pastoral leaders becomes crucial in developing ways to transform the interpretations of "self" and take advantage of parish diversity as a learning and growing activity. Rather than loving just the tasks they perform, small groups should learn how to love the "what" they can learn about themselves in a caring and nurturing environment with a diversity and plurality of others.

Creating new knowledge of the relational paradigm is best, not so much through rational ways alone (reading, analyzing, extracting lessons to be learned), but through "relational learning." In this way, the paradigm used to gain knowledge about relationships models the object of the learning. Being open and able to integrate from those cultures that already enjoy dominant relational attributes is one way to create awareness and overcome the cultural biases against relational learning. In their book "Culture, ethnicity, and personal relationship processes," Gaines, Buriel, Liu, and Rios (1997) suggest that Hispanic, African-American, and Asian cultures in North America have much to contribute to "relational learning." In fact, Catholic theologians have already noted that "U.S. Hispanics, with their focus on family and community values, can bring a much-needed balance to U.S. culture" (Schaeffer, 2000, p. 4). African-American culture (Nicotera, Clinkscales, & Walker, 2003) and Asian cultures (Park, 1998) have similarly contributed their relational values, traditions and practices. It therefore seems reasonable that rather than treating these cultural sectors as "recipients" of hospitality or as "guests," we should instead seek to learn from these cultures by "making a home" for them (Matovina, 2001) as a way to foster relational learning and a broader understanding of self, community and spirituality.

In summary, the shell of individualism, competition and rational dominance are identified by scholars and researchers as attributes of the North American culture that may be placing artificial limits on the understanding of self and community within parish life. Needless to say, much is at stake here. The richness of parish life is tied to the extent to which the leaders in the parish are able to reform their sense of self. It is here that the pastoral leader has an important and significant task in finding ways to penetrate this "shell" and promote "community competency" through more intense relational frameworks.

Pursuing Community Competency

One of the most recognized research projects on the value of small groups as transforming U.S. communities is a work conducted by Robert Wuthnow. In his book, "Sharing the Journey: Support Groups and America's New Quest for Community" (1994, Free Press), Wuthnow describes the results of an extensive study based on quantitative and qualitative data collected from close to 2,000 individuals. Among his conclusions, he observes that 40 percent of the adults in the United States (about 75 million Americans) claim involvement in a "small group that meets regularly and provides caring and support for those who participate in it" (Wuthnow, 1994, p. 45). Most of the small-group involvements occur in a church setting. Here, Wuthnow confirms through his sober assessment of small groups that the "thirst for community" emerges as a reaction to the purely rational and privatized approach to community:

> The small-group movement has emerged as a serious effort to combat the forces of fragmentation and anonymity in our society and to reunite spirituality with its roots in human community (Wuthnow, 1994, p. 40).

The historical development, significance, anatomy, operational dynamics and implications of this movement to Church and society in the United States are extremely relevant to leadership development programs designed to develop leaders capable of fostering community competencies. Wuthnow's research is a sound foundational context for presenting successful techniques, identifying shortfalls and measuring effectiveness of leader skills in developing true community. Likewise, a recent study by Bernard and D'Antonio (2000) entitled "The Catholic experience of small Christian communities" offers a comparable analysis within the Catholic Church context and contains more specific pastoral recommendations.

So how is community defined and what mental models can we use to help penetrate the "shell" of cultural biases and promote community competencies that are better aligned with relational dynamics that can lead to deeper spiritual experiences in parish life?

Defining "Community" in Parish Life

In defining parish groups and ministries both as a "community" and as a "community within a community" within parish life, we prefer to emphasize the relational framework presented in the previous chapter. Therefore, we define "community" as a nursery of relationships.

The term "nursery" is a very deliberate attempt at recognizing the organic, experimental and protected nature of relational dynamics in the group setting. Nurseries, by definition, are spaces carefully designed for the fostering of skills, behaviors and growth within a protected and supervised environment. Children's nurseries, for example, are places where children are cared for in a safe and stimulating environment. These are typically for children between the ages of 3 and 5, staffed by qualified teachers and other professionals who offer supervised activities directed at developing character, social behaviors and creativity. A plant or tree nursery is also a protected environment, but in this case designed for the propagation and care of seedlings and young plants. Here, plants or trees are provided protection and a controlled environment designed to maximize the growth potential of the plants. As such, these nurseries are a place where plants are allowed to grow or heal before being transferred to more unpredictable or even hostile environments. In effect, the plants are prepared to thrive in a less accommodating environment.

The strategy we suggest for building community competency is simple, and it is based on applying this *Nursery Effect* to every small group or team in parish life. Said in a more elaborate way, the common functions of a nursery—that of a protected place, a place of renewal, a place of healing—is what we are suggesting pastoral leaders provide small groups. A small group (or a community) as a nursery of relationships is a *safe space* where participants feel free to interact and explore deeper and more meaningful relationships, develop a capacity for forgiveness, better understand diversity and trust, and build confidence in life and spirit as a single connected reality and not as two worlds that need to be managed separately. Workplaces, television, movie theaters, bars or shopping centers are unlikely places to help with the deeper social and spiritual pursuits of adults who seek more meaningful depth that faith provides. A small group as a nursery of relationships is also a *place of renewal*, a place to develop a language of the heart, to practice discernment, to experience love in action, to challenge childhood beliefs or misunderstandings of Church, to resolve moral dilemmas and to acquire a better understanding of life and death issues. A small group as a nursery of relationships is also a *place of healing*, of encouragement, of celebration and of courage when we face difficult decisions and need emotional support for family issues, loneliness, problems at work, a place to rebuild fragmented lives in the company of others, to learn how to give up personal interests and pay more attention to the needs of others, and a place to feel wanted despite brokenness and fragility.

In our experience, too many pastoral groups come about more as a way to get something done than as a source of relational support. Yet ministry groups as nurseries of relationships are more than just ends in themselves. They are also the setting in which participants have the opportunity to broaden their understanding of themselves as individuals, to find themselves, to rediscover what was lost and to seek answers to complex questions. Nurseries of relationships are spaces that provide highly personal and informal interactions and forms of intimacies not found elsewhere. Nurseries of relationships teach how to transcend our self-centered interests and ways to satisfy the quest for deeper spirituality needs. The alternative is to conform to the secular models of teams and groups and lose our capacity to grow meaningfully.

To be sure, we are not advocating a new Walden, based on a romantic and utopian vision of heaven on earth. No community on earth will exist in total bliss, even those that adhere most ardently to the principles of the spiritual nursery which we advocate. What we propose is that our life as church, especially within the Church, should be lived by the Gospel values established by the primordial Founder of our Church. To do otherwise is to ignore the principle that grace builds on nature. All earthly communities will struggle relationally to some extent. However, by remaining focused on the other, we will continue to help ourselves and others to focus on who we are becoming and on who we were made to be. Getting the job done simply cannot trump those values.

In summary, a community is nursery of relationships that offers a *safe-place*, a place of *renewal* and a place of *healing*. Community is a place where transactional, assurance, identity, nurturing and transformational forms of relationships grow safely, evolve into formative renewal, and offer effective healing. In assessing the role of the leader with respect to this perspective, Wuthnow (1994) notes,

> The role of leaders as sources of information and advice, therefore, must not be overlooked as a factor in the spiritual development of group members. (Wuthnow, 1994, p. 267).

Since we have been arguing throughout this book that pastoral leadership is a spiritual practice, it follows that each group—as a small community of faith within the larger community of parish life—becomes more a *safe place*, a place of *renewal*, and a place of *healing*.

If there is a priority for leaders in ministry, improving their *community competency* skills becomes more relevant and crucial than learning how to adopt secular leadership theories and practices. It is here that we are convinced that much is at stake.

The Potentials of Community

Any group—in parish ministry or in a business setting—has the potential to become the type of community described above. Teams and groups may be largely defined by tasks in any sector in any industry, but there is always room in the internal dynamics of a group to include a nursery of relationships. It is always possible to develop the relational dynamics of a group. Even in the highly disciplined, highly task oriented and highly effective world of military special operations teams—as an extreme case—there is always room for language of the heart and spirit. The experiences we have shared with military commanders and chaplains at their home bases and in the battlefields give credence to the possibilities of developing the "softer side" of any type of team and group. So essentially, becoming community is a choice.

Here again, the leader plays a crucial role. More to the intent of this chapter, the pastoral leader plays a crucial role in recognizing the potential of the group and findings ways to guide the group into a more relationally oriented set of behaviors. But how can this be accomplished without the assistance of mental models based upon relationships?

As an easier approach to promulgating a richer relational environment in ministry for both the leader and the group participants—and drawing from formal research on the sociology of group dynamics—we suggest *all teams and groups* have the potential to grow along three fundamental behavioral dimensions: a community of task, a community of practice and a community of spirit. In fact, most groups in ministry tend to navigate freely among these three dimensions of interpersonal behaviors, although with a tendency to emphasize *community of tasks* dimension. We intend to present a clearer view of the implications of each dimension as a way of identifying a path to building community competency. In this way, we hope to generate a fuller picture of possibilities to help pastoral leaders become more aware of the spiritual yearning of those who are entrusted to them in ministry. The increased role of spirituality in the American culture and the quest for community are at the core of why people come to a parish community. By providing within parish ministries what other groups—clubs, social gatherings, workplaces, etc.—cannot fully address, the pastoral leader becomes more aligned with the mission of the Church in the world.

A way to visually illustrate the *dimensions of community potential* is by means of a diagram in the form of a trifold sheet of paper, in which each face of the trifold corresponds to one of the dimensions and the "natural" relational emphasis becomes a function of the "angle of view" (See Figure 4). So for a team or group that adopts the *community of tasks* dimension, the direct angle of view for this trifold model is directly focused on transactional and assurance relationships, and the angles for the other views of the trifold are too acute to influence the observer. Such a focus is typically what is expected from a "high performance" team or work group in the business or for-profit sector. As the trifold on the following page indicates, the "higher level" relational dynamics are always present and thus able to influence the group, but the focus on tasks reduces the potential of these influencers.

In contrast, the angle of view for a *community of practice* is wider and thus potentially more influential in nurturing relationships— perhaps even transformational relationships. This is the case of many nonprofit organization teams or groups (humanitarian services, hospitals, ministry services related) for which the tasks (group objectives) themselves are people-oriented.

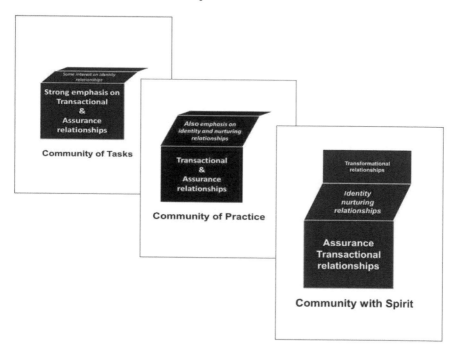

Figure 4, Trifold view, Dimensions of Community

Here is where the team or group realizes the value of spirituality—albeit in different forms—and this is where the group or team can become a *nursery of relationships*. The convergence of broader angles of view of the team (or group) indicates that generative potential of *leadership as*
a spiritual practice.

In the next paragraphs, each of these three potentials of community are defined in more depth and are analyzed against the hierarchy of relationships and the pastoral leadership model. Also, examples are offered to assist in the better understanding of each potential.

Community of Tasks

The dimension of community potential referred to as *Community of Tasks* describes dynamics that are heavily focused on an orientation on tasks. Here, the "harder" side of leadership prevails, albeit with some potential for "higher level" interpersonal interactions. Within this dimension, the terms "team" and "group" are more interchangeable because the natural common ground among them is the emphasis on completing tasks and achieving goals. Here, the classical definitions of both team and group show minimal differentiations, as Lussier and Achua (2007) demonstrate:

> A team is a unit of two or more people with complementary skills who are committed to a common purpose and set of performance goals and to common expectations, for which they hold themselves accountable; share responsibility; leadership is participative and empowered-oriented; performance measures create direct accountability for the team and incentives are team-based. A group is a collection of people working together that focus on individual performance and goals,

189

and reliance on individual abilities, sometimes work independently with greater motivation to achieve personal goals; the leadership style tends to be very hierarchical; performance is characterized by individual self-interest, with a mindset of (what's in it for me)." All teams are groups, but not all groups are teams. A manager can put a group of people together and never build a team.

The central elements in a comparison of these definitions illustrate the team's fundamental social essence (*working together*), its purpose (*goal-performance*), and the expected roles, responsibilities and contributions of the members. It's interesting to observe how the definition of team quoted above softens its task focus by suggesting relational means, whereas the definition of a group—perhaps by nature a bit looser in task focus and more open to relationships—calls for a hierarchical style of leadership to ensure that things get done. But again, the driving force in both definitions is "getting things done."

This predominance of task orientation provides the framework that defines the multiple forms of teams and groups in the business setting, such as functional teams (a group of employees belonging to the same functional department), cross-functional teams (composed of members from multiple functions or disciplines), high-performance teams (team members recruited on the basis of their expertise). The latter exhibit a sense of ownership for whatever the group is doing, possess the ability to work together effectively to resolve conflicts; use win-win negotiation strategy; communicate openly and supportively, and collaborate on problem-solving tactics. Another type of task-oriented team is the self-managing team (SMT). It's key characteristics include: operates relatively autonomously, the team members share or rotate leadership responsibilities, and they hold themselves mutually responsible for a set of performance goals. Despite the unique names and the different operating modes of these teams or groups, they all share the essential characteristic of being a communities of tasks, and thus focused principally on the task.

To be sure, parish activities must include some element of task orientation, otherwise little will ever be accomplished. Accordingly, some orientation to a *Communities of Tasks* is essential in parish life. For example, projects, such as capital campaigns, parish finances, fund raisers, facility scheduling, maintenance, management of information systems and technology and natural disaster planning, will require a high task orientation to make it possible to conduct parish life. Additionally, *Communities of Tasks* in parish life make it possible for the parish to use its resources appropriately, to identify and obtain needed skills and to provide the necessary structures to carry out the mission of the parish. In effect, without an appropriate respect for getting things done, a parish will eventually devolve into a community of chaos. So it seems necessary to engender an appropriate level of *Communities of Tasks* in the community of the parish.

But in ministry it is also imperative that we recognize that *Communities of Tasks* represent only one dimension of community potential. To limit the development of *community competency* to the dynamics of a task orientation neglects the potential that relational experiences bring to parish life and also ignores the unique treasures of what parish life and the Church have to offer our society.

In recognizing the value of the *Communities of Tasks*, the leader and the group operate on the lower end of the hierarchy of relationships. That level of the relational hierarchy is largely transactional in nature and is designed to protect the institution and its achievements. The difference between the secular and the pastoral leadership models—as we have presented earlier—reside in the value of creating the nursery effect, that is of building community capacity, of promoting interpersonal relationships and nurturing the spiritual life. In this sense, the pastoral leader must be committed to forming others by helping them become aware of the shortcomings of our culture and to discover the great potential in their lives.

Community of Practice

The second dimension of community potential is the *Community of Practice.* It is a relatively new term in organizational development. The term is an outgrowth of the knowledge management movement, which seeks to develop more flexible types of organizations that "learn" how to manage diversity —and in the case of for-profit organizations— become more competitive. This business strategy has also been used by nonprofit organizations and other organizations in the public and private sectors as a way to enhance performance, foster ownership and perpetuate a continuous improvement effort.

A *Community of Practice* refers to teams or small groups that thrive on *learning and capability development,* both personal and collective (Wenger & Snyder, 2000). Knowledge—and how knowledge affects practice—is the expected outcome of a community of practice. Communities of practice tend to be more informal and self-organizing. As a result, they are oriented to learning and discovering. Because the "output" or results of a community of practice are intangible (*learning* and *capability development*), more intense relational dynamics and introspection are prevalent. (Refer to "*The knowledge creating company*" by Nonaka & Takeuch, 1995). As such, this type of community provides the beginnings of what we have called *the Nursery Effect*, of creating the protected spaces for new ideas and experiences.

In the case of high-performance teams, or *Communities of Tasks*, we noted that the team is highly structured and goal-oriented. Belbin (2004, 2007) referred to this structure as a "set framework"—or as we said, an angle of view—with strict guidelines for the team's internal activities. This rigidity can often stifle creativity and personal growth of the team members, while facilitating the performance of tasks. Also, team members tend to substitute their sense of commitment to themselves for commitment to the tasks at hand. But when organizations give teams higher levels of responsibilities in an effort to earn their trust and engage them more in organizational processes, the organization is valuing team learning and building. Under the newly acquired levels of trust, team members form communities of practice for various reasons ranging from peer-to-peer connections, responses to external influences, or to adjust to challenges presented when company strategies are realigned. Snyder, Wenger, & de Sousa Briggs (2004) described this dimension of community as "social learning systems" designed to develop relationships within the peer group as well as with stakeholders, to solve problems, to share ideas and to build toolsets to effect change. Team members take ownership of processes and brainstorm ways to improve day-to-day and long-term operations that will sustain growth in and of the organization.

The concepts that describe *Communities of Practice* may be new to Western culture, but have always existed in tribal communities. These communities share similar concerns, interests and passions that allow them to collectively evolve the necessary structures and processes to deepen their expertise and knowledge through engaging one another in an ongoing basis (Barab & Duffy, 2000). In many ways—and from the social construction perspective—communities of practice are mutually sustaining communities where members share overlapping histories, values and beliefs. Over time they develop a repertoire of artifacts that embody learning. They are organized in ways that maximize opportunities for interactions, for active participation of all and for the development of meaningful relationships. Finally, growth and renewal processes are made available to new members using past and present persons within the community (Hung et. al., 2006). Today these principles of *Communities of Practice* include all kinds of enterprises, professional organizations, medical disciplines and religious and educational communities, as well as other networks of people with the desire to share and learn.

We cannot emphasize enough the differences between *Communities of Tasks and Communities of Practice. Communities of Tasks* are tightly integrated units that coalesce by the nature and importance of the tasks they are to complete. They are defined by the focus on managing task completion and bound together principally by the collective commitment of its members to results. *Communities of Practice*, on the other hand, are loosely knit groups driven by the shared value they provide to members. They are defined by the opportunities to learn, to interact and to discover. *Communities of Practice* are driven by shared values, while *Communities of Tasks* are bound by task deliverables. Unlike teams, *Communities of Practice* almost never have specific tangibles to deliver to the organization. They are driven by the value they provide for individual members. *Communities of Practice* arise out of people's natural desire to share ideas, get help, learn about new ideas, verify their thinking and hear about the latest professional terminologies. As a result, to start and develop communities of practice is much more difficult that developing a team, because communities of practice are organized around knowledge, rather than output. Whether the organization supports them or not, *Communities of Practice* arise naturally in most organizations. A known and proven key success for building and sustaining *Community of Practice* is of course, the leader (McDermott,1999).

As noted earlier, the angle of view for a *Community of Practice* is wider and thus is more focused on personal identity and on nurturing relationships, maybe even transformational relationships. This is the case of many nonprofit organization teams or groups (humanitarian services, hospitals, ministry services) for which the tasks and group objectives are people-oriented. Examples from the for-profit, military, nonprofit and ecclesial sectors should help clarify the value and the angle of view corresponding to the *Communities of Practice* dimension.

In the for-profit sector, the Society of Human Resource Management (SHRM) is a community of human resources (HR) professionals working for numerous types or organizations across all major industries. SHRM members act as a professional network of individuals who share the knowledge and experience they have gained through white papers, forums, blogs, conferences and personal and business contacts, among other things. Knowledge is defined as "relevant information that is applied and that is based partially on experience (Zarraga-Oberty and Saa-Perez, 2006). The knowledge is shared across industries and business functions. There is no hierarchy in the community; the person with the most knowledge on a specific subject and the ability to share the knowledge effectively is generally the leader for the moment. In the case of SHRM, the organization acts as a conduit for information and is structured as the resource, and thus leader, for human resource professionals. The SHRM community operates as a community of practice by sharing "information, insight, experiences, and tools about an area of common interest" (McDermott, 1999, p. 33).

In the military sector, the After Action Review (AAR) sets the stage for organizational learning after field exercises. For example, at the Army's Joint Readiness Training Center (JRTC) in Louisiana, at the end of an exercise rotation, all significant observations of strengths and deficiencies from each participating unit are collected and evaluated in a cross-functional forum. The objective of the forum is to seek out and demonstrate best practices and "learning events" that can be applied to future exercise rotations.

An example in which *Communities of Practice* apply to the non-profit sector is in the use of Community Health Partnerships (CHP). These partnerships are made up of diverse community organizations that have joined forces on a volunteer basis to explore and address many of the complex issues in healthcare and to seek better ways to improve community health (Mitchell & Shortell, 2000). In fact, some colleges and universities are already offering leadership certifications or degree programs for managing and sustaining non-profit *Communities of Practice*. Examples of such certification programs come from the Texas Association of Non-profit Organizations (TANO) and Austin Community College.

In the ecclesial sector, parish councils may be seen as *Communities of Practice*. In these groups, learning about parish life is fostered, and the opportunities for improvement are investigated, reflected upon and considered for action. The more common—and misguided—concept of a pastoral council is that of a board of directors. In a study that compares parish council guidelines from thirteen different areas of the Catholic Church in the United States, Fischer (2010) argues that a pastoral council that behaves as a coordinator of parish ministries misses a central aspect of parish life:

> The council is not pastoral because it prays, uses consensus, or avoids administration. It is pastoral because it helps the pastor by its study, reflection, and recommended conclusions.

As parish councils go beyond the "board of directors" model and become more engaged in identifying and articulating the vital signs of parish life, they explore, study and reflect on the "signs of the times" and formulate a "collective wisdom" as guidance for the pastor. In doing so, they are in fact using *Communities of Practice* principles, if only inadvertently. As an example, the following description is from the Diocese of Sacramento Pastoral Council guidelines (November 2005) stating (with our emphasis in italics):

> The Parish Pastoral Council is a consultative body, pastoral in nature, because it strives to *discern* the movement of the Holy Spirit among God's people in the parish. A Parish Pastoral Council gives its help to the pastor in *fostering pastoral activity*; it *investigates*, under the authority of the pastor, all those things which pertain to pastoral works *to ponder them*, and to *propose practical conclusions* about them. It is essential that Council meetings occur in the context of prayer and openness to the Holy Spirit, so that at all times the common good will prevail.

Another—and most unique—example of *Community of Practice* is the INSPIRE program. It is a joint venture of the Archdiocese of Chicago and The Institute for Pastoral Studies (Loyola University-Chicago), sustained by a grant from the Lily Endowment. As a program designed to address pastoral learning and individual learning within the parish leadership teams (primarily parish staffs), the director sought out and recruited a cadre of experienced consultants with experience in secular models of leadership and organizational development and team dynamics, balanced by substantial experience of Church and parish life. Each of these parish consultants served as change agents who promoted reflection, awareness, discovery and interventions to give the parish teams new perspectives about themselves and their contributions to parish life. Detailed team and individual learning plans were crafted by each parish team, with team and individual learning resources allocated accordingly. Over a period of about nine years, close to forty parishes within the Archdiocese of Chicago benefited from this program.

What is remarkable about this program is its natural setting for creating *Communities of Practice*. Project INSPIRE's purpose was to focus on team and individual learning in ministry as a path to pastoral excellence. Such a purpose is consistent with the definition of *Communities of Practice*. More importantly, the cadre of consultants met periodically not only to report the status of their activities but also to ponder the commonalities, the potential and the best practices that emerged from their own parish consulting experiences. The learning from these interventions over time benefitted the consultants, but also provided the continuous framework for topics of interest and for communicating best practices to all participating parishes during the general assemblies, or INSPIRE convocations. These convocations became opportunities to set up conferences and workshops with some of the most recognized experts on Church and parish life. They were designed as a place to create more awareness among parishes, and a forum for formal and informal sharing among parish teams. In fact, the interest in researching and publishing a book dedicated to pastoral leadership at the service of parish life is driven largely by the learning that emerges from this project and from all the parishes that one of the authors was privileged to consult and develop over the nine years of the grant period.

The INSPIRE experience was not only a validation of how communities of practice can promote pastoral learning in parish teams and how that learning emerges and is shared, but more importantly, it was a confirmation of the need, desire and value of becoming a commu-

197

nity with spirit as a pathway to pastoral excellence. As the team and individual learning became intertwined with the spiritual, a number of caring, nurturing and safe space activities emerged as a transformational force within the teams and groups. Within this emerging dimension of community, tasks, learning and spiritual concerns converged to create a community with spirit. Understanding the fundamentals of communities with spirit is the topic of the next section.

Community with Spirit

The third dimension of community potential we refer to as *Community with Spirit.* It is within this dimension that a group acknowledges the significance of "safe spaces," of a fuller scale of interpersonal relationships and where active participation in spiritual endeavors is a constant and evolving practice. As indicated earlier, the potential for teams or groups as *Communities with Spirit* suggests an angle of view that embraces a fuller spectrum of relationships and transformational possibilities. Here is where the team or group realizes the value of spirituality in its variety of forms, and where the group or team becomes a *nursery of relationships* along *with the Spirit.* The team (or group's) angle of view encompasses all three dimensions. The team remains aware of all dimensions and this recognition, practice and synchronicity with the Spirit. It is in this dynamic that the uniqueness of *leadership as a spiritual practice* has its most generative effects.

If one could make a case that the for-profit sector is responsible for demonstrating the value of *Communities of Tasks* and the eventual evolution into *Community of Practice,* we would also have to acknowledge their role in the evolution of *Communities with Spirit.* As employees of business organizations implemented *Communities of Practice*, they eventually began to form relationships that nurtured the careers of their colleagues through the teaching of best practices, the sharing of industry-related knowledge. As a result, they eventually became genuinely concerned for the personal and professional well-being of each participant (McDermott, 1999; Zarraga-Oberty and Saa-Perez, 2006).

These atypical forms of relationships then transcended into forms of more personal relationships of *care and concern*. In discovering the competitive advantage rising from these new relational dimensions, Novell Corporation implemented a leadership program that instilled a "community of nurturing" approach to leadership development. And when the community approach was applied to the program, the corporation was able to develop leaders who had the desired organizational culture and the leadership skills required to lead teams in a more positive and nurturing manner (Klein, 2005). In the healthcare industry, as another example, the leaders who are most successful display an "interconnectedness" to their spiritual self and project that upon the team (Strack & Fottler, 2002; Klein, Ziergert, Knight, & Xiao, 2006). These nurturing behaviors were built around relationships such as a "trust-in, and loyalty-to, centers of value that are of ultimate concern..."

Inevitably, this same momentum also triggered an interest is relationships within a spiritual context, therefore generating the Spirit at Work Movement. Consequently, research has acknowledged that leaders who are more spiritually centered in their ways achieve better results in their organizations, especially as they become what secular leadership is calling "transformational leaders" (Strack & Fottler, 2002).

However, pastoral leadership has the potential to communicate and achieve a deeper understanding of transformational leadership. In secular leadership theory, leaders who become "transformational" basically implement Kouzes and Posner's *Five Practices of Effective Leaders*: (1) challenge the process, (2) inspire a shared vision, (3) enable others to act, (4) model the way, and (5) encourage the heart (Strack & Fottler, 2002). A leader who operates within his or her spiritual center, realizes his or her "fundamental state" and extends that spiritual center into the leadership role. Quinn (2004) calls this *a fundamental state of leadership*. The fundamental state of leadership suggests that an individual must realize the fullness of self-in relation (to others and to the Divine) and be open to *deep change* (Quinn, 2004). In other words, transformation comes from the leader's initiatives.

Yet different than the secular models, the pastoral leader—as we intend—is not the primary cause of the transformation, but is more a "steward of transformation." Pastoral leaders—as stewards of transformation—hold something in trust for another person (the Divine), make choices of service to others over self-interests and make a visible and genuine commitment to the community and to the broader "community of communities." If the group is to become a *nursery of relationships*, then the leader's role, as a "steward of transformation," is akin to the gardener's role. Stewardship is a spiritual value, and as such, it fits nicely into the continuous mantra of this book that 'leadership is a spiritual practice."

Another difference between the secular and pastoral views of spiritual transformation is the depth and breadth of proven schools of "spirituality available to parish life. The secular understanding of transformation is at this point, too narrow and for the most part, untested. In fact, one of the objections of secular transformational leaderships is the question, "What are you transforming me into?" On the other hand, the pastoral leader recognizes "transformation" as one of many other words used by spiritual authors throughout the life of the Church:

> The word transformation is part of a richly varied semantic field: to form, malform, reform, be conformed and transform. Throughout the centuries spiritual authors have used this semantic field to bring out the inner logic of the spiritual way. For them this semantic field—and within it especially the term "transformation"—refers to the most significant transitions into the divine-human relational process. (Waaijman, 2002, p. 455)

We can also consider a third difference between the secular and pastoral views of spiritual transformation in relation to the group, or community, which is the reality of *communio* within the Church. *Communio* is a central principle of community competency in the Church. It is absent from secular literature because of its origins in the Divine. In fact, in *Novo milleniuo ineunte (January 6, 2001)*, Pope John Paul II gives a broad topography of the meaning and significance of *communion:*

> A spirituality of communion indicates above all the heart's contemplation of the mystery of the Trinity dwelling in us, and whose light we must also be able to see shining on the face of the brothers and sisters around us. A spirituality of communion also means an ability to think of our brothers and sisters in faith within the profound unity of the Mystical Body, and therefore as "those who are a part of me." This makes us able to share their joys and sufferings, to sense their desires and attend to their needs, to offer them deep and genuine friendship. A spirituality of communion implies also the ability to see what is positive in others, to welcome it and prize it as a gift from God: not only as a gift for the brother or sister who has received it directly, but also as a "gift for me." A spirituality of communion means, finally, to know how to "make room" for our brothers and sisters, bearing "each other's burdens" (*Gal* 6:2) and resisting the selfish temptations which constantly beset us and provoke competition, careerism, distrust and jealousy. (NMI, 43).

These differences alone—the definition of transformation, becoming a *steward of transformation*, the variety of proven *schools of spirituality* within the Church and the reality of *communio*—lead us to conclude that pastoral leadership has a unique potential to express and achieve a deeper understanding of what secular theory is calling "transformational leadership" possibilities. Of course, transforming individuals, groups and even organizations will always be topics of interest to

A PLACE...

... where everyone *feels at home.*

... where everyone *feels the presence of God.*

... that also tends to *emotional* needs.

... of *trust* and *respect.*

... of *celebration.*

...of *balanced informality.*

... that emphasizes the *important things in life.*

Table 1, Design Rules for Placemaking

scholars, researchers, practitioners and consultants across many disciplines. But such efforts inevitably pale in comparison when compared to the incalculable fruits of the Spirit and the two millennia of Church life experience with transformation.

In fact, the wealth and depth of "*Community with Spirit*" examples within the Church—as they parallel the evolution of and maturation of humanity and society —cause us to reflect on a general misconception about *Communities with Spirit*. Such a misconception considers this type of community as a "perfect society," impossible to achieve, free from adversity and suppressing diversity in order to sustain internal coherency. But what makes a group a *Community with Spirit* is the drive to *transcend*, to *go-beyond,* to *elevate and* to *lift-up.* Disagreements, conflicts, dissonance and growth pains become opportunities to embrace a higher level of possible solutions that is inclusive of the Spirit, and hence, of life. Situations of internal imbalance within a *Community of Spirit* affords them sources to seek new levels of awareness, new discoveries and new opportunities for increased interaction. Bad things also happen in nurseries despite many protective measures, so being a member in a nursery of relationships is no guarantee of insulation from the same internal and external pressures that occur in any social structure. What makes a difference is *Communities with Spirit* is the drive to go-beyond, the conviction that growing with the Spirit is the right way, if not the only way, and a desire to discover self through others, to adapt, to learn, to heal and to learn love.

Without a doubt, these are difficult topics to address and apply even in the pastoral setting, given some of the cultural biases and misconceptions about *Communities with Spirit.* Yet in our parish staff consulting, leadership workshops and pastor coaching sessions we have used a series of resources that proved to be effective in building community competencies that can lead to the *Community with Spirit* dimension. Among printed resources that we have used in the past are *The Catholic Experience of Small Christian Communities* (by B.J. Lee, Paulist Press, 2000) and *Sharing the Journey: Support Groups an America's*

New Quest for Community (R. Wuthnow, The Free Press, 1994). These resources can be used for personal development, but we find greater impact when groups (teams) read and study them as a group project. Also, we also used *Building Team Spirit* (B. Heermann, McGraw-Hill, 1997) as a priceless tool box of group activities and language to help communicate and build *Community with Spirit*.

There are two other practices we have used that when adopted, tend to help foster a deeper appreciation of community and the possibilities of *Community with Spirit*. These are placemaking and overnight group activities.

Placemaking refers to the practice of creating and maintaining a climate of spiritual community in small groups, and is based on the concept "sense of place:"

> The concept of 'sense of place' typically is used to refer to an individual's ability to develop feelings of attachment to particular settings based on combinations of use, attentiveness, and emotion. Despite the assumed positive values of a sense of place, critics point out that places are more than simply geographical sites—they are also fluid, changeable, dynamic contexts of social interaction and memory, and they "'contain' overt and covert social practices that embed in place-making behaviors of notions of ideology, power, control, conflict, dominance, and distribution of social and physical resources" (Stokowski, 2002, p. 368).

"Place" here is understood as the "intersection between people's lives and the physical world they inhabit" (Howe, 1996).

In many ways, both physical space and environmental or climate space differentiation have traditionally been functional in nature; for example, sacred spaces (Williams, 2002), learning spaces (Buchen, 2003) and workspaces (Becker, 2002). In a typical parish, for example, it is easy to recognize the music spaces, liturgical spaces and youth spaces, in addition to the child development, classrooms, office and meeting spaces. Each of these spaces is configured to optimize a specific task-relationship set. Placemaking refers to creating environmental conditions (e.g., physical, social, spiritual) that enhance the transformational (not transactional) potential of relationships (Michel & Wortham, 2002).

Again, using the parish context, some examples of questions that could be asked to assess placemaking include: Where are the "community building spaces" in our parishes and institutions, and what should they look like? Are ministry spaces too "functional" (business or classroom configured) and unintentionally discouraging *relational* activity? Do we have physical spaces that foster relational activities? Are our leaders trained to emphasize *relational learning*? The point here is to assess if individualism, competition and rationality have affected the construal of "community space" in the Church setting. In this sense, *placemaking* is not exclusive to lay ministry leadership, rather pastoral leaders are seen as facilitators of small groups that enhance a "sense of community."

Placemaking consists of creating and maintaining relational spaces conducive to building spiritually based communities (Mankowski & Rappaport, 2000). As a way to start placemaking initiatives, seven suggested *Placemaking Design Rules* are listed in Table 8. Each design rule was derived from the discoveries of Robert Wuthnow's *Sharing the Journey: Support Groups and America's New Quest for Community* (1994).

The first design rule of "feeling at home," is supported by many observations in the Wuthow survey. The desire to "see each other socially" (95% of respondents, Table 6.2), the need to support and encourage (86%, Table 9.1) and the relevance of welcoming newcomers (92%, 5.2) all point to the sense of comfort, belonging and care contained in this first design rule. These table numbers are from the Wuthnow book.

The second design rule operationalizes in small groups the value of "feeling the presence of God among us" (86% of respondents, Table 4.5).

The third design rule addresses the empathic component of spiritual communities, in which emotional support is given (92% of re-

205

spondents agreed that supporting each other emotionally was an important small group activity; Table 6.2).

Respondents valued trust (90%) and respect (89%) when evaluating small groups (Table 5.2), observations that are captured in the fourth design rule.

The fifth rule captures the expressed desire of being able to share gifts (71%, Table 6.2) and being able to celebrate something (51 %, Table 6.1) as activities "that mattered" in small groups.

The next rule captures how Wuthnow synthesizes the success of small group structure, activity and member satisfaction (Wuthnow, 1994, p.125-161).

Finally, rule seven emphasizes the group's role in satisfying "the expressed need to figure out the important things in life" (51%, Table 4.6).

The reader can observe that each of these design rules can be expanded and addressed as separate skill sets within this placemaking model. In fact we encourage curriculum developers, educators, consultants and seasoned pastoral leaders to practice placemaking skills in their current ministry assignments as a pathway to community experiences.

A second practice that is valuable in promoting a climate of community is living together and sharing a common lifestyle over an extended period of time. In its most basic form, these conditions translate into sharing meals, praying together and sleeping "under the same roof," a community-building principle available to religious communities and secular institutes, yet not as simple to accomplish within the parish setting. Although some ministries incorporate within their spirituality programs frequent three-day retreats that offer the basics of eat—pray—sleep as foundational to fostering community, for other parish ministries it may be considered nearly impossible. For youth groups or ministries that are associated with spiritual movements (e.g., Christ Renews His Parish-CHRP), overnights are an integral expectation. But for parish staff, a group that already works together most of the week, asking for an overnight may be impractical. Yet these types of time constraints may explain why many parish ministries have opted for a one-day retreat or a day of reflection (4-6 hours), which allows for eating-praying, albeit without the benefits of an overnight stay. Nevertheless, the benefits of an overnight experience of sharing meals and praying together, along with the overnight experience, cannot be underestimated. Perhaps in limiting the availability of eat-pray-sleep opportunities for parish ministries we have also inadvertently provided limitations to making a sense of true community more vivid as a parish life value. Certainly, this is a pastoral planning factor in sustaining a sense of community within parish life.

In defining "community" and in presenting three dimensions of community, we have managed to extend the application of the pyramid of relationships discussed in the previous chapter beyond just a leadership skill set. In this chapter, we examined the dynamics of spiritual intelligence in the small-group setting, and argued a case for an interpretation of group dynamics inclusive of the spiritual component, which we define as a "sense of true community." Then we identified three dimensions of community potential, namely, the potential as a *Community of Tasks*, a *Community of Practice*, and the potential for becoming a *Community with Spirit*, which are dynamics derived from the hierarchy of relationships. Although we believe any group, team or small community, either in the secular sector or in ministry, can achieve these dimensions, we consider the choice and the harmonizing of these dimensions to be most appropriate for the pastoral setting. Finally, we offer practical applications to pastoral leaders on how to inspire teams and small group communities into the choice of becoming communities with spirit.

Since communities are not isolated phenomena but subsets of a wider sense of community, and in defining groups (and teams) as "communities" and as "communities within communities" a *context*— preferably one inclusive of spiritual dynamics—now becomes the next topic of discussion. Here, an interesting overlap occurs, because *community* requires a clear context (Kegler, Rigler, & Honeycutt, 2010) but so does *spirituality* (Temane, & Wissing, 2006) and *leadership* (Zigarmi, Lyles, & Fowler, 2005).

This shared need for *context* represents the vantage point in time and culture that conditions a person's and community's experience of the world, interpretation of the world, and mission in the world. Although there can be multiple interpretations of this wider context—or *worldview* to be more precise—and since our pastoral interests are focused on pastoral leadership and parish life, the next chapter is dedicated to providing a fuller understanding of the intent, value and effects of leading small communities within the larger community of parish life.

Case Study

For the past eighteen months Dr. Martina Joya has been temporarily assigned as the parish life coordinator to Our Lady Queen of the Apostles pending the eventual assignment of a priest as pastor. Father Mark Brennan, the previous pastor had suddenly become seriously ill, and without any other priest available, the bishop asked if Martina could help administer the parish until a replacement for Fr. Mark could be found. Circumstances were such that it seemed likely that Martina would serve as parish life coordinator under the supervision of Father John Swagert for at least another year.

Martina has sufficient credentials to justify her selection as one of the few parish life coordinators in the diocese. She has a doctorate in ministry (DMin), is a certified Lay Ecclesial Minister (LEM) for the diocese, has served as a theology professor for the last eleven years; before that was the DRE for a very large parish in the diocese, has served before in diocesan positions. She is the mother of two sons, one of them a priest in the diocese the other a business executive living in Chicago. Martina has been married for 28 years and her husband is a retired Army colonel currently serving as director of diocesan social services.

The parish of about 820 families has done quite well under Martina's tenure as parish life coordinator. Father John offers the only Mass at Our Lady Queen of the Apostles, which is at 11:00AM on Sunday. He also has a full workload at the neighboring parish for which he is the pastor and only priest. Despite the liturgical constraints of not having a full time priest, Martina has been able to find help from retired priests and deacons. The revenue from Sunday collections and other small investments remain steady and predictable. The facilities are in good condition; parishioner and facility needs are properly tended to by the nine-person parish staff. The 18 recognized ministries in the parish are not growing but remain healthy. The parish has good relationships with the surrounding non-Catholic churches, the mayor's office, and the surrounding parish communities.

Yet despite these successes, Martina has observed behaviors among the members of the parish ministries that are inconsistent with building and maintaining a proper sense of community. Her concerns are focused primarily among three leadership groups and their perceptible inability to work together and recognize the broader reality of belonging to a community. Specifically, Martina notes that parish staff, the parish council, and the finance council work well as autonomous entities but remain largely isolated from each other. Martina observes a serious tendency in some of the ministry leadership to compartmentalize, thereby developing "stove pipes" or "silos" within the parish community. Stove pipes or silos refer to structures that are very hierarchical (top/down) in their thinking and narrow in their actions.

Martina has tried individually and in groups over the past months to encourage these groups to consider the value of working within a broader scope of understanding—that of a leadership community for the parish. The reaction to her efforts has largely been one of resistance to breaking these three silos by working with each other within the context of a community. From the parish staff she often hears the comment: "We only work from 9 to 5 so we just don't have any more time left to deal with the Parish Council". From the Parish Council she hears phrases like: "We have higher priorities..." From the Finance Council she hears "Our primary concern is with the finances of the parish ..." But Martina knows that if these leadership teams are able to create a sense of community as parish leadership, they would become an invaluable example to the rest of the ministries and community and thus spur the growth of the parish as a functioning community of believers.

Questions for reflection

1. Research and describe in your own words (or share in group) the multiple definitions of "stove-pipes" or "silos" within organizations. What seem to be the common elements among these definitions?

2. Using the common elements described in the first question, what are examples in business organizations that illustrate the consequences of stove-pipes (or silos)? What are the typical areas of conflict that emerge when stove pipes (silos) are perpetuated within organizations? You can use personal experience or examples by way of newspapers, magazines, or scholarly journals as sources to respond to this question.

3. How is the concept of stove-pipes enacted at Our Lady Queen of the Apostles given the mindset and commentaries from the parish staff, parish council and finance council?

4. What is the implication of stove-pipe behaviors among ministries of a parish to the potential of being able to build true community in Our Lady Queen of the Apostles? What kind of actions can help resolve the issues of stove pipes (or silos) among these three ministries?

5. Discuss other possible behaviors (e.g., competition, excessive autonomy, group think, etc) in parish ministry that may hinder the forming of true community within a parish.

6. Discuss how creating a true sense of community is a prerequisite for creating spiritual community.

7. Is creating spiritual communities within the parish a realistic goal? What helps in achieving this as a goal, and what doesn't help?

Workshop Activities

1. Read the case and distribute roles among the group participants. Allow six to eight minutes for each participant (in silence) to prepare for their role. Conduct a 30-minute role play along the assigned roles, in which the merits and risks are explored, discussed and debated. Compose a strategy for which the group can unanimously agree to implement.

2. Then in a plenary session, compare the different approaches from each group. To what degree was the approach based upon the *Community of Task dimension*? To what degree was the approach based upon to *Community of Practice* dimension? To what degree was the approach based upon to *Community with Spirit* dimension?

3. Why is it so difficult to sustain the dimension of *Community with Spirit* within parish ministry groups? Create a list of reasons and address possible solutions to fostering and sustaining community competency and spiritual life within parish ministry groups.

Personal Reflective

1. In analyzing Tuckman's (1965) group development discussed earlier, it's conceivable that a leader may not have the right skills to manage a specific stage and help transition into a next stage. Which stage best fits your current leadership style? Which stage of group development do you

suspect you will not be as good as someone else in the group? Again, the stages are *Forming* (establishing a common understanding), *Storming* (emerging conflicts and disagreements), *Norming* (developing friend-ships), *Performing* (achieving goals) and *Adjourning* (disbanding or mourning).

2. Conduct a visual inventory of the spaces you use for meetings with your pastoral group or ministry team. Is the layout conducive to open dialogue and "safe space" topics? Validate your findings by privately asking a few participants. Are there simple solutions that can enhance the climate of openness and dialogue?

3. Re-read the section on *Community with Spirit*, this time taking inven-tory of the potential you have to make this happen in your group or team. What strengths do you bring as a leader? What areas of develop-ment would you consider to improve?

Chapter References

Anderson, S.M., & Chen, S. (2002). The relational self: An interpersonal social-cognitive theory. Psychological Review, 109, 619-645.

Barab, S.A., & Duffy, T.M. (2000). From practice fields to communities of practice. In D. Jonassen & S. Land (Eds.). Theoretical foundations for learning environments. Mahwah, NJ: Eribaum.

Becker, F. (2002). Improving organizational performance by exploiting workplace flexibility. Journal of Facilities Management, 1, 154-162.

Belbin, R. M. (2004). Management teams: Why they succeed or fail. Elsevier Butter-worth-Heinemann.

Belbin, M. (2007). Managing through empowerment: Getting the most out of team-work, Day 11. The Daily Telegraph.

Buchen, I.H. (2003). Education in America: The next 25 years. The Futurist, 37, 44-50.

Chickering, A. (2003). Encouraging authenticity and spirituality in higher education. Journal of College and Character, 4(8), 38-53.

Cima, L.R., & Schubeck, T.L. (2001). Self-interest, love, and economic justice: A dialogue between classical economic liberalism and Catholic Social Teaching. Journal of Business Ethics, 30, 213-231.

Cook, T.D., & Campbell, D.T. (1979). Quasi-experimentation: Design and analysis issues for field settings. Boston: Houghton Mifflin.

Cooper, C. R., & Denner, J. (1998). Theories linking culture and psychology: Universal and community-specific processes. Annual Review of Psychology, 49, 559–84.

Cross, S.E., & Morris, M.L. (2003). Getting to know you: the relational self construal, relational cognition, and well-being. Personality & Psychology Bulletin, 29, 512-523.

D'Antonio, W. V. (1985). The American catholic family: Signs of cohesion and polarization. Journal of Marriage & Family, 47, 395-405.

Ditomaso, N., Parks-Yancy, R., & Post C. (2003). Structure, relationships, and community responsibility. Management Communication Quarterly, 17, 143-150.

213

Eagly, A.H., & Karau, S.J. (2002). Role congruity theory of prejudice toward female leaders. Psychological Review, 109, 573-598.

England, J.T. (1992). Pluralism: Building community for the 21st century. Counselor Education & Supervision, 32, 83-89.

Fischer, M.F. (2010). Making pastoral councils pastoral. Mahwah, NJ: Paulist Press

Gaines, S.O., Jr., Buriel, R., Liu, J.H., Rios, D.I. (1997). Culture, ethnicity, and personal relationship processes. New York, NY: Routledge.

Garvey, J. (1993). The protestant moment? Religion in the United States (how individualism affects the Catholic Church and other religions). Commonweal, 120, 910.

George, J.M, & Jones, G. R. (2007). Understanding and managing organizational behavior (5th ed.). Upper Saddle River, NJ: Prentice Hall.

Gillis, C. (1999). Roman Catholicism in America. New York: Columbia Press.

Hay, I. (2000). Gender self-concept profiles of adolescents suspended from High School. Journal of Child Psychology and Psychiatry 41(3), 1469-7610. doi.org/10.1111/1469-7610.00618.

Heron, J., & Reason, P. (1997). A participatory inquiry paradigm. Qualitative Inquiry, 3, 275-294.

Hewitt, J.P. (2002). The social construction of self-esteem. In Handbook of Positive Psychology. Oxford University Press, 2002. (Ed. Snyder & Lopez) pp. 135-147.

Howe, L. (1996). Placemaking. Journal of the American Planning Association, 62, 396-398.

Hung, D., Chen, V., Koh, S.T. (2006) The reverse LPP process for nurturing a community of practice. Educational Media International, 43(4), 299-314, DOI: 10.1080/09523980600926267.

Huusko, L., (2007). Teams as substitutes for leadership. Team Performance Management, 13(7), 244-258.

Johnson, L.J., Zorn, D., Yung-Tam, B., Lamontage, M., Johnson, S.A. (2003). Stakeholders' views of factors that impact successful interagency collaboration. Exceptional Children, 69(2), 195-210.

Kaufman, J. (2002). The political economy of interdenominational competition in late nineteenth-century American cities. Journal of Urban History, 28, 445-466.

Killen, M., & Wainryb, C. (2000). Independence and interdependence in diverse cultural contexts. In Harkness, S., Raeff, C., et.al. (Eds.). New directions for child and adolescent development, 87, 5-21.

Kegler, M. C., Rigler, J., & Honeycutt, S. (2010). How does community context influence coalitions in the formation stage? A multiple case study based on the Community Coalition Action Theory. BMC Public Health, 1090-100.

Lawler, M. G. (1995). Family: American and Christian. America, 173, 20-22.

Lee, S.M., & Peterson, S.J. (2000). Culture, entrepreneurial orientation, and global competitiveness, Journal of World Business, 35 (4)401-416. DOI: 10.1016/S1090-9516(00)00045-6.

Lussier, R., & Achua, C. (2007). Leadership: theory, application, & skill development. Mason: Thomson South-Western.

Mankowsi, E.S., & Rappaport, J. (2000). Narrative concepts and analysis in spiritually-based communities. Journal of Community Psychology, 28, 479-493.

Matovina, T. (2001). Hispanic Catholics. Commonweal, 128, 19-21.

McCarthy, J. (2000). Communion without community? America, 183, 6.

McDermott, R., (1999). Learning across teams: The role of communities of practice in team organizations. Knowledge Management Review, 8, 32-36.

McMullen, B. (2003). Spiritual intelligence. Student BMJ, 11, 60-64. Retrieved from http://proquest.umi.com/pqdweb?did

Michel, A.A., & Wortham, S.F. (2002). Clearing away the self. Theory & Psychology, 12, 625-650.

Mitchell, S.M., & Shortell, S.M. (2000). The governance and management of effective community health partnerships: A topology for research, policy and practice. The Millibank Quarterly, 78(2) 241-289.

Nicotera, A.M., Clinkscales, M.J., & Walker, F.R. (2003). Understanding organizations through culture and structure: Relational and other lessons from the African-American organization. Mahwah, NJ: LEA Publishers.

Park, S.W. (1998). Turning to God in Asia: Renewing the understanding of community. International Review of Mission, 87, 497-503.

Ratzinger, J. (1992). Communio: A program. Communio, 19(3), 436-49.

215

Russell, J. (1999). Counseling and the social construction of self. British Journal of Guidance & Counseling, 27, 339-352.

Schaeffer, P. (2000). Scholars say religious institutions ignore growing 'latino reality'. National Catholic Reporter, 36(20), 4.

Snyder, W., Wenger, E., & de Sousa Briggs, X. (2004). Communities of practice in government: Leveraging knowledge for performance. The Public Manager, 32(4), 17-21.

Stewart-Allen, A. Doing business the American Way. Business Strategy Review 14(1), 1467-8616. doi.org/10.1111/1467-8616.t01-1-00244

Stokowski, P.A. (2002). Languages of place and discourse of power: Constructing new senses of place. Journal of Leisure Research, 34, 368-381.

Temane, Q., & Wissing, M. P. (2006). The role of spirituality as a mediator for psychological well-being across different contexts. South African Journal of Psychology, 36(3), 582-597.

Thompson, D., Socolar, R., Brown, L., Haggerty, J. (2002). Interagency collaboration in seven North Carolina Counties. Journal of Public Health Management & Practice, 8(5), 55-64.

Tuckman, B. W. (1965). Developmental sequence in small groups. Psychological Bulletin, 63, 384-399.

Waaijman, K. (2002). Spirituality: Forms, foundations and methods. Leuven, Paris: Peeters.

Wenger, E., & Snyder, W. (2000). Communities of practice: The organizational frontier. Harvard Business Review, 78(1), 139-145.

Williams, H., Parker, S., & Turner, N., (2010). Proactively performing teams: The role of work design, transformational leadership, and team composition. Journal of Occupational and Organizational Psychology, 83, 301-324.

Wuthnow, R. Sharing the journey: Support groups and America's new quest for community. New York, NY: Free Press.

Zaccaro, S., Rittman, A.L., Marks, M.A. (2001). Team leadership, The Leadership Quarterly, 12(4), 451-483. doi:10.1016/S1048-9843(01)00093-5

Zane, N., & Yeh, M. (2002). In Kurasaki, K.S., Okazaki, S. (Eds.), Asian American mental health: Assessment theories and Methods. International and cultural psychology series. San Diego State University.

Zarraga-Oberty, C. & Saa-Perez, P., (2006). Work teams to favor knowledge management: Towards communities of practice. European Business Review, 18(1), 60-76.

Zigarmi, D., Lyles, D., & Fowler, S. (2005). Context: The Rosetta Stone of leadership. Leader to Leader, 2005(38), 37-44.

"Leadership is the capacity to translate vision into reality."
Warren G. Bennis

CHAPTER 7

Envisioning as Spiritual Influence

In previous chapters of this book we described ministry leadership as having distinct forms of influence, in many ways similar but in other ways quite different from the business or non-profit models of leadership. Leadership is about a variety of forms, perspectives and situations in which influence is used to achieve the hard side and soft side of the leadership function. Leadership—at least in the ministry setting—is seen primarily as a portfolio of *spiritual practices* that use spiritual influences; in this book we have highlighted only a few.

In many ways, what we present in this book is also widely discussed in scholarly publications. Specifically, we emphasize the gifts of each one's calling as an influence (also referred to in the leadership sector as the *charismatic leadership model*), and the effects that result from strength of character (called by different names, such as *leading by example, ethical leadership or values leadership*). We also presented the dynamics of relationships as persuasion (e.g., *relational leadership*), and the influences that emerge from the forces at work within a true community (e.g., *spiritual leadership, servant leadership*). In focusing on the principle of *leadership as a spiritual practice*, we have established inter-connections among an array of spiritual practices and with the evolving models that parallel secular leadership models but that adopt practices more oriented to the spiritual development of the individual and the community.

Although we emphasized that there are many practices that have their origins in the secular sector that can benefit ministry, we find it in-teresting that some specific forms of influence widely used in business settings seem to transfer to the pastoral sector with difficulty. One such case is that of "envisioning." Envisioning appears in multiple forms (e.g., worldview, vision statement, etc.), and is also known in the secular world as visionary leadership. It has been traced back to Mary Parker Follett's work on leadership, group membership, contribution, participa-tion and cooperation (McLamey & Rhyno, 1999).

In the next sections, we will discuss the nature of the envisioning influence in its various forms, how it is associated with spiritual activi-ties (and is therefore a spiritual practice), and what the elements are that make up effective envisioning. Finally, we offer some specific examples of how envisioning has worked in the pastoral setting.

The Nature of the Envisioning Influence

For our purposes, *envisioning* refers to "picturing yourself" and the team (or group, community) out of a "current" state and using that "picturing" as a form of influence to direct efforts toward the achieve-ment of a "new state." Envisioning is the seed of "strategic planning," it's more like the influence an explorer has on an expedition—that of moving into new territory with a vision and some navigation tools. Kouzes and Posner (1996) offer the following images to express the in-tent and effects of *envisioning*:

Even armed with techniques, though, the leaders find that there's no freeway to the future, no paved highway to the future from here to tomorrow. Nor are there roadmaps or signposts. Instead, the explorer must rely upon a compass and a dream. The vision of an organization acts as its magnetic north. It possesses the extraordinary ability to attract human energy. It invites and draws others into it by the force of its own appeal (Kouses & Posner, *Futurist,* p. 19).

Envisioning, in practice, is not really as hard as it seems. We use it more than we think. Take the example of the different stages in preparing for a vacation. What are the mental processes involved in getting ready for a vacation? At first your options are too spread out (which country, which city, which mode of travel, which tours, which activities, etc.), and over time you develop an appeal for a certain series of events that you believe optimizes your vacation time against your scattered desires. Then you start your research by looking into websites, travel guides and maps, and seek the alternative that best suits your aspirations for your vacation. Then you start looking at the details of seasons, climate, food, lodging, transportation, etc. as a way to provide continuity in your travels. Then you consider optimal dates, consulting with others who have visited the desired places. Eventually, you make the required deposits. So the dream starts with the desire for a simple vacation, and in time evolves into an energizing opportunity. In this sense, preparing for a vacation is a form of envisioning, since you are creating a picture of what you expect to accomplish, and that "picture" sustains your focus and energies.

The *envisioning* influence, although carrying different names, has fundamentally the same effects of "painting a clear and compelling picture." The term for "worldview," for example, refers to a philosophical outlook of reality, sort of an ideological landscape, by which reality is interpreted through an overarching set of principles that provides a sense of meaning and value with guidelines for action. Worldview is also called a "philosophy of life" either conscious or unconscious—that provides a sense of coherency to the past, present and future.

> Our worldview forms the context within which we organize and build our understanding of reality...Our beliefs and values are imbedded in our worldview...(Kim, Fisher, McCalman, 2009, p. 116).

This is significant to leaders because as individuals go through the maturation process they gather a myriad of life experiences, which assists them in formulating, developing and changing their worldview. This means that the perspective from which a leader sees the world changes. Moreover, this developing worldview affects not only the leader, but also other people as well, including the organizations around them. "A worldview shapes our culture and expresses itself in all social institutions including the arts, religion, education, media and business. In the academic arena, the researcher's worldview has enormous implications in that it affects the way studies are designed and how conclusions are drawn" (Kim et al, p.116).

Another form of envisioning is the "vision" of an organization. Here, "vision" is used as an artifact to communicate the new (or clearer) direction and mobilize people into action (Galbraith & Lawler, 1993; Gardner, 1990). In this sense, vision becomes the deepest expression of what the members of the organization want to work on together. Some examples of business vision statements include "To develop the perfect search engine" (Google), "Apple is committed to bringing the best personal computing experience to students, educators, creative professionals and consumers around the world through its innovative hardware, software and Internet offerings" (Apple Computer), "At the heart of The Chevron Way is our vision ...to be the global energy company most admired for its people, partnership and performance " (Chevron), and "To be the number one athletic company in the world" (Nike).

Envisioning is not limited to the organization's "vision statement" narrated in a few sentences. It can also take the form of a motto, a slogan or a catchphrase. In the business sector, the *envisioning* of services, products, brands and company dreams is very common and helps demonstrate the power of this from of influence. Phrases like, "Be all that you can be" (US Army), "To enrich women's lives" (Mary Kay), "Just Do It" (Nike) and "Taking Care of Business" (Office Depot) give a clear picture of product or service intent. Other, less common, phrases such as CISCO's "Empowering the internet generation," the Red Cross phrase, "The greatest tragedy is indifference," the Johnson & Johnson statement "The Family Company" and USO's "Until everyone comes home..." are phrases that make it easier for leaders within these organizations to "paint a big picture" of where the organization is expected to be and do in the future.

Similarly, non-profit organizations also take advantage of the power of "picturing" their futures. Some examples are "Aggressive discovery. Global outreach" (from the Minneapolis Heart Institute Foundation), "Building a strong foundation for the future of our Region" (Northland Foundation), "Joining forces to fight hunger" (Second Harvest Heartland), "Giving voice" (Women's Cancer Resource Center), and "We build strong kids, strong families, strong communities" (YMCA of Metropolitan Minneapolis). Each offers a "clear picture of intent." More examples of non-profit envisioning include "Connecting people. Enriching lives" (Community Volunteer Service), "We help teens take charge of their lives." (Inwood House), "Mentoring works. The internet connects. The combination changes lives." (iMentor), "Improving life one breath at a time" (American Lung Association), and "Helping many by helping one" (AIDS Service Center NYC) convey very powerful messages to the organization and its clients.

In searching the Web for envisioning statements of diocese and parishes in the United States, we also found some valuable examples to continue illustrating the power of the envisioning influence. On occasion, we have seen parishes using the envisioning influence for special projects, such as a capital campaign. One example is "United, the vision continues" (Notre Dame Church, Diocese of Galveston-Houston). Other examples we found on the Web include "A Catholic compass: follow the direction" (Our Lady of Wisdom Catholic Church & Student Center, Lafayette, LA), "Pray, Build, Celebrate Together," St. Sylvester Catholic Church Pensacola Beach, FL), "Growing Together – Building in Faith" (St. Sabrina Parish, Belton, Mo) and "Etched in Our Hearts, Who we are, what we can be." (St Francis Xavier, Phoenix, AZ).

A troubling trend noted during these Web searches on the use of envisioning within parish life in the United States was that envisioning efforts seemed more prevalent in capital campaign programs or special parish projects than in the ordinary ministries of parish life. In an effort to validate this finding, we inserted additional exercises in our parish leadership workshops. One of the exercises was to select among nine secular definitions of leadership (for this exercise we use Table 1-1, Yukl, 2002). Invariably, the participants selected the definitions of leadership that had "vision and mission" words in them. Yet when we inquired during the workshop's plenary session what the parish "vision" was and what the current pastor's top three priorities were, we noted hesitation, lack of clarity and contradiction. We conclude that these pastoral leaders had a clear understanding of the value of envisioning, but were unable to articulate the key priorities of their parish and how they related to the ministries entrusted to them. At least for us, this confirmed our suspicions that although many parishes have mission and vision statements readily available (websites, parish bulletin, bulletin boards, etc.), the "picturing" as a form of influence to direct efforts toward the achievement of a "new state" was not as strongly evident in the parish setting as in the for-profit and non-profit sectors.

Essentially, this demonstrates the value of envisioning and emphasizes the conviction that, just as envisioning works in the business and non-profit sectors, it also has value in the pastoral sector when effectively formulated and lived, albeit with some differences. In the for-profit and non-profit sectors, the envisioning process is focused on the human dimension, whereas in the pastoral setting, the envisioning includes a spiritual dimension.

Envisioning Influence as a Spiritual Practice

The researchers that study the process of envisioning in leadership use some very interesting terms to characterize its effects upon followers--terms that are comparable with those employed when describing spiritual matters. First and foremost, researchers indicate that *envisioning* has a transformational quality, an ability to inspire a move from the current "state of affairs" to a higher or more satisfying "level of affairs." Conger and Kanugo (1998) observe that managers tend to use transactional influences by means of hard targets and goals, but that leaders use transformational influences such as creating a vision.

Researchers also agree that envisioning is associated with *meaning-making*. "For leaders, a vision is not a dream; it's a reality that has not yet come into existence... Leaders create meaning for people by amassing large amounts of information, making sense of it, integrating it into a meaningful vision of the future, and communicating that vision so people want to participate in its realization" (Snyder & Graves, 1994). Yet interestingly, spirituality is also related to meaning-making. Researchers have also established that meaning-making can be understood as one of three dimensions of spirituality, along with identity and transformation: "Meaning-making is the language of personal identity and spiritual rootedness" (Seicoi, 2005, p. 295).

Envisioning in this sense carries a transformational quality that not only shows a new possible state, but also enables a renewed sense of commitment, enthusiasm and purpose (Christenson & Walker, 2004). Yet is transformation not also an attribute of spirituality? In fact Waaijman (2002) notes that transformation indicates the intentionality of the spiritual way. The use of *envisioning as a transformative influence* in fact carries a spiritual connotation, many times associated with conversion (moving ways from…), conformation (a selected model of trans-formation in behavior, thinking and willing), and discernment (*diakrisis* or the critical-reflective movement of transformation in God).

A third attribute of envisioning that parallels spirituality is that it provides a sense of direction. In secular organizations, envisioning pro-vides a common perception of organizational direction and objectives (Lloyd, Braithwaite, & Southon, 1999). Also J.P. Kotter's research (1996) points out that an authentic vision unifies diverse participants around a shared aspiration and clarifies direction in the face of turbu-lence and confusion. Here, the connection between envisioning and dis-cernment meet again, because envisioning means transcending, and tran-scendence is a spiritual attribute.

From the attributes used by academics and researchers to de-scribe the effects of the *envisioning* influence, there is an evident con-nection between *envisioning* and three specific dynamics of spiritual de-velopment and growth. The underlying dynamics *of meaning-making*, a clear *sense of direction*, and the expected *transformation* that results from a good sense of identity and a clarity of purpose and direction sug-gest that envisioning is not just a function of one spiritual dynamic, but a result of a mutual interlinking of these three (or perhaps even more) spir-itual dynamics. The origins of *envisioning* stem from the spiritual stir-rings awakened by meaning-making (identity), which when combined with other circumstantial variables provides a direction (clarity of path) to move from one state to a higher state with transformation as the ob-jective. But it's also true that as transformation occurs, the path opens to new possibilities, and meaning-making becomes more focused, just as taking steps in the initial direction can affect meaning-making and trans-formation. Perhaps it is the synergistic effect of at least these three spir-itual dynamics that makes *envisioning* such a powerful influence in leadership dynamics.

Next, we explore the elements that make up an effective envi-sioning. Having identified the main elements that make up effective

226

ways to "paint a picture," we can address some of the spiritual practices that seem to best support envisioning in the parish setting.

Elements of Effective Envisioning

What makes an effective envisioning? What are the most relevant attributes of an envisioning dynamic that influences the conduct of the discipline of leadership? What is the process? To answer these questions, we draw again from the academic research and then interpret the observations within the context of "leadership as a spiritual practice."

The most reported characteristics of an effective visioning include establishing *brevity* and *clarity*, by limiting the vision statement to no more than 20-22 words, and the degree to which "painting the picture" addresses a *direction*, not a goal (Baum, et.al, 1998; Jacobs & Jacques, 1990). The envisioning also should have a certain degree of appealing abstractness or *idealism* so it can't easily be made obsolete (Baum, et.al, 1998; Jacobs & Jacques, 1990). Also, an envisioning statement has a *future orientation* that helps "see" the future condition, environment or dynamics (Kotter, 1990; Lipton, 1996; Senge, 1990). The envisioning statement should also propose an *inspiring challenge* that engages a majority of participants (Locke et. Al, 1991; Sims & Lorenzi, 1992) and remain *stable* over time (Baum, et al 1998). In summary, the seven attributes of an envisioning statement most noted within the published research are summarized in the Table 2.

One crucial variable to remember when looking at effective envisioning—as well as when applying the leadership function in general—is the topic of generational differences. Within parish life there are a variety of age groups and experiences that are characteristic of different generations that need to be considered. Generation is described as an "identifiable group that shares birth years, age location and significant life events at critical developmental stages" (Cennamo & Gardner 2008,

p. 892). Murphy, Gibson and Greenwood (2010) define generations as cohorts of individuals born in the same period and raised in a similar social and historical environment. Although there is some discrepancy among researchers regarding the exact name and beginning and end dates for each generation, generally, the dates vary by only a few years.

The scholarly literature on this subject identifies four distinctly defined generations in our society, and therefore also in parish life. The generation identified as veterans are individuals born between 1922 and 1945 (Cennamo & Gardner, 2008, p. 891). The U.S. Census Bureau identified the baby boomer generation as individuals born between 1946 and 1964. The generation identified as Generation X or Gen Xers are individuals born between 1962 and 1979 (Cennamo & Gardner, 2008, p. 892). The generation identified as Generation Y or the Millennials, are individuals born between 1980 and today. (Cennamo & Gardner, 2008, p. 892).

As demarked by the year of birth, each generation entered society during a significant period in history. There were events that helped shape the names identified with each generation. For example, the baby boomers are the offspring of adults born after WWII. Differences between each generation range from differences in age, education, family, career paths, career expectations, financial status and their understanding of Church. Therefore, value that each generation places on education, family, career, finances etc. differs greatly.

Veterans, or traditionalists, are the individuals who lived through several war years. World War I, World War II and the Great Depression were integral times within their lives. Eisner (2005) states that "this generation was socialized through economic times of scarcity and hardship." They are mature, disciplined, have a great deal of respect for authoritative figures, are the authoritative figures, are consistent and methodical in their daily activities and are uncomfortable with change. Many have retired and the few who are still around are proficient in their duties and are comfortable in their surroundings. This generation is most comfortable with a structured, traditional, hierarchical approach. Veterans do not see the value of teamwork and in allowing others to aid in the decision-making process. Veterans will provide or share information to others on a need-to-know basis. Veterans are limited in their use of technology and prefer a hard copy of information verses an electronic version.

Baby boomers are identified as the offspring of the veterans. They were born after World War II, and according to the U.S. Census Bureau, baby boomers comprised the largest generation in U.S. History. According to the 2006 census, baby boomers numbered 78 million and compromised 26.1 percent of the total U.S. population. Baby boomers believe in growth, change and expansion (Eisner, 2005). Baby boomers have a core set of beliefs that focus on hard work and achievement in their personal and professional lives, a value shared with the veterans. Baby boomer core beliefs are generally based on their personal values, beliefs and ideals as dominant during their upbringing or formative years. They are optimistic, confident and believe in value-free expression and social reform (Eisner, 2005). Baby boomers tend to work long hours, show loyalty and many are extending their work life. They are likely to respect authority, but want to be viewed and treated as equals (Eisner, 2005). The core set of beliefs that baby boomers have can be considered extrinsic or intrinsic factors (Cennamo & Gardner, 2008). Baby boomers are the generation holding most management or positions of control within the public, private and religious institutions. The baby boomer thrust is toward larger systems, team-based learning, and decision-making and rewards (Sirias et. al 2007). Many baby boomers will remain employed and in authoritative positions well after their designated retirement period. Their desire to remain employed is a result of a number of factors such as second stage of parenting, children in college, financial stability or instability or health reasons. This generation is in employment competition with the fast growing Generation X, the third form of generation.

Generation X are the individuals coming of age as the children of the baby boomers. This generation consists of persons who were beginning to see the demise of the "stay at home" mother. This generation has an attitude much different from that of the baby boomers. As a generation born between 1962 and 1979, this group thrives on independence, the need for technology and an attitude of "knowing it all." Generation X is a group without a clear identity, with members who generally have diminished expectations and feelings of alienation, pragmatism, cynicism, conservatism and detachment (Sirias, Karp, and Brotherton, 2007). According to Wieck (2007), Gen Xers have lived with social, corporate and cultural volatility; have little trust in the corporate America or loyalty to it. Generation X is entering the workforce with values, education, a need for technology, a clear bottom line mentality, a great need for independence and a focus upon less socially supportive environments (Sirias et al., 2007). The loyalty of Gen X is not tied to work. Gen X, according to Salauddin, (2010) have a work ethic characterized by adaptability, independence and creativity and are not intimidated by authority. Gen X does not have the same work ethic or loyalty to an organization as baby boomers, because they seek opportunity, are impatient and seek instant gratification and flexible working conditions.

Generation Y or millennials, born after 1979, is the group whose ideals were shaped during the war on terrorism and the attack on the Twin Towers. Currently, Gen Y appears to be the largest generation according to De Meuse and Mlodzik (2010) with a population of 80 million in the United States. Gen Y is composed of a very diverse group. According to Morton (2002), 34% of Gen Y are minorities and are tolerant of diversity in their public and private lives. Like Gen X, the Gen Y is a product of latchkey, but in this instance, single parents are raising more Gen Y. The non-traditional family setting is becoming the norm for Gen Y. In addition, like Gen X, Gen Y does not respond to the traditional work ethic as the baby boomers. Gen Y has more of a practical understanding of technology and has a greater level of expectation regarding where they see themselves in the work environment.

Gen Y is optimistic and they are at ease with putting their emotions on display and participating in decisions (Wieck, 2007). Because

Attribute	Source
Is the envisioning statement brief?	(Baum, et.al, 1998; Jacobs & Jacques, 1990).
Is the statement clear?	(Baum, et.al, 1998; Jacobs & Jacques, 1990).
Does the envisioning statement provide direction?	(Kotter, 1990; Lipton, 1996; Senge, 1990).
Is the statement sufficiently abstract?	(Baum, et.al, 1998; Jacobs & Jacques, 1990).
Does the statement provide a future orientation?	(Kotter, 1990; Lipton, 1996; Senge, 1990).
Does the statement seem to inspire challenge?	(Locke et. Al, 1991; Sims & Lorenzi, 1992)
Does the envisioning statement seem stable?	(Baum, et al 1998).

Table 2, Attributes of an effective envisioning statement

231

of advancements in technology, according to Morton (2002), Gen Y does not respond to the traditional training method or lecture method. Training and information can be conducted electronically or remotely. Gen Y seeks leaders who are open, positive and allow for flexibility.

As can be inferred from reading the generational differences, a leader cannot continue with a "one size fits all" style in dealing with multi-generations in parish life. As indicated in the generation descriptions above, varying degrees of beliefs, values and Church experiences are determining factors in how a generation will work with a leader and with other generations. The veteran may want to be left alone, as long as the goals and objects are met. The baby boomer may seek opportunity for advancement. The Gen X may want to lead a team or begin to mold their leadership skills and Gen Y may seek projects that will allow them to work independently from others. This makes the pastoral envisioning process more difficult, but once a common vision is achieved, it bridges the gap between generations and provides uniformity of effort. Regardless of generational differences, spirituality remains a common thread, and envisioning can make help sustain this awareness.

In the studies we reviewed and the observations offered by the consultants we interviewed on the subject of the *envisioning* process, we found many great examples of ways to reinforce the many opportunities that exist to meaningfully use envisioning in the pastoral setting. We share some of these examples below. The first examples come from parish life. These are followed by a discussion of the effects of envisioning on a *spiritual worldview.* Next, we discuss how envisioning can be used effectively in parish life. Lastly, we explore some ideas on how to conduct the envisioning process as a spiritual practice.

Examples of Envisioning in Pastoral Work

After reviewing some of the main elements of the envisioning influence presented in formal research, we offer some examples of this form of influence applied to typical parish ministries.

Whether the envisioning statements presented below meet each or any of the criteria expressed above is hard to assess outside of the group or ministry context. Yet there is value in sharing some of the statements we have encountered or have helped construct, since many of these ministries are common throughout parishes in the United States. If nothing else, they offer opportunities for constructive critique, they reinforce what has been discussed to date, and they may offer insights into envisioning possibilities you may have as a reader and leader of a parish ministry.

Good examples of using envisioning in parish life were somewhat difficult to find, but they nevertheless provide valuable insight into the power or envisioning. For instance, a leader of the Extraordinary Ministry of Holy Communion (EMHC) ministry in a

parish suggested envisioning the ministry as "*Resolved to undertake the giving the Body and Blood of the Lord to our brothers and sisters, and so serve to build up the Church.*" In another parish, the leader of the Sacristans sees the ministry as "*Silently making ready for Christ's love*" not only in the preparations for the Mass, but also as a spiritual guideline and point of reflection from week to week. A third leader, this time of Lectors, emphasizes to those entrusted to her the following statement: "*Reading* your holy Word to the glory of your name" A group of altar servers has selected the following statement to guide their ministry: "*We are here to serve the Lord!*" A youth minister from a large suburban parish has this way of envisioning evangelization for the youth they serve: "*If Christ's love is to be, it must start with me.*"

A team of hospitality ministers is guided by a simple phrase they composed and opted to follow in the exercise of their ministry: "*Love and kindness in welcoming to Christ's banquet.*" Finally, a Director of

233

Religious Education is focused on making sure each catechist approaches the classroom with the thoughts of *"Inflaming their hearts with living faith."*

In most of these cases, the envisioning statements were intended to visualize beyond just the acts of performing the tasks of the ministry. They were also meant to be opportunities for personal and community growth.

Envisioning and Movements

The Merriam Webster Collegiate Dictionary (2001) defines *"movements"* as loosely organized, sustainable and campaigning collectivities, intrinsically seeking changes from a current status to an improved and better state of affairs. The Britannica Encyclopedia (2001) adds that members of *movements* undergo a psychological reorganization in which the new sense of direction, security and value obtained through the newly envisioned state is acquired at the expense of personal autonomy (changes made by a new ideology or worldview). Thus, in *movements*, the power of envisioning carries the attributes of identity, direction and subsequent transformation.

In the past decade, social movement theorists have identified three major theoretical approaches or components that explain the dynamics of *movement* phenomena: (1) the envisioning or framing processes, (2) the mobilizing of supporting structures, and (3) leveraging of opportunity (Johnston & Klandermans, 1995; McAdam, 1996). Framing processes refer to the way individuals and groups identify, interpret and express their grievances. Ideological framing for *movements* is akin to our discussion on *envisioning*, in which a scheme of collective interpretations and ideological meanings are packaged and operationalized by activists. Through the envisioning of a newer and better state, movement participants communicate and legitimize their actions. An example of this envisioning is the case of Martin Luther King's "I have a dream"

234

speech (August 1963) in which more than 250,000 people heard the dream at the Lincoln Memorial and millions others watched it played and replayed on television. The power of this leader's "vision" is still felt today throughout American society.

The second component or theoretical approach that characterizes movements is their mobilizing of supporting structures; it specifically consists of networks and resources that account for the actions and participation in the movements. Interpersonal ties, organizational membership, efficacy and identity salience are some of the factors that influence these networks and movements (Taylor, 2000). As an example of this second approach used in *movements,* consider the consumer protection movement. This movement started as a grassroots reaction to product adulteration, product safety, corporate greed and unreasonable increases of prices. Independent watch-dog institutions, local and regional volunteer organizations, and even government agencies evolved as supporting structures that subscribed to the vision of the consumer protection movement and were instrumental in pushing back the tide of abuses.

Finally, the third component that characterizes the dynamics of movements is related to leveraging situational opportunities. Here is where groups of participants are able to access and leverage circumstances to their advantage (Taylor, 2000). For example, situations such as the Bhopal disaster (1984), the Exxon Valdez oil spill (1989), Chernobyl (1986), Iraqi oil spill (1991), the Deepwater Horizon oil spill (2010) and the Fukushima Daiichi nuclear disaster (2011) were examples of situations in which the environmental movement was able to leverage circumstances—in this case media coverage—of their vision.

The purpose of *movements* as expressed by these three major components or theoretical approaches is to identify macro issues in our society and exercise influence and direct pressure on established structures (Bradley & Howells, 1994). Movements behave as supra-organizational influences capable of creating awareness and influencing desirable outcomes. Movements are an unstructured reaction to a specific need, wrong, injustice, dissatisfaction or cultural omission. In many

235

ways, Church movements "exercise" a supra-organizational influence upon the injustices, corruption and anomalous social behaviors.

Examples of transforming movements in the United States include the civil rights movement (Van Buren III, 1998), the labor movement (Hannigan, 1998), the feminist movement (Hoggart, 2000), the green consumer movement (Valley, 1992), and the environmental protection movement (Blowers, 1997). The Catholic Church also benefits from movements, such as the Charismatic Movement, Opus Dei, Schoenstatt, Focolare, Sant'Egidio, Taize and Emmanuel Community movements. Yet among these Church movements, one specifically caught our attention in the way envisioning had become a powerful influence in sustaining unity of efforts and in obtaining specific formative outcomes. Because of its abundant use of interconnected envisioning at personal, group, community, national and international levels, sustained in most cases by thoughtfully discerned outcomes (e.g., Practical Faith in Diving Providence), the Schoenstatt Movement provides an example in which envisioning is effectively used within Church movements.

The Apostolic Movement of Schoenstatt is a Catholic Marian movement founded in 1914 by Father Joseph Kentenich. The core of their efforts include Christian personality development, orientation after ideals and a deep sense of community. The Schoenstatt Movement exists in about 42 countries, and has a unique form of devotion to the Blessed Mother that is closely linked to their original shrine in Germany, for which there are over 200 replicas of around the world.

Among the formation principles of Schoenstatt is what can be described as a cross-layering of integrated and mutually supported envisioning processes. At the personal level, formation processes are centered around the "personal ideal," which is essentially an original envisioning of how God "sees" each person. This continuous discovery of the personal ideal (i.e., "ontological name") places God in the center of the discovery process, has the Church and the movement as a source of inquiry for this discovery process, and directs the discoveries of one's uniqueness to one's unique calling to the service of others. Personal ideal then becomes a continuous encounter with God through day-to-day life, a subject of dialogue and prayer, and a main theme in the lifelong search of a personal, axial life-principle. Yet in the Schoenstatt movement, the personal ideal is also related to the group ideal. Because developing a strong sense of community (i.e., family) is another core value, formation also takes place in small groups (i.e., a group "ontological name.") These personal and group ideals are also interconnected with guiding ideas (envisioning) at diocesan, national and international level across all branches, guilds, federations and secular institutes of the movement. The leaders and formulators of the movement are very keen at formulating these ideals and mottos by means of well elaborated discernment processes.

Although there are other movements and religious groups within the Church that use envisioning based on discernment, Schoenstatt's integrated philosophy, its mottos and other forms of envisioning that serves the ends of formation, provides a good example of effective visioning.

Envisioning within Spiritual Worldviews

When viewing personal and community envisioning as a "shared philosophy of life," there is a clear relationship between "worldview" and spirituality (Beyer, 2011; Hedlund-de Witt, 2011). Worldviews as an "envisioning" influence from a spiritual perspective have the ability to either perpetuate personal and community-level biases and crisis (L. Po, 2011) or promote positive intra- and interpersonal connectedness that can help overcome "current state" dissatisfactions (Pesut, B. (2003). Spirituality as worldview serves as a practical and theoretical template with holistic capacity to process and offer direction to reality (Gangadean, 2006; Haynes, 2009), provides depth of relationships with the divine in relationship to day-to-day life activities (Meraviglia, 1999), offers capacities to cope with life ambiguities (Pickard & Nelson-Becker, 2011) and presents "pictures" for a growth journey with abundant shared opportunities and critical examinations (Watson, J. (2006). Here again resonate the three results of "envisioning" stated earlier; they seem to be tied to the same outcomes expected of spiritual development and growth, that of *meaning-making*, developing a clear *sense of direction*, and ending up with the expected *transformation*. It is no surprise that appeals of spirituality as "imagery of spiritual development" (Tale & Parker, 2007) are considered among the most powerful influences of spiritual leaders (Jones & Mason, 2010).

Just as in the case of *movements*, Church spiritual traditions—also called *schools of spirituality*—originate from socio-cultural turmoil of their times. The following definition highlights the basic elements of a *school of spirituality*:

> We define a school of spirituality as (1) a spiritual way that derives from a Source-experience around which a (2) inner circle of pupils takes shape which (3) is situated within a socio-cultural context in a specific way and (4) opens a specific perspective of the future; a second (5) generation structures all this into an organic whole, by means of which (6) a number of people can share in the Source-experience.; when the Source-experience, the contextual relevance, and the power to open up the future are blocked, (7) a reformation is needed (Waaijman, 2002, p.118).

In many ways, schools of spirituality originate from social-cultural turmoil that exist within a historical context and express themselves by "painting a picture" that promotes a set of spiritual values that exercise influence on established structures (Bradley & Howells, 1994). Spiritual schools, as movements, also exercise *supra-organizational* influences upon the injustices, corruption and anomalous social behaviors of historical proportions. For example, the early monastic schools of spirituality (circa 300-1150) were considered a reaction to the problems of major early medieval times, and became like "escape pods" from the effects of a collapsing Roman Empire, barbarian invasions and the emergence of new kingdoms. In many ways, it was the envisioning and *supra-organizational* influences of the monastic paradigm that shaped early medieval civilization by offering a sense of security in a world that seemed always on the brink of collapse, by promoting literacy and study and by offering a praxis for economic, religious and cultural change (Sheldrake, 2007).

Similarly, civil society and Church were shaken again by different—although equally profound—cultural and religious changes that took place during the latter part of the middle ages (circa 1150-1450). The rebirth of major cities, emergence of intellectual centers (universities), the corruption caused by power and wealth, and the Gregorian reforms created another major disturbance of historical proportions. From here, another worldview emerged—that of the mendicant paradigm—such as the Franciscan school of spirituality. Equally so, other schools of spirituality formed as reactions of the age of Reformation as well as during the early centuries of modernity as a result of clashes between science, the industrial revolution and spirituality (Sheldrake, 2007). Our point is to demonstrate that schools of spirituality originate from social-cultural turmoil in a historical context and express themselves by envisioning spiritual practices that promote spiritual values capable of widespread influence on established structures.

As a way to illustrate the influence of envisioning with a school of spirituality, we present in more detail the Benedictine worldview.

St. Benedict of Nursia is credited with developing his Rule, what later became known as The Rule of St. Benedict (heretofore "The Rule"), sometime around 540 AD, near the end of his life. (Skrabec, 2003) The Rule was to guide monastic life and its "fundamental premise [is] that whatever authority we have is for the common welfare. Leaders are but trusted servants." (Skrabec 2003, p.70) The notion of trustworthy servanthood as applied to leadership in The Rule is consistent with the ecclesiology of the Second Vatican Council, which occurred over 1,400 years after The Rule was written. Any concerns about the precepts of The Rule being post-modern inventions that should therefore be approached with caution and suspicion should be allayed by the long and venerable history of this way of life. The Rule seems to transcend both history and theology. "The Rule of St. Benedict is not concerned with a single time and place, a single view of church, a single set of devotions, or a single ministry. [It] is concerned with life; what it's about, what it demands, how to live it. And it has not failed a single generation" (Chittister 1992, 19). History suggests that The Rule would be as effective as a way of life outside of the monastery as it is inside. " ... Pope Gregory the Great was one of the first to apply the Rule to organizations. Using Benedict's Rule, Gregory defined requirements for church leaders such as bishops" (Skrabec 2003, 43). In approximately 590 AD, Gregory developed his church manual, Pastoral Care, which provides guidance as to the care of souls to Church leaders and ministers. One of the principles in Gregory's "Pastoral Care" is: "Those should not take on the office of governing who do not fulfill (sic) in their way of life what they have learned by study" (Davis 1950, pp. 23-24). It appears that the notion of leading by example in the Church can be traced to 590 AD. Clearly, it is not a post-modern invention.

As noted earlier in this book, one of the constitutive factors of sound ecclesial leadership is the leader's sense of vocation, which is related to the leader's identity as a person of faith. The ecclesial leader's style will emerge from the person's perspective of self as person and as leader. The Rule demands that "the head of the monastery will not be a chief or a queen or a feudal lord. The superior of a monastery of Benedictines will be a Christ figure, simple, unassuming, immersed in God, loving of the marginal, doer of the Gospel, beacon to the strong" (Chittister 1992, 36). Such a view of self and leadership is a strong antidote to a feudal model of leadership, especially during difficult times. Moreover, the humility implicit in this view of leadership ensures that the ecclesial leader will be prone to remain a student of the times as well as a teacher. Such a leader would be capable of reading the signs of the times with clarity and depth.

With regard to getting things done, the Rule reflects Benedict's conviction that "he does not want people in positions simply to get a job done. He wants people in positions who embody why we bother to do the job at all" (Chittister 1992, 42). This thinking supports our contention that in the ministry sector, the person is to be accorded a higher status than the task.

The *sine qua non* of effective leadership anywhere, but most certainly in the Church, is the leader's ability to listen beyond the words to the message behind the message. Certainly, such a skill is a prerequisite to an effort to read the signs of the times. Benedict acknowledged the importance of this skill in The Rule by requiring that a leader demonstrate the capacity to be a "holy listener" (Chittister 1992, 42). Perhaps Benedict envisioned that the world would eventually be run by holy listeners. Could one imagine what the Church would be like if it were run by holy listeners? A holy listener would, by definition, seek to understand before seeking to teach. A holy listener would focus on loving the other rather than on protecting an institution. A holy listener would seek the medicine of mercy rather than the weapon of condemnation. A holy listener would seek holiness by entering into the mind and heart of Jesus in search of the requisite humility to be a good servant of the Gospel.

Ecclesial leadership is to be focused on the person, as well as the institution. After all, an institution, properly managed, can be a source of stability and resources for doing the Lord's work. But the focus on the person is primary, for it is the person who is an integral part of the Body of Christ and who is a temple of the Holy Spirit. To ignore the person for the sake of an institution is to turn away from God and toward idolatry. It is to implicitly reject the integrity of the person as God's creation. So it is not surprising that "personalism" is a constant throughout the Rule of Benedict. ... There is no room in Benedictine spirituality, though, for bloodless relationships between people in authority and the people for whom they have responsibility. Benedictine authority is expected to have meaning It is to be anchored in the needs and personality of the other person" (Chittister 1992, 43).

"Humility is at the heart of managing, while pride requires heavy supervision" (Skrabec 2003, 37). This is a fundamental tenet of The Rule. Great, if not herculean, humility is demanded of the ecclesial leader by The Rule. There is great wisdom in this non-negotiable demand of The Rule, for humility is the heart and soul of sound leadership, ecclesial or otherwise. Humility orients the individual to the other; it allows the leader to listen well; it instills the value of learning in the teacher; it rejects self-serving ideas and behaviors; it seeks unity in diversity; it fosters a worldview that seeks to understand rather than dominate, to love rather than to condemn, to courage rather than to dissimulation. "Again as in all of Benedict's thoughts, humility was the cornerstone of community. Administrators and managers were to be what Pope Gregory the Great called himself -- 'servant of the servants of God.' More importantly, managers were to love their job but not its trappings" (Skrabec 2003, 35). Such is the worldview required of those in pastoral leadership positions.

In this chapter we defined the *envisioning* forms as "picturing yourself and the team (or group, community) out of a "current" state and using that "picturing" as a form of influence to direct efforts toward the achievement of a "new state." For this we reviewed how *envisioning* was enacted in the business, non-profit and pastoral sectors. We also demonstrated how the envisioning influence is a spiritual practice, as well as some of the elements that make up effective envisioning. In the final parts of this chapter we analyzed the envisioning influence in social and Church movements as well as the envisioning that takes place within some of the traditional schools of spirituality within the Church.

Yet interestingly enough, the topic of how to go about formulating and sustaining the envisioning process has not been discussed in the literature. Although there are training programs and techniques available from the business and nonprofit sector that would help any leader develop the envisioning influence, we believe most of them miss a crucial dynamic that cannot be ignored for a pastoral leader—that of *discernment.*

242

One thing is for a leader to "paint a picture" based solely on a fact-finding intuitive process, and the other is to envision along God's promptings.

In the next chapter, we will address the topic of discernment—not only as an envision technique—but also as a leadership spiritual practice that helps vs. understand how all of these spiritual influences are interwoven.

Case Study

Every year, the Academy of Management (AoM, also see www.aomonline.org) conducts a convention that gathers 12,000-15,000 scholars, researchers, practitioners and graduate students as a forum to publish, present, critique and improve the understanding of multiple management disciplines. The annual convention activities are divided among its divisions and special-interest groups some of which include conflict management, entrepreneurship, healthcare management, management consulting, public and non-profit management, technology and management education. One of the newer special-interest groups within the Academy of Management is Management Spirituality and Religion.

Father Dan is a late vocation, and prior to his formation as a diocesan priest he was a top-level manager at a major U.S. manufacturing corporation. Because of his secular executive functions, he remained interested in the development of management theories and models, and since his day-to-day manufacturing activities kept him away from reading, attending workshops and being able to purse graduate education in management, he would use vacation time to attend the Academy of Management conventions and refresh his knowledge and become more effective. Even upon entering the seminary for late vocations and after ordination, he remained interested in the topics of management, more so

243

now that after only five years after ordination he is a pastor of a suburban parish of about 4,800 families. As you can imagine, attending the Academy of Management conventions become a lower priority.

However, Father Dan just discovered that the Academy of Management convention for this year would be held in a major city close to the parish. He also noticed that he had a couple of days available in which he could actually attend some of the paper presentations and discussion sessions. Upon making arrangements to attend, he decided to participate in some of the sessions presented by the *Management, Spirituality and Religion* special-interest group. During the sessions it was evident to him that some of the more common "buzzwords" being used included various forms of "envisioning" (e.g., vision statements, envisioning skills, implications of envisioning to the organization).

A few days after the convention, Father Dan was at a Vicariate meeting, and during one of the breaks he started a conversation with some other pastors just as a way to see how they would value the "envisioning" influence when implemented in parish life. Many of his peers observed that certain ministries seem to be better suited than others for establishing and using vision statements. Also within the discussion, other pastors lamented that out of all the possible groups and teams in parish life, the parish leadership team (parish staff) seemed to be among the ministry groups less likely to be influenced by a parish vision. Father Dan was somewhat stunned at this observation and decided to give it some more thought. He also decided to continue consulting with other pastoral leaders on this topic.

CASE STUDY QUESTIONS

1. Think about what is needed to get started with an envisioning process. What kind of prerequisites do you think are essential to the envisioning process? What factors seem to help facilitate an effective *envisioning* in the pastoral setting? What behaviors would hinder the process?

2. For sure, Father Dan in his secular position as a manager would have used some form of *envisioning* (e.g., vision statement). Based on what you have read in this chapter, how would you convince him that envisioning also works in ministry? What arguments would you use?

3. Father Dan has asked you how to go about starting an envisioning process for Religious Formation and the group of catechists. In a group setting, enact the process based on the realities of your parish and formulate a vision statement for Religious Formation.

Discussion Questions

1. Conduct a group discussion on trying to understand why on one hand, pastoral leaders have a clear appreciation of the value of envisioning, yet the effects of envisioning seem not as evident as they are in the for-profit or non-profit sectors. What are some possible causes? What are some possible remedies?

2. Search the web for envisioning statements from other diocese, ministries or parishes. Do any of these resonate with your own ministry? Do any of these awaken new ideas or possibilities for the ministry group you lead?

3. We said that schools of spirituality are (1) a spiritual way that derives from a Source-experience around which an (2) inner circle of pupils takes shape which (3) is situated within a socio-cultural context in a specific way and (4) opens a specific perspective of the future; a second (5) generation structures all this into an organic whole, by means of which (6) a number of people can share in the Source-experience; when the Source-experience, the contextual relevance, and the power to open up the future are blocked, (7) a reformation is needed (Waaijman, 2002,

p.118). As a group, take the parish vision statement and analyze it against these criteria? What criteria are met, and which are not fully met?

4. What are some of the traditional *schools of spirituality* that are present in your parish? How do those schools of spirituality contribute to help keep alive the parish envisioning process within the different ministries?

5. When envisioning at the parish level, you are not alone. There are other pastoral leaders who are also aligning the "picture" or vision of their ministries with the parish vision. Yet what kind of events or activities may be missing at the parish level to ensure pastoral leaders and the pastor are all communicating the same vision?

Personal Reflective

1. Some spiritual traditions suggest each person have an *envisioning* statement or sort of a personal vision statement. Many envisioning statements emerge from what we said in previous chapters about vocation as influence. Take the time to formulate through journaling what you believe is your own personal envisioning statement.

2. As a pastoral leader, to what degree are you able to use envisioning as a spiritual influence on the group or groups you lead? What works? What is not working?

3. Can you think of specific cases in which *envisioning* was used in the Old Testament or the New Testament? How did these cases hold up to the elements that make up an effective envisioning? How would some of these be related to your own personal vision statement?

Chapter References

Baum, I.R., Locke, E.A., & Kirkpatrick, S.A. (1998). A longitudinal study of the relation of vision and vision communication to venture growth in entrepreneurial firms. *The Journal of Applied Psychology, 83,* 43-54.

Beyer, A. (2011). A whole world: The personal is the global. *Journal of Spirituality & Paranormal Studies, 34*(1), 48-58.

Cennamo, L., & Gardner, D. (2008). Generational differences in work values, outcomes and person-organization values fit. *Journal of Managerial Psychology, 23*(8), 891-906. doi:10.1108/02683940810904385

Chittister, J. (1992). *The rule of St. Benedict: Insight for the ages.* New York: Crossroads.

Choi, J. (2006). A motivational theory of Charismatic Leadership: Envisioning, empathy, and empowerment. Journal of Leadership & Organizational Studies,13(1), 24-43.

Davis, H. (1950). St Gregory the Great: Pastoral care. In Ancient Christian Writers: The works of the Fathers in translation. J. Quasten & J. Plumpe (Eds.) Volume 11. Washington DC: Catholic University of America.

De Meuse, K., & Mlodzik, K. (2010). A second look at generational differences in the workforce: Implications for HR and talent management. *People and Strategy, 33*(2), 50-58.

Eisner, S. (2005). Managing generation Y. *S.A.M.Advanced Management Journal, 70*(4), 4-15.

Gailbraith, J.R., & Lawler, E. (1993).*Organizing for the future: The new logic for managing complex organizations.* San Francisco: Jossey-Bass.

Gangadean, A. K. (2006). Spiritual transformation. *Zygon: Journal of Religion & Science, 41*(2), 381-392.

Gardner, J.W. (1990). *On leadership.* New York: Free Press.

Haynes, C. J. (2009). Holistic human development. . *Journal of Adult Development, 16*(1), 53-60. doi:10.1007/s10804-009-9052-4

Hedlund-de Witt, A. (2011). The rising culture and worldview of contemporary spirituality: A sociological study of potentials and pitfalls for sustainable development. *Ecological Economics, 70*(6), 1057-1065. doi:10.1016/j.ecolecon.2011.01.020

Jones, C. A., & Mason, W. (2010). Leadership among spiritual teachers. *ReVision, 30*(3/4), 28-36. doi:10.4298/REVN.30.3.4.28-36

Kouses, J.M, & Posner, B.Z. (1996, May). Envisioning your future: Imagining ideal situations. *Futurist*, pp 14-19.

Kotter, J.P. (1990). *A force for change: How leadership differs from management.* New York: Free Press.

Kotter, J.P. (1996), *Leading change,* Boston, MA: Harvard Business School Press (pp. 68-70).

Lipton, M. (1996). Demystifying the development of an organizational vision. *Sloan Management Review, 37*(4), 83-91.

Lloyd, P., Braithwaite, J., & Southon, G. (1999).Empowerment and the performance of health services. *Journal Of Management in Medicine, 13*(2/3), 83-94.

L. Po, S. (2011). Awakening community: The need to reinvent the social dimension of Religion. *International Journal of Religion & Spirituality in Society, 1*(2), 47-55.

Meraviglia, M. G. (1999). Critical analysis of spirituality and its empirical indicators: Prayer and meaning in life. *Journal of Holistic Nursing, 17,* 18-33.

McLamey, C. & Rhyno, S. (1999) . Mary Parker Follett: Visionary leadership and strategic management. *Women in Management Review, 14*(7), 292-304.

Molvig, D.. (1996, April). Envisioning leadership. *Credit Union Management, 19*(4),14.

Morton, L. (2002). Targeting generation Y. *Public Relations Quarterly, 47*(2), 46-48.

Murphy, E., Gibson, J., & Greenwood, R. (2010). Analyzing generational values among managers and non-managers for sustainable organizational effectiveness. *S.A.M. Advanced Management Journal, 75*(1), 33-43.

Pesut, B. (2003). Developing spirituality in the curriculum: Worldviews, intrapersonal connectedness, interpersonal connectedness. *Nursing Education Perspectives, 24*(6), 290-294.

Pickard, J. G., & Nelson-Becker, H. (2011). Attachment and spiritual coping: Theory and practice with older adults. *Journal of Spirituality in Mental*

Health, 13(2), 138-155. doi:10.1080/19349637.2011.565239

Salahuddin, M. (2010). Generational differences impact on leadership style an organizational success. *Journal of Diversity Management, 5*(2), 1-6.

Sheldrake, P. (2007). *A brief history of spirituality.* Malden, MA: Blackwell Publishing.

Shelton, K..(2009, June). What's right with this picture? Leadership Excellence, 26(6), 2.

Skrabec, Q.R. (2003). *St. Benedict's rule for business success.* West Lafayette: Purdue University Press

Seicol, S. R. (2005). A pastoral understanding of positive aging. In H. R. Moody (Ed.), *Religion, spirituality and aging: A social work perspective* (pp. 293-300). New York, NY: Haworth.

Senge, P.M. (1990). *The fifth discipline: The art and practice of the learning organization.* New York: Doubleday.

Sims, H.P., &Lorenzi, P. (1992). *The new leadership paradigm: Social learning and cognition in organizations.* Newbery Park, CA: Sage.

Sirias, D., Karp, H., & Brotherton, T. (2007). Comparing the levels of individualism/collectivism between baby boomers and generation X. *Management Research Review, 30*(10), 749-761. doi:10.1108/01409170710823467

Tale, Y., & Parker, S. (2007). Using Erikson's Developmental Theory to Understand and Nurture Spiritual Development in Christians. *Journal of Psychology & Christianity, 26*(3), 218-226.

Yukl, G. (2002). *Leadership in organizations* (5th ed.). NJ: Prentice Hall.

Waaijman, K. (2002). *Spirituality: Forms, foundations and methods.* Leuven, Paris: Peeters.

Watson, J. (2006). Spiritual development and inclusivity: The need for a critical democratic approach. *International Journal of Children's Spirituality, 11*(1), 113-124. doi:10.1080/13644360500504405

Wieck, K. (2007). Motivating an intergenerational workforce: Scenarios for success. *Orthopedic Nursing, 26*(6), 366-71; quiz 372-3.

The "soft" side of leadership

Framework that guides our choices

Discernment
Envisioning (Worldview)
Spiritual community
Primacy of relationships
Building Character
Your Calling

PASTORAL LEADERSHIP

Goals
Processes
Working together
Getting things done
Exercising influence & power

Framework that guides our actions

The "hard" side of leadership

To discern a difference is essential to spiritual life, especially when it concerns the difference between a dead-end road and the road of life.
(Kees Waaijman, 2002, p.486)

CHAPTER 8

Discernment as Influence

In the previous chapter, we discussed the *envisioning* influence, that of "painting a clear and compelling picture," a worldview or a philosophical outlook of reality. It is like an ideological landscape, by which reality is interpreted through an overarching set of principles that provides a sense of meaning and value with guidelines for action. The underlying dynamics *of meaning-making*, a clear *sense of direction* and the expected *transformation* that results from a good sense of identity and a clarity of purpose and direction, suggest that envisioning is not just a function of one spiritual dynamic, but a result of a mutual interlinking of these three (or perhaps even more) spiritual dynamics. The "envisioning" influence—from a spiritual perspective—has the ability to either perpetuate personal and community level biases and crisis (L. Po, 2011) or to promote positive intra- and interpersonal connectedness that can help overcome "current state" dissatisfactions (Pesut, 2003).

But that interpretation of reality, through an overarching set of principles that can serve to make a difference between perpetuating biases and the status quo, or sustain a growing sense of interpersonal connectedness, requires making choices. The *envisioning* influence provides inspiration, shows the way and unites, but the journey still needs to be traveled. And making the journey throughout day-to-day life at home, at work or in parish ministry, requires choices. Yet choices that sustain a sense of meaning and value with guidelines for action within the "vision" requires a reflective process, a formulation of best courses of action and the courage to take those courses of action.

Given that we have used a considerable number of ideas from the secular leadership field (and sometimes even the management discipline), the easiest way to fulfill this need to select optimal choices would have been to use the variety of problem-solving techniques available in these fields. Here, we could have considered grid analysis, conjoint analysis, Pareto analysis, decision tress, matrices and utility theory, force field analysis, cost benefit analysis, break-even analysis, risk management—and many others—all within the perspective of either the leader as the decision maker or the group as a decision-making body. But in doing so, we would be betraying the fundamental principle that *leadership is a spiritual practice.*

All the spiritual influences we have discussed in this book require choices, and decision-making is the quintessential leadership task. Accordingly, our selection of methodology for satisfying this natural next step, which stems from the *envisioning* influence, is to suggest spiritual forms of decision making, or more specifically, *discernment. Discernment* is the process of assembling and sorting out knowledge with respect to the way toward God. It tests the ends and the means and creates a critical center. *Discernment* also ties together all of the spiritual influences we have mentioned in this book, since all spiritual practices demand day-to-day choices within a broad "vision" or worldview. Then it is through *discernment* that a leader and the group (team, community) is able to enhance knowledge, critical thinking and receptivity to God's will and ways (Grothe, 2008; Valk, 2009). In this sense, *discernment* provides a "contemplative wisdom" that looks at a person's and community's life journey and *envisions* its perfection through the divine (Waaijman, 2002). Therefore, in this chapter we present *discernment* as the choice of spiritual decision making for the pastoral leader.

The Meaning of Discernment

One of the most difficult challenges of this chapter was to find a definition of discernment and a discernment methodology that would be simple enough to communicate and practice without affecting the breadth and depth of its fundamental spiritual significance as presented in scripture, tradition and teachings. What follows is a brief analysis of *discernment,* first from a secular perspective, then clarifying the need for inclusion of the divine and finally a simple discernment methodology we and other leaders have used successfully over the past few years. Our intent in presenting this methodology is not to interfere with those leaders who already have strong discernment skills—especially those leaders formed along the lines of the traditional schools of spirituality—but to provide a simple, but valuable, technique for those leaders not yet as skilled. For us, there cannot be a true pastoral leader without discernment as a central skill and spiritual influence.

Interestingly enough, the workshops we have conducted along the lines of spiritual influences have convinced us that *discernment* is a crucial first step for pastoral leadership development. In this book, the order of topics build upon each other as the ideas move from the individual (vocation, character development), to others (relationships and community), to the broader view of ideology and from there to the *envisioning* of life (vision, worldview). But in the workshops we found it more valuable to conduct an awareness exercise followed by a brief overview of the spiritual influences and then focus on *discernment* as the first spiritual influence. This way, the discernment module as the first spiritual influence skill became a theoretical presentation as well as a skills practice session in which the participants were charged with discerning the next training module according to their reflection and prayerful dialogue.

The group and plenary discussion on this topic—as well as the results of the workshop pre-assessments—gave us the impression that leaders have some awareness of the need to apply discernment, but they showed a confusing mix of secular and religious interpretations of the term, and had some difficulty implementing discernment as an influence skill in the team (group) setting.

This mixing of secular and religious understandings was not surprising. From the secular point of view, the term *discernment* is not new to leadership theory and practice, albeit difficult to relate these definitions to scripture, tradition and teachings. In fact, there have been some recent attempts in formal research to operationalize "discernment" in the business sector and even efforts to measure its effectiveness. In a study by Traüffer, Bekker, Bocârnea, Winston (2010), discernment was characterized by three variables—courage, intuition and faith. The project was a mixed-method research project, with a qualitative component consisting of in-depth interviews conducted with eight purposively selected leaders about their decision-making processes and followed by a quantitative component with data from 240 leaders, generated via an online survey. In this study, a survey was administered measuring the effectiveness of these variables, all resulting in high Cronbach alpha values (0.85, 0.89, 0.85) suggesting that discernment was a significant factor with these leaders. Although the conceptualization of "discernment" used in this study is narrow in scope, it shows that *discernment* has value in contemporary leadership and organizational praxis and starts a unique line of research inquiry on the topic.

To confuse matters more between the secular and religious, some researchers in the business sector suggest drawing from the traditional schools of discernment as a valid method for business decision making. For example, Moberg and Calkins (2001) suggest spiritual practices by St. Ignatius Loyola as an organizational development technique and a tool in dealing with and training for business ethics. In another case, the

Rule of St. Benedict is presented as a crucial lesson for leaders, a Rule that has "discernment" as one of the virtues (Chan, C., McBey, K., & Scott-Ladd, B. (2011). In this case, discernment was defined as **a** more involving kind of approach to decision making for the leader. Discernment not only relies on precedents, best practices or benchmarking, but it compels leaders to understand the self and organization in a holistic way, inviting constant self-evaluation and adjustments to make good judgments that serve the greater whole. It is not clear if in this case the authors intended "holistic" to also mean an openness to the divine. In another publication, Tredget (2010) also uses the Rule of St. Benedict for defining the leadership function and argues that *discernment* is an integral and indispensable part of practical wisdom, a reality of a leader's core spiritual and religious beliefs and practice. Other authors also associate *discernment* in business as a way leaders can exercise "practical wisdom" at the service of the organization (May, 1999).

This movement from the secular to the religious and vice versa represents an interesting turn of events, because the original discussion on secular leadership research regarding discernment was able to "loop back" at methods and practices from the traditional schools of spirituality. From the secular setting we returned to the religious setting. The references about St. Ignatius and the Rule of St. Benedict mentioned above allude to what we said earlier about some of the confusion in using secular and religious language in defining *discernment*. This prompts us to address some of these differences, clarify terminologies and settle on a definition of discernment.

Elements of Discernment

Significant elements of the popular definition of the term *discernment* include: "to see distinctly; to perceive by the eye; to see or understand the difference; to distinguish mentally; to see or understand the difference" (Webster's New Twentieth Century Dictionary, Unabridged 2nd Edition). The definition suggests that discernment requires the ability to see beyond the apparent. As a result, insight into matters small and large, simple and complex, is a key product of discernment. Engaging in discernment is essentially a "movement toward insight" (O'Connell Killen & De Beer, 1994). Writing about theological reflection, a close kin of discernment in the spiritual sense, O'Connell Killen & De Beer note that:

> Becoming aware of [the] movement [of insight] in our own lives can strengthen and refine our habit of reflection. It puts us in touch with how, at times in our lives, we have come to significant understandings that allowed us to choose more freely among options or that strengthened or shifted our sense of who we are in relation to God, self, other, and the world." (1994, p.21).

What the authors stated about reflection also applies to discernment in the spiritual sense of the word. Spiritual discernment requires awareness, honesty and an authentic sense of self. Without these, discernment becomes an exercise in self-delusion. To the extent that we deny the authentic self, we move away from authentic discernment. If meaningful insight is to result from discernment—authenticity more than technique—is a basic requirement.

Through his book *Decision Making and the Will of God* (1980, 2004), Garry Friesen suggests two branches of discernment thought that are useful in setting the foundation for the discernment of voice methodology we recommend for pastoral leadership. The first school, called the traditional approach, is based on the premise that God reveals his plans through specific different individuals (e.g., prophets). The second approach, also called "the way of wisdom" relies on the individual and community's God-given reasoning abilities, wise counsel and a clear assessment of their strengths, talents and abilities. This approach to *discernment* is built upon on biblical scripture wisdom or a pragmatic wisdom—one that is based on the use of wise counsel and use of common sense. A review of some of the Scriptural passages referring to the wisdom of discernment is helpful to develop greater insight into this form of discernment. For example,

> And I tell you, ask and you will receive; seek and you will find; knock and the door will be opened to you. For everyone who asks, receives; and the one who seeks, finds; and to the one who knocks, the door will be opened (Luke 11:9-10)

There is no evidence in this Scripture passage from the Gospel according to Luke that it is necessary to knock down the door or to make loud demands to be heard. Instead, the passage indicates that the person discerning should take the initiative to ask, to seek and to knock—and then listen for the response. Impatient demands and loud knocking on doors result in a lack of attention to the gentle promptings of the Spirit that lead us inevitably to insight. Accordingly, sound pastoral leadership calls instead for a reflective attitude toward the many demands of pastoral life.

Consider a second example of scripture in relation to discernment:

> The Pharisees and Sadducees came and, to test him, asked him to show them a sign from heaven. He said to them in reply, "In the evening you say, 'Tomorrow will be fair, for the sky is red'; and, in the morning, 'Today will be stormy, for the sky is red and threatening.' You know how to judge the appearance of the sky, but you cannot judge the signs of the times. (Matthew 16:1-3:)

As the authentic "self" interacts with the culture, it is critically important that one remain sensitive to reading the signs of the times. By *culture* we refer to more than the values, world-view and traditions of a community. Culture also refers to the same dynamics of the local Church and the parish. Without a good sense for the local social, economic and political currents, the pastoral leader will have difficulty moving toward an insight that promotes the spiritual life of the community.

In summary, the second approach presented by Friesen (2004) called "The way of wisdom" relies on biblical scripture wisdom as well as pragmatic wisdom—one that is based upon the use of wise counsel and common sensing with others. Because we offered some of the Scriptural passages referring to the "wisdom" of discernment, we should also offer examples of what we mean by use of wisdom stemming from others.

The other interpretation to the "way of wisdom"—rather than based on scripture wisdom—argues that that God remains actively involved in the world and the decisions people make (Willard, 1993; Smith, 2005; Main, 2007). Discernment is not focused primarily on decision making. It is focused on gaining insight and on seeing matters through eyes that transcend the moment. As such, discernment leads to thoughts and actions that support the common good and that bring life to difficult situations that seek growth rather than results. On the other hand, a presumption that discernment is mostly about making decisions, likely results in a utilitarian and lifeless dynamic. To be sure, a decision-making approach to discernment could lead to a good result. The important distinction to bear in mind is that a utilitarian approach to discernment reduces significantly the opportunities for growth. A substantially utilitarian approach to discernment largely ignores human growth needs and tends to approach the person as a means to an end (even a good end).

After addressing some of the elements and approaches to classifications and forms of reflective decision making, we define *discernment* here as a process of prayerful reflection of "voices" that leads a person and a community to an understanding of the ways toward God at a given time or in a particular circumstance of life. It involves listening to God's voice in all the ways God communicates with us: through personal and community prayer, Scripture, tradition, Church hierarchy and teachings, the world, personal experience and other people.

258

In this sense, it may be said of *discernment* that it is more than an activity or process. Certainly, there are excellent processes for engaging in discernment. One example is the process for Ignatian discernment. Without a roadmap for discernment, it is unlikely that one will move toward insight. A process or roadmap is helpful to find one's way through a process that requires stillness, humility and introspection. On the other hand, discernment is not the particular process or roadmap that one may use. Discernment is more a state of being. That is, it requires an internal attitude of humility, expectation, alertness and vigilance. Discernment requires a still heart so that the urgings of the Spirit can influence the person. The urgings of the Spirit don't usually manifest themselves in great sound and much fury, so it is the still heart that is able to discern those gentle urgings.

Discernment also requires a developed "language of the heart" (Rojas, 2009), which allows for a fuller understanding, interpretation and communication of what one is noticing in the urgings of the Spirit. A language of the heart consists of a lexicon that is rich in relational words and ideas of community. While rational, the language is mostly relational. As such, it allows the one who is discerning to articulate to others what is being noticed. The fuller the articulation, the richer the experience. A language of the heart also allows the individual to see beyond the apparent. It provides the means to notice opportunities and meaning where they are not obvious. Linguists note that language both reflects and influences a culture's worldview. A language of the heart similarly influences the person to a deeper and fuller awareness of what is real, yet not evident. And so, the movement toward insight is facilitated. Efficiency is not the goal; depth is the intention.

For this approach to *discernment*, the argument is that God's will and ways are attained when individual and community spiritual maturity govern the choices made, and they develop a sense of taking responsibility for making decisions within the framework of an intimate divine-human relationship. It is this third approach from which we opt to adopt a simple, yet effective, discernment method that we call *discernment of voices.*

Discernment of Voices

In reviewing the possible ways that God "speaks" we suggest three major categories of "voices" that can help focus the collection of data toward discovering God's will and ways. Essentially, discernment is the seeking of God's voice, the voice of self and the voices of others (Giallanza, 2006). This form of discernment is illustrated by the Samuel Calling (1 Samuel 3):

> During the time young Samuel was minister to the LORD under Eli, the word of the LORD was scarce and vision infrequent. One day Eli was asleep in his usual place. His eyes had lately grown so weak that he could not see. The lamp of God was not yet extinguished, and Samuel was sleeping in the temple of the LORD where the ark of God was. The LORD called to Samuel, who answered, "Here I am." He ran to Eli and said, "Here I am. You called me." "I did not call you," Eli answered. "Go back to sleep." So he went back to sleep. Again the LORD called Samuel, who rose and went to Eli. "Here I am," he said. "You called me." But he answered, "I did not call you, my son. Go back to sleep." Samuel did not yet recognize the LORD, since the word of the LORD had not yet been revealed to him. The LORD called Samuel again, for the third time. Getting up and going to Eli, he said, "Here I am. You called me." Then Eli understood that the LORD was calling the youth. So he said to Samuel, "Go to sleep, and if you are called, reply, 'Speak, LORD, for your servant is listening.'" When Samuel went to sleep in his place, the LORD came and stood there, calling out as before: Samuel, Samuel! Samuel answered, "Speak, for your servant is listening." (1 Samuel 3).

Pastoral Leader and Discernment of Voices

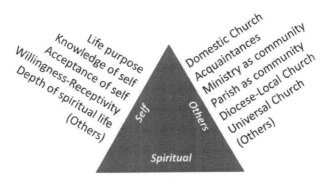

Practical faith in Divine Providence
Depth of prayer life (Originality)
Image-relationship with God
Sensitivity to the effects of grace
(Others)

Figure 5, Discernment of Voices

As noted earlier, discernment requires, among other things, a stillness of the heart, humility and an attitude of listening. These are required so the person is able to notice, interpret and respond to the gentle urgings of the Spirit. Typically, the gentle urgings of the Spirit manifest themselves in the various voices that speak to the person. Although one cannot place restrictions on how God chooses to communicate with a person, the long record of history indicates that God usually chooses to communicate his hopes and dreams to us through the voices of the prayerful people in our life. As we shall see, the voices are not always overtly vocal ones, but they are expressive voices nonetheless. We identify three groups of voices: personal, spiritual and external.

The graphic (Figure 5) depicts the elements of each voice and their relationships.

Personal Voice

Referred to as 'self' in the diagram, the personal voice reflects our impressions and responses to the urgings of the Spirit. It is the connection that we maintain between ourselves and the divine. While the objectivity (i.e. freedom from significant distortion) of any one of the voices is a consideration, this voice can present substantial questions about that matter. The human psyche seems to have an inexhaustible capacity to convince itself that what it wants, God wants just as much. Ascertaining a reasonable degree of objectivity is a challenge for this voice. This is why it is important to be able to harmonize all of the voices. We will discuss this point at the end of this section. Integral to the personal voice are:

  a. Clarity of life's purpose
  b. Knowledge of self
  c. Acceptance of self
  d. Desire to be formed
  e. Depth of one's spiritual life

Clarity of life's purpose refers to the extent to which we are aware of our ultimate purpose and of some of the possibilities for our life in light of our God-given gifts and interests. To be sure, most of us spend a lifetime seeking a perspective on our ultimate purpose while on this earth. Questions about who to marry, which profession to pursue, whether or not one is called to a Church vocation, and what ministries to engage in are among the many matters that a person who lives a reflective life ponders. It is the rare individual who enjoys absolute clarity about such matters. Most of us spend a lifetime engaged in the questions. This is precisely the point about discernment. We seek not clarity as much as we seek a journey toward clarity. It is in the willingness to humbly and with an open heart learn what hopes and dreams God has for us that we remain open to others and their journey. A preference for quick answers, absolute certainty and simple solutions make a movement toward insight impractical. Moreover, one with such preferences will only add noise as an external voice to someone seeking insight.

Knowledge of self refers to the extent to which one is open to knowing oneself—not just the aspects of self that everyone seems to like, but also those less-positive aspects of our personality and behavior. All of the elements of this and other voices of discernment relate to one another. None stand alone. Accordingly, knowledge of "self" influences the extent to which we are able to develop some clarity of life's purpose. It relates to authenticity. By seeking insight into ourselves, we learn to be authentically who we are. Adopting a masquerade of a false self, we understand ourselves less. Tragically, we learn to know our masks better than we know the person on whom the mask rests. Lack of authenticity masks our God-given gifts and enslaves us to our ego-given illusions. Under such circumstances, we become functionally incapable of discerning the urgings of the Spirit for us, especially when they are not consistent with our illusions about ourselves.

Acceptance of "self" posits that knowing oneself adequately is not possible if one is unable to accept who one is. At the same time, ac-

263

ceptance of one's less desirable traits can lead to stagnation and denial. Without acceptance of the authentic self, knowledge of self is short-circuited. Sometimes, it is necessary to seek professional help to learn to accept oneself. Such acceptance requires a degree of maturity and trust. Maturity leads to an understanding that no one is all-knowing, all-powerful or consistently virtuous. Our weaknesses may be seen as God's way of making us strong. We become stronger when we learn to trust that God showers us with more gifts than we can fully use and that our failings can and should lead us to greater dependence on the source of our life. Emotional and spiritual immaturity inevitably leads us to a childish vision of ourselves as all-powerful. This and similar distortions of self significantly increase the difficulties of moving toward insight. Similar distortions of "self" include being too readily accepting of our less-desirable traits. The results are the same—we become unable to humbly listen, honestly reflect and consistently trust. Such a milieu is inconsistent with spiritual growth and the ability to discern appropriately.

A desire to be formed indicates that without a willingness to be formed by the Lord it is impossible for one to discern God's will. Instead, the exercise to discern becomes a self-fulfilling prophecy. Formation involves conforming the person emotionally, psychologically and intellectually to the gifts that God has given us. At a minimum, a sense of self in harmony with reality, acceptance that God has created us in his image and likeness, and a sincere desire to live according to our God-given gifts, are required for growth to occur. If, for whatever the reason, we are not able to allow ourselves to seek growth, we do not benefit very much from our gifts. The general lack of openness to anything not coming from within that characterizes this lack of interest in growth makes a movement toward insight unlikely. Whether the voices emerge from within or outside the person, lack of openness shuts the door to authenticity and objectivity. The urgings of the Spirit usually cannot get the person's attention in such a situation.

Depth and breadth of one's spiritual life indicates that a deep, adult relationship with the Lord is both a requirement for and goal of discernment. It is simply essential. Much of what could be said here has already been said. It is important to note, though, that the goal of discernment is not reaching a decision; it is deepening the spiritual life of the person discerning as well as the person who might be the object of the discernment. Looking at discernment from the perspective of the person discerning, one can readily see how, approached properly, the journey of discernment inevitably deepens the person's relationship with the Lord. Similarly, the goal of discernment is to enrich the spiritual life of those who are directly or indirectly the objects of the discernment process. For example, if the pastoral leader is discerning how to structure the process for engaging in volunteer ministry at the parish, the key goal of that reflection is to implement a process that enhances the spiritual life of the ministers. The goal is not to develop the most efficient and cost-effective process, although those are important values. Properly done, discernment would approach these as secondary values, at best.

Spiritual Voices

These voices may seem to be the most self-evident of all. After all, if discernment is movement toward insight resulting from a response to the urgings of the Spirit, then these should be the voices to whom one first turns. To be sure, the spiritual voices are primary and significant. But, as we have seen, they are not the only voices. Listening to the spiritual voices requires that we develop a sensitivity to the integral elements of these voices; it also requires that we remain sensitive to the elements of the other voices. Nevertheless, maintaining the ability to quiet our frantic hearts and listen to the gentle urgings of the Spirit depends in large part on our honoring the importance of the following integral elements of the spiritual voices. Integral to the spiritual voices are:

       a. A "practical" faith in divine providence
       b. Depth of prayer life
       c. Image of and relationship with God
       d. Relationship with other key people
       e. Awareness of and sensitivity to grace

Faith in divine providence is another way of expressing the need for faith in God. It refers to the extent to which we have faith that God will lead us to what is best for us. It is faith in the goodness of the Lord. The insights gained from discernment are often counter-intuitive, seren-dipitous and striking. It is easy to ignore such insights. They may be too far from our expectations to believe they come from a God who cares about us. When we believe that we are being taken far from our expected path, we can convince ourselves that the more conservative path must be the divine one. Of course, experience tells us that we should be suspicious of such conclusions. It is faith that enables us to trust in the goodness of God enough to strike out on a journey that seems out of character for us. The movement toward insight often takes us outside of our comfortable expectations and into a deeper mystery in which we find new life and hope.

Depth of prayer life refers to the fact that God often speaks to us in whispers and through others. It is through prayer that we connect with the appropriate voices; through prayer we also remain connected to the genuine whispers from God. Prayer is not intended to make God present to us but to make us present to God. Our Lord is always with us and present to us. Often, it is we who are distracted, unaware and semi-conscious. As long as we remain so, it is difficult for us to detect and listen to the gentle urgings of the Spirit. Under those circumstances, discernment becomes impractical. In prayer, the discerning person strives to gently, gradually and gratefully become increasingly aware of God's presence. As that occurs, one more fruitfully enters into the gentle movements to insight.

266

The image of and relationship with God calls us to critically examine our images of God. It is common to have developed an image of God early in life that has not been examined and may not be serving the individual well today. We at times domesticate God so he more conforms with our expectations and with our need for control. The following diversity of our domesticated and false gods is adapted from a work by Kerry Walters (2001, pp. 27-40).

> **God of Logic:** This is the god of clarity and of the mind. He is borne from a dislike of ambiguity. The implicit expectation is that God is to be clear about everything at all times. God becomes an abstract thought—an idea rather than an encounter. As such, God becomes safe, satisfying, predictable.

> **God of Experiences:** This is the god of intense feelings and experience. God exists only to the extent that he can be experienced intensely and often. This domesticated god is an experience, but an experience that is everywhere thrilling and safely choreographed. The choreography is important because it heightens the experience of God and at the same time keeps him predictable. After all, even God will follow a script, they believe.

> **God of Laws:** This is the god of laws, lots of them. The worshippers of this god seek haven in a deity who reveals himself in clear and precise laws that disallow ambiguity or exception. This god is the cosmic codifier, the celestial bookkeeper, the consummate censor. This domesticated god tells us exactly what to do and not to do. Righteousness is defined by fidelity to an inflexible list of dos and don'ts. Fidelity is measured by unerring adherence to a never-ending list of rules.

God of Accomplishments: This is the go-getter god. Busyness and efficiency are its cardinal virtues. As a result, this god enjoys widespread popularity in this culture. Devotees have no time for impractical theologizing or for foolish expenditures of energy that could be put to better use. What counts for them is quantity: how many church committees served on, how much money raised, how many old ladies helped across the street. One's worth becomes proportionate to the number of one's achievements.

Discernment calls us to a relationship with the one, true God. Anything less simply won't do for an adult who strives to be a Christ-centered pastoral leader. When we listen to the urgings of these gods, we engage in an encounter with a lifeless god, who leads us away from insight and into darkness.

Relationship with others reinforces the notion that spirituality is relational, just as God is relational. The depth and character of our relationships with others inform us about our spiritual and emotional maturity. Discernment occurs within the context of the "other." To be in relationship with God and others requires us to be aware and to remain awake.

> Spirituality is basically the art of being awake; it is the discipline of being aware. Spiritual growth is essentially becoming more and more conscious. The biggest handicap to our personal development is that we live almost unconsciously. We become so immersed in our habits and routines that we don't notice obvious solutions to our dissatisfactions and golden opportunities for growth. In like manner, we don't sense the presence of God because we are half asleep. Our need, therefore, is to wake up and take notice of what is going on in our lives moment to moment (Kent 1996, p. 4).

268

To the extent that we remain unaware and sub-optimally conscious, we are unable to progress in the movement toward insight on the urgings of the Spirit in our life and the life of those entrusted to us.

Awareness of and sensitivity to grace enables us to be open to the movement of the Spirit in our life. God's grace calls us to love more, listen more and give more. Discernment calls us to humility and gratitude for this unmerited gift from God, who fills us with his love even when we have done nothing to earn it. We move toward insight that the urgings of the Spirit bring with a constant attitude of gratitude and awareness. Giving thanks is an integral part of worship and community life for Catholics. It is also an integral part of discernment, for without it, we remain outside of our full potential as a person and as a pastoral leader.

External Voices

These voices involve a dialogue with others, but especially with elements of the Church. In the case of a spouse, it is the domestic church with which the dialogue occurs. With regard to the parish and the larger Church, the voices to which one should attend are numerous as they are important. Integral to the external voices are:

> a. Dialogue with spouse (or significant person)
> b. Dialogue with parish
> c. Dialogue with the Church

Dialogue with spouse (or significant person) for a married person is key to engaging in a meaningful discernment. Significant people for one who is unmarried would include a parent or older sibling, grandparent, godparent, teacher, coach or anyone who knows the person well and is deeply concerned about the individual. It should be said that the significant person would also deeply love the person who is discerning. The connection between the significant person and the person who is discerning should be one of love and mutual respect. Such a person, no matter the relationship, would know the person discerning at a deep level. In this way, the significant person or spouse is able to prayerfully reflect and engage the individual in a dialogue characterized by honesty, integrity and love. A dialogue such as this would inevitably reflect the urgings of the Spirit and thus help the person notice what may not yet be evident.

Dialogue with the parish includes one's pastor and ministry associates, who can often be a source of guidance when one is attempting to discern an appropriate course of action. Individuals who engage in discernment as a spiritual practice in their own lives can be indispensable to one seeking wisdom in difficult circumstances. The notion of collaborative ministry is usually proffered to those addressing difficult and complex situations at times almost reflexively. Perhaps the highest level of collaborative ministry occurs when ones seeks the wisdom of ministry colleagues in a situation that requires discernment. It is at those times that differences in role and responsibility become less important than the opportunity to grow as community by seeking to discern together the urgings of the Spirit.

Dialogue with the Church is typically necessary when the discernment involves a question about a person's participation in a formal Church ministry. Whether it is possible ministry as a priest, permanent deacon, vowed religious, youth minister, faith formation director or stewardship director, a dialogue with members of the diocesan staff is at times necessary, and always advisable. But even outside of these situations, the pastoral leader who must discern a complex matter may be well advised to seek the wisdom of other individuals experienced in such matters. Humility will often lead such a person to consider consultations with those who are outside the immediate circle of pastoral associates.

Harmonizing the Voices

Thirteen different types of voices multiplied by possibly several individuals for each voice could yield a cacophony of voices. To be sure, it is also unlikely that the voices will be speaking at once, but the individual seeking to know the urgings of the Spirit may have to listen to many voices. It is unlikely that all of the voices will agree or provide a unified perspective. However, many voices may be involved in the discernment, and they will need to be harmonized. Differences in perspective must be understood; contrary courses of action must be reconciled; divergent assessments of risk and possibilities must be evaluated. In the end, a course of action, or a decision for inaction, must be taken; new knowledge may need to be integrated; fresh wisdom may have to be acknowledged.

Discernment involves much more than adopting the majority view or averaging the common elements of the perspectives offered. Discernment requires an application of wisdom to gain new wisdom and insights. No single process or procedure will suffice. No formula will guarantee the optimal outcome. Accordingly, the voices of discernment are harmonized in prayer, reflection and humility. By adopting a stillness of the heart and by learning to listen humbly, one begins to notice the urgings of the Spirit in the many voices of discernment. If, on the other hand, we allow ourselves to be driven by arbitrary deadlines, self-imposed limits and inflexible processes, we become frozen by the resulting lack of freedom and are unable to notice God's grace-filled urgings.

Harmonizing the voices of discernment requires that we free ourselves (with God's help) from the shackles of our pre-conceptions and self-imposed limitations. We do that by humbly and completely turning ourselves over to God's grace. This is not a one-time turning over of ourselves. We will need to do so over and over again. As we learn to free ourselves in and through God's grace, we become freer

The Challenges of Pastoral Leadership

and thus able to harmonize the many voices in which the urgings of the Spirit speak to us.

Discernment and Leadership

We started this chapter by stating that the interpretation of reality through an overarching set of principles (envisioning) requires making choices. And making the journey throughout day-to-day life at home, at work or in parish ministry requires choices. We also indicated that choices that sustain a sense of meaning and value with guidelines for action within the "vision" requires a reflective process, a formulation of best courses of action and the courage to take those courses of action. Despite all the methods and techniques available in the secular disciplines of leadership and management, we decided to remain loyal to the central theme of this book—that *leadership is a spiritual practice*—and chose discernment as the preferred tool.

Again, in delivering the workshop module on discernment of voices and conducting a few exercises within the groups, we discovered an urgent need and a powerful opening to look at leadership as a spiritual practice. In doing so, we also were able to illustrate the connections between leadership and the spiritual practices. One's personal calling or vocation is the dimension of pastoral leadership that addresses the origin and fulfillment of one's life plan. This dimension connects the exercise of the leadership function to one's fundamental identity. Building character is also related to personal identity. However, it also relates to self-regulation, resilience and maturity. This dimension is associated with "interior conversion" and provides some measure of protection against corruption and making poor choices by engaging in unethical behaviors in exercising the leadership function. The primacy of relationships is the dimension that emphasizes the value of connections among individuals, which are many times more important than tasks. Spirituality is fundamentally relational, and therefore this dimension allows for a natural flow of values such as love and forgiveness, while honoring the relation-

272

ship with the dynamics of the supernatural (e.g., divine providence) in performing the leadership functions—exercising leadership to create and nurture spiritual communities rather than just organizational development. Rather than focusing mainly on team or group performance, the optional objective is to recognize and nurture a sense of *communio*. The dimension of envisioning allows the pastoral leader to work, make decisions and interact with others from a framework that includes the best articulation of what it means to be Church. In this way, responsible stewardship and an enduring evangelization is maintained.

Yet envisioning and discernment within the group (or team) setting must also follow the growth and maturity of the ministry and parish life. Different ministries within parish life develop at different rates of growth and have different needs throughout time. Therefore, in the next chapter we will look at stages of growth and the implications of these stages to pastoral leadership as a spiritual practice.

Chapter References

Barry, W. A. (2008). Communal discernment as a way to reconciliation. *Human Development*, *29*(3), 10-14.

Chan, C., McBey, K., & Scott-Ladd, B. (2011). Ethical leadership in modern employment relationships: Lessons from St. Benedict. *Journal of Business Ethics*, *100*(2), 221-228. doi:10.1007/s10551-010-0676-x

Friesen, G. (2004). *Decision making and the will of God* (rev. ed.). Sisters, Oregon: Multnomah Books.

Giallanza, J. (2006). Living with discernment in times of transition. *Human Development*, *27*(2), 15-21.

Horton, D. J. (2009). Discerning spiritual discernment: Assessing current approaches for understanding God's Will. *Journal Of Youth Ministry*, *7*(2), 7-31.

Kent, M. R. (1996). *Bringing the Word to Life: Scripture messages that change lives*, Twenty-Third Publications.

Main, B. (2007). *Holy hunches: Responding to the promptings of God*. Grand Rapids: Baker.

May, W. F. (1999). Persuasion and discernment: The gifts of leadership. *Christian Century*, *116*(8), 282.

Moberg, D.J., & Calkins, M. (2001). Reflection in business ethics: Insights from St. Ignatius' Spiritual Exercises. *Journal of Business Ethics,2 33*(3), 257-270.

O'Connell Killen, Patricia & De Beer, John. *The Art of Theological Reflection*, Crossroad: New York, 1994.

Rojas, R. (2009). *A Relational Identity for Deacon Spirituality: Exploring the Spirituality of the Permanent Diaconate in the United States.* San Diego, CA: Aventine Press.

Seidman, A. N. (2011). Listening for the Sacred Within—and at work. *OD Practitioner*, *43*(3), 36-43.

Smith, C. (2005). *Soul searching: The religious and spiritual lives of American teenagers.* New York: Oxford University Press.

Traüffer, H. V., Bekker, C., Bocârnea, M., & Winston, B. E. (2010). A three-factor measure of discernment. *Leadership & Organization Development Journal, 31*(3), 263-284.

Traüffer, H. V., Bekker, C., Bocârnea, M., & Winston, B. E. (2010). Towards an understanding of discernment: a conceptual paper. *Leadership & Organization Development Journal, 31*(2), 176-184.

Tredget, D. (2010). Practical wisdom and the Rule of Benedict. *Journal Of Management Development, 29*(7/8), 716-723. doi:10.1108/02621711011059158

Valk, J. (2009). Knowing Self and Others: Worldview Study at Renaissance College. *Journal Of Adult Theological Education, 6*(1), 69-80. doi:10.1558/jate2009v6i1.69

Walters, K.. *Soul wilderness: A desert spirituality*, Paulist Press: Mahwah, 2001

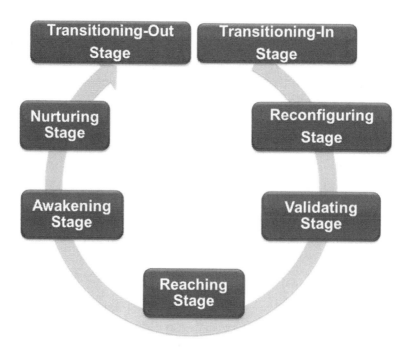

Figure 6, Pastoral Team Life-cycle

The unexamined life is not worth living.
Socrates (469 BC - 399 BC), *in Plato-Dialogues, Apology*

CHAPTER 9

Leading within Pastoral Life-cycles

After the strong emphasis on the spiritual skills of the pastoral leader, the focus now shifts toward the situational realities and needs of the ministry group (team) and how best to address them with spiritual influences. Here, we introduce pastoral life-cycles, where regularities or patterns of behaviors that seem to occur over time in ministry groups are segmented into discrete stages of organizational development. In doing so, we rely again on the application of mental models.

We indicated in previous chapters that mental models have a significant influence on the way leaders establish priorities, address internal and external forces, and assess effectiveness of alternative courses of action (Zaccaro, Rittman, & Marks, 2001). Although using mental imported models from other sectors into ministry is quite inevitable, there are benefits as long as the models are used with discretion and flexibility. Here, we were sensitive about properly addressing desirable faith and spiritual values into the group dynamics because either the desired values are incongruent with the "imported" mental model or the mental model is "blind" to or discourages certain values. Therefore, our intent in composing a model that describes pastoral life-cycles was to help view priorities, be able to recognize the elements that are "holding back" the group's growth, and offer a repertoire of possible ways for the group to continue developing. The idea was to provide a "structured landscape of possibilities," not a prescription.

Out of the experiences of working as parish consultants and drawing from the academic research on life-cycles within small businesses and non-profit organizations, seven stages of development are formulated for the pastoral life-cycle model. Each stage of this model is discussed, and best-observed spiritual practices are paired with each of these stages. The combination of the life-cycle model and what was presented earlier on leadership as a spiritual practice provides a wider landscape of possibilities and options, all embedded within the parish life context.

Although organizational life-cycle modeling has demonstrated to be a valuable framework to both for-profit and non-profit leadership effectiveness in general, the question of its direct applicability to the pastoral setting remains a topic in need of further analysis and validation. As a result of this need, a qualitative research project using the research process called "grounded theory" was performed on the yearly progress reports of 32 parish leadership teams (parish staffs) over a five year period participating in a *Sustaining Pastoral Excellence* grant awarded to a Catholic archdiocese in the mid-western United States. Narratives from the performance of these parish teams against specific learning objectives were coded and analyzed for characteristics that typify stages of development from the non-profit sector, and then were adapted to the pastoral setting. From this analysis emerged a life-cycle model with seven distinct stages that suggest practical guidance in the use of spiritual influences that typify pastoral leadership modeling.

Background on Life-cycle Modeling

Because using life-cycles in ministry is quite unique—and in remaining faithful to our caution of using new models in ministry—we opt to provide some background on the research process we used, the rationale for using non-profit life-cycles as a starting point, some of the research methodology, and finally, details on how the model was generated.

First of all, non-profit life-cycle models (rather than business models) were chosen as a baseline for pastoral life-cycles, since non-profit organizations—although they are also concerned about financial issues—are largely driven by factors that are different from those that drive the for-profit sector (Kamaria & Lewis, 2009) and are very similar to those of the pastoral sector:

> In terms of context and leadership challenges, the many differences between for-profit, government and non-profit organizations make it inappropriate to assume that research and findings in for-profit contexts apply to non-profit contexts (Dandridge, 1979; Westhead & Cowling, 1998). Moreover, it is also inappropriate to assume that research findings in non-profit contexts such as education or medicine apply to religious or church-based non-profit contexts. Moreover, the vision and mission of for-profit organizations and non-profit organizations are vastly different in terms of their underlying motives, where one is largely earnings driven, and the other is driven by a social mission (Quarter & Richmond, 2001). This difference suggests that effective leadership in a non-profit organization is likely to differ to leadership in a for-profit organization. (McMurray, et al, 2010, p. 437).

More to the point, the McMurray, Pirola-Merlo, Sarros, & Islam's (2010) study concludes that many of the operational and mission oriented attributes of a non-profit organization are also evident in church–based organizations, such as parish leadership teams. This gives us some margin to believe that theories developed for the non-profit sector are closer to the realities and mission objectives of the pastoral sector than models available from the business sector. In other words, since research on the specific subject of pastoral life-cycles seems lacking, using the research available for non-profit life-cycles is a reasonable starting point for reflecting on possible life-cycle patterns in the pastoral environment.

Now that the academic literature points to a reasonable parallel between non-profit and church–based mission oriented attributes, the next step is a more in-depth look at the various forms of life-cycle models used in the non-profit sector. In being able to understand these models, we set the stage for considering their use as a template for research in pastoral organizations.

Again, the formal research and academic publications show that organization life-cycle modeling for nonprofit organizations has been used as a framework to analyze organizational development, performance and for anticipating and leadership effectiveness (Clifford-Born, 2000). This concept is based on an organic view of organizations that acknowledges a succession of developmental stages, learning opportunities and performance strategies which—at a minimum—typically address stages of birth, growth and maturity (Milliman, Gilnow & Nathan, 1991). Life-cycle frameworks in nonprofit organizations have been used for research on leadership stability and growth (Alexander, Fennell & Halpem, 1993), in characterizing a founder's leadership and manager's style (MacNamara, 1998), leadership styles and changes in service-oriented organizations (Scmid, 2006), in searching for causes of organization mortality (Fernandez, 2008), in characterizing senior leadership performance (Dart, Bradshaw, Murray, & Wolpin, 2006) and assessing nonprofit development and capacity (Schuh & Leviton, 2005).

Despite the popularity of organizational life-cycle modeling within the non-profit sector, there seems to be some degree of divergence with respect to the number and naming of stages applicable to non-profits. For example, in her book *5 Life Stages of Nonprofit Organizations* (Wilder Foundation, 2001), Judith Sharken-Simon identifies five stages of development (Imagine and Inspire, Found and Frame, Ground and Grow, Produce and Sustain, Review and Renew). Yet in *Trade secrets for non-profit managers* (Wiley & Sons, 2001), Thomas A.

280

McLaughlin presents six stages for a non-profit life-cycle (Forming, Growing, Coalescing, Peaking, Maturing, Refocusing). Furthermore, in *Non-profit Life-cycles: Stage-based wisdom for non-profit capacity* (Stagewise Enterprises, 2002) Susan Kenny-Stevens recognizes seven distinct stages (Idea, Start-up, Growth, Maturity, Decline, Turnaround, Terminal). The variety in the number of stages in these examples seems to be a function of organizational structure, size and mission. In spite of these differences, each of these models illustrates the significance of a life-cycle dynamic to the development of nonprofit organizations and how leadership styles are related to performance in each developmental stage.

On the other hand, Church-based organizations, such as the parish leadership teams, often have a series of situations somewhat different than traditional nonprofits, something that may very well affect the dynamics of organizational growth and life-cycle dynamics. For example, the emerging literature has established that organizations tend to assume the personality of the leader (Giberson, Reisck & Dikson, 2005; Schmid, 2006). So in a pastoral setting for instance, it is understandable that a change in pastor would result in organizational adjustments relevant to life-cycle modeling of the parish leadership team. In this case, the transition and the effects of newly assigned pastors is more dramatic when considering the effects of the charisms they bring and variable degrees of leadership skills they possess (Hernandez & Leslie, 2001). Added to the special circumstances of Church-based or religious organization is the pastor's and pastoral team's understanding of the business operation within a pastoral setting, a phenomena comparable similar to bringing in a for-profit executive into a nonprofit organization (Bowen, 1994). The inseparability of a faith-based mission and business dynamics presents a series of challenges and ambiguities different than experienced in traditional non-profits. In many cases, business operational decisions may be overturned in preference of religious values, such as trust, forgiveness and mercy (Fleckenstein & Bowes, 2000). As another difference, it could also be observed that pastors may tend to resolve conflicts between business processes more in favor of values based on sacred beliefs (Duncan & Morris, 2003). For many pastors, the dual role of spiritual leader and business executive represents a stressor, since they find themselves continuously switching roles from one meeting to the next (Cnaan, 2007). The relevance of these and other experiential factors of parish leadership—although primarily anecdotal in nature—are crucial to effectively bridging gaps between nonprofit and Church-based modeling.

After understanding the possible similarities and differences that may affect the application of nonprofit life-cycle modeling within a Church-based setting, what follows is a fuller explanation of the theoretical methodology, the specifics of the target sample used, and a basic presentation of how the model was generated. Once this is accomplished, the model is presented in full and is then analyzed against the spiritual influences of pastoral leadership discussed in previous chapters.

The Research Process: Grounded Theory

Although this is not the place to fully narrate the research methodology used to formulate the pastoral life-cycle model, it is necessary to discuss—albeit minimally—some of the background, rationale and processes in order to build confidence in the model's value. This discussion also has value for those researchers, scholars and consultants who would be inclined to continue developing research projects along these or similar lines of inquiry.

The basic approach used here to compose and formulate the model of pastoral life-cycles from basic observations is called "grounded theory." In formal research, grounded theory is a qualitative method that provides a systematic generation of theory from data obtained by very specific protocols and is used in understanding the realities of everyday interactions of human behavior through a process of discovery and induction rather than by surveys, quantitative data and deduction (Creswell, 2003). For this research method and this project, theoretical sampling is used, which is defined as:

> ...the process of data collection for generating theory whereby the analyst jointly collects, codes and analyzes his [sic] data and decides what data to collect next and where to find them, in order to develop his [sic] theory as it emerges (Glaser & Strauss, 1967, p. 45).

The sample for this research consisted of 32 pastoral teams that had participated in a five-year grant from the Lilly Endowment), which focused on providing organizational development resources for qualifying pastoral leadership teams. The final reports are proprietary to the grant provider and therefore unavailable to the public, although one of the authors was also a consultant to the project and was able to receive consent to access the information from the reports and conduct the research.

Specifically, the goals of the grant were to develop capacity for pastoral leadership excellence among qualifying parish leadership teams. With the assistance of professional consultation specialized in parish life, each team wrote personal and team learning plans. Consistent with the terms of the grant provider, financial resources, consultation and organizational development services were offered to support each parish team's distinctive learning commitments. Each team shared ways to grow personally and spiritually. They, in turn, shared their experience with the parish at large in order to contribute to their organizational mission and parish life objectives.

All the official yearly progress reports and final outcomes of the 32 pastoral teams selected over the five-year grant became the source of qualitative data for this research project. A pastoral team is typically composed of the pastor as leader, members of the clergy, a business manager, a director of religious education, a manager of youth programs, a facilities supervisor, a manager of liturgy and music, a finance and accounting member, and if applicable, the principal of the school. Pastoral teams under the same diocese have the added advantage of being guided by the same administrative policies and procedures, a factor that helps reduce the amount of process variability among the sampled pastoral teams and enhance the potential transferability of final outcomes. Additionally, pastors are periodically transferred among parishes, allowing more frequent opportunities to analyze and validate the impact of the crucial outgoing and an incoming leadership transition on the pastoral team life.

Once sample of parish leadership teams and source documentation was identified, the next step was to start the analysis. The analysis process was based on "open coding," which is a method of sorting data into categories to identify themes (Bird et.al, 2009). Descriptive characteristics from two nonprofit life-cycle models were used as a starting point. These were *5 Life Stages of Nonprofit Organizations* (Wilder Foundation, 2001) and *Non-profit Life-cycles: Stage-based wisdom for nonprofit capacity* (Stagewise Enterprises, 2002). What followed was a three-month systematic coding on these reports to discern preliminary patterns of team relationships with the pastor as leader that may represent organizational regularities that could be segmented into discrete states (Dodge & Robbins, 1992). During the analysis, the keywords and stage names were modified to better accommodate the language and situations of these parish teams as addressed in the report narratives. Once preliminary life-cycle stages were identified, they were triangulated with other sources, such as the pastoral team learning plans, consultant assessments, documented stories of growth experiences and vitality indicators for the parishes (DeLambo, 2002). Table 3 illustrates the final version of this iteration process.

Reliability and Validity Parameters

For this project, the validity and relevance of a grounded theory approach was based on the credibility of the sources, their degree of transferability, dependability of the data and confirmability of the results (Lincoln & Guba, 1985). Credibility of the sources was established by the rigor and controls of the parish reports to the grant, where the leadership team learning was certified by the pastor of each parish. Transferability of the experience to other leadership team situations is considered very high, especially within the same diocese where the grant was applied. Pastoral teams under the same diocese have the added advantage of being guided by the same administrative policies and procedures, a factor that helps reduce the amount of process variability among the sampled pastoral teams, which enhances the potential transferability of final outcomes. Therefore, transferability to other diocese may well depend on the policies and preferences, as well as variances in the team composition and experiences of the leadership team. Dependability of the data stems from the fact that the outcomes of this first round of 32 parishes served as justification for an extension to the grant, where comparable monies were awarded to additional parish leadership teams (different than these first 32 teams) for an additional four-year period. Confirmability was formed by triangulation with other sources, such as the pastoral team learning plans, peer consultant assessments, documented stories of growth experiences, and vitality indicators for the parishes (DeLambo, 2002). Table 3 illustrates the final version of this iteration process.

Another way to enhance confidence in understanding the findings is to provide evidence as to how the researcher's own a priori assumptions may have molded the research process and the analysis (Murphy, et al, 1998). In this case, some of the assumptions made a priori where non-profit life-cycles would apply in one way or another to the pastoral setting better than the business-generated models. Another assumption was that through the research project we would be able to discover particularities and rename some of the stages. A third assumption was to maintain the number of possible stages to not less than five but no more than seven.

Because qualitative research is fundamentally interpretative, it's also essential to provide some degree of the inquirers' qualifications, professional experiences and preferences (Creswell, 2003). Succinctly

Table 3, Research Keywords and Phrases for Coding

STAGES	SAMPLE KEY WORDS AND KEY PHASES FOR CODING
Transitioning-In (TI)	Pastor and pastoral team forming the relationships, sensing of each other, building trust. Sharing of past performance and eliciting expectations from new leader. Part "Letting go…" and part "welcoming." Transforming (change into something different) rather than "forming" (to make). Composing a "new landscape" to fit new Pastor and finding "my place." Applies to any changes in the pastoral team, but most significant is the change of pastor. Pastor finds ways to understand and be understood: part operational, part spiritual since it is the mission.
Reconfiguring (RC)	A time to assess, acknowledge, adjust and accept. Discovering what stays, what changes, what stops. sorting out the ambiguities, comparing & contrasting. Re-examination of processes, duties and responsibilities. Some sorting out of the "Good, the Bad and the Ugly." An opportunity to "dig in the heels" or to "discover new ground." A test of each pastoral team member's ability to adapt. Relationships turn to negotiations, addressing sensitivities, re-addressing expectations. Pastor's opportunity to align team dynamics with personal worldview.
Validating (VA)	Heavy focus on individual tasks more than on pastoral team relationships: "Individual" spaces are much larger that "team" spaces. Individually proficient, but relationships with others need significant improvements. Delegation is very hard, team power struggles seem frequent. Perceived scarcity of time, feeling overloaded, risk of isolation, burn-out. Suppression of sensitive issues, a sense of frustration in working with others on team. Pastor "casting a long shadow," high risk for micromanagement.
Reaching (RE)	Moving from individual tasks to pastoral team processes requires some facilitation: Increasing willingness to consider the value of "team." General acceptance of basic teambuilding (effective meetings, team prioritizing, working together, communications, conflict management). Emerging attempts at conversation and dialogue. The "elephant" in the room (an obvious truth that is being ignored or goes unaddressed). Pastor focus on relational skills and dynamics.

	(Continuation of Table 3)
Awakening (AW)	A palpable awareness of trust, shared awareness of mission: Authentic interest in envisioning, integrating, sharing. Increasing interest in the value of "dialogue" (beyond communications). Ability to create "safe spaces." Bringing issues to light, active listening. Storytelling and dialogue emerge as values. Cooperation becomes a working value. An emerging conviction that the "Elephant" needs to be addressed.
Nurturing (NU)	Relational achievement in pastoral team becomes an enhancer of task performance. Mission becomes evident in team operations: Spiritual common ground rising: prayer, forgiveness and healing are part of team dynamics. Appreciative awareness of each other's spiritual lives. Storytelling is a way to established shared meaning and team growth. The "elephant" is recognized, accepted and tamed for now. True collaboration becomes a working value. Pastor as nurturer and protector of pastoral team growth.
Transitioning-Out (TO)	Rising uncertainty comes to the forefront as current pastor starts the exit process. Apprehension, fear, loss emerge in the work climate and need to be addressed. A rising destabilization of working relationships within pastoral team. A time to reflect on what has been achieved and what remains to be done. Exiting pastor focuses on transitional readiness of the pastoral team.

stated, the researcher for this project has a terminal degree in business (Doctorate in Business Administration) and teaches research at graduate level (MBA and DBA programs), has over 18 years of experience as a nonprofit consultant, is of the Catholic faith and is an ordained member of the clergy (permanent deacon), and participated as a consultant for six of the 32 pastoral teams within the sample.

Naturally, and as with all research, there are a series of limitations to consider when using the outcome of this research project. First is the interpretative nature of qualitative research, meaning that although the outcome of this project could be verified by other researchers, it's also possible that other researchers may come up with different viewpoints of life-cycle stages. For example, some ministries may confront an "end-of-life stage," which was not a consideration in the model researched.

What matters here is the fact that life-cycles in ministry could be established as a tool for better applying pastoral leadership influences. A second consideration was in relation to the sample—that of parish staff. Because of time constraints, the researcher was unable to validate the life-cycle model directly with any other major ministry in the parish setting. A third limitation was related to factors of diversity, parish geographical location (urban, suburban, rural) and parish affiliation (religious order or diocesan). We recognize these as variables that may also affect the interpretation of life-cycle phenomena, yet were not possible to clearly discern given the sample. Nevertheless, we submit that—at least a priori—the seven stages of life-cycle presented have value in stressing different pastoral leadership influences given different developmental stages of ministry groups.

Now that we have explored an explanation of the theoretical methodology, the specifics of the target sample used and how the model was generated, what follows is a more detailed presentation of each stage, followed by a discussion on how these life-cycle stages relate to the spiritual influences of pastoral leadership discussed in previous chapters.

The Pastoral Life-cycle Model

The seven stages of a religious nonprofit life-cycle that emerged from this study are transitioning-in, reconfiguring, validating, reaching, awakening, nurturing and transitioning-out. These stages are illustrated in Figure 6.

A task orientation prevailed in the first three stages of the pastoral life-cycle in leadership teams. As a new pastor came into the pastoral team, there was an observed urgency to share past performance and elicit the new expectations, to understand and to be understood not only from the operational perspective but also from a spiritual perspective since the mission of religious nonprofits is fundamentally spiritual. This is characterized by the *transitioning-in* stage.

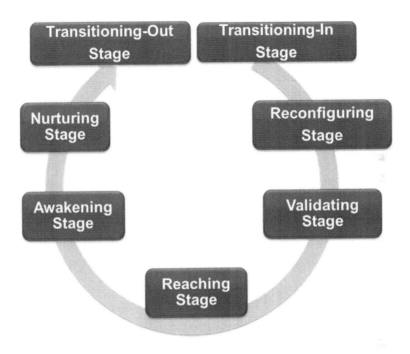

Figure 6, Seven Stage Pastoral Team Life-cycle

The next stage is *reconfiguring*, in which each staff or pastoral team member internalized the changes and the perceived personality image of the pastor and adjusted processes, duties and responsibilities accordingly. Here, the leader-team relationships focused on negotiations, sorting out ambiguities and sensitivities, and readdressing expectations as changes were implemented.

The *reconfiguring* stage was followed by the *validating* stage. Here, each team member matured in fulfilling the expected changes, yet the focus still remained more on task performance than on relationships and team performance.

Yet once team members develop improved levels of confidence and trust in the changes affecting the tasks each team member performs individually, there seemed to be an emerging willingness to re-address team processes. As a transition stage between task and relational orientation, the *reaching* stage represented a shifting of interests from individual performance to team performance, in which developing the basic team-building skills (e.g., effective meetings, communications, envisioning, conflict management, etc.) became a team value. In this context, teamwork in the secular sense became a topic of discussion and of common interest. However, the degree of relational activity remained at the "business level" alone, despite the possibility of a continued learning and growing that may be afforded by the spiritual mission. Here, specific interventions by parish consultants and other external resources proved valuable to most of the 32 pastoral teams in discerning the spiritual opportunities of pastoral team growth.

The final three stages of *awakening, nurturing and transitioning out* embodied the more *relational* stages of the pastoral team life-cycle. *Awakening* was a natural step from "team" to "spiritual community," in which the organization's mission and the religious vocation of the pastor converged. The *awakening* stage was very much about the awareness of relational values beyond just work, where communications turns into dialogue, cooperation turns into collaboration, and authentic "safe spaces" were created that effectively addressed even the most sensitive of common concerns. When the awakening stage was properly cultivated, it lead to the *nurturing stage*, where relational fulfillment became an enhancer of task performance, and collaboration became the dominant value. Finally, the time arrived for the leader to transition out, and in doing so, a series of instabilities emerged and the team drifted back to the more task-oriented stages and increased levels of apprehension, caution and the sense of loss that began to reappear within the pastoral team and religious organization. Each of these stages is also explained in Table 4.

In re-assessing the effects of this life-cycle perspective on the 32 pastoral teams sampled, some additional observations should be noted. First of all, not all pastoral teams moved through the life-cycle in linear fashion. In fact, some pastoral teams moved very quickly into the relational stages, whereas some had actually stagnated or even regressed. Secondly, although the effects of life-cycle changes seem most dramatic when a new pastor was assigned; it was also evident in the turnover and replacement of one or two other members of the pastoral team. Finally, there was clear evidence that leadership and managements styles of the pastor as leader had significant influence on the team's pastoral ability to mature and grow.

Relating Pastoral Leadership to Life-cycles

Now that a model of pastoral life-cycle stages has been composed from a qualitative research project, the main objective of this chapter can be achieved—which is to relate the spiritual influences of pastoral leadership described in previous chapters to the different stages of pastoral life-cycle. In doing so, we anticipate the model will help pastoral leaders recognize some of the internal group dynamics and have a template to better adjust leadership influences to circumstances. Again, in doing so, the pastoral leader is dependent on the discernment process, such as the method discussed in the previous chapter.

In attempting to align the spiritual influences to the stages of pastoral team life-cycles, we observed two specific influences that in

Table 4, Life-cycles and influences

PASTORAL LIFE-CYCLE STAGES	DIMENSIONS OF COMMUNITY	CORRESPONDING LEADER INFLUENCES
TRANSITIONING-IN STAGE *Urgency to share past performance and elicit the new leader (pastor) expectations, to understand and to be understood not only from the task perspective but also from a personal point of view. Climate of uncertainty and expectancy.*	Primarily a Community of Tasks	Primarily a climate of transactional relationships with opportunities to start building assurance and identity relationships through envisioning. *Leader emphasis mainly on clarifying expectations for task and relations, not just tasks.*
RECONFIGURING STAGE *Each staff or pastoral team member internalizes the changes, the perceived personality image of the leader (pastor) and adjusts processes, duties and responsibilities accordingly. Climate of adjustments and negotiations.*	A Community of Tasks, with emerging tendencies toward Community of Learning	Transactional relationships with more opportunities for assurance and identity relationships. *Leader emphasis is primarily on openness for negotiations and behavior-reinforcing relationships.*
VALIDATING STAGE *Each team member is complying with the changes, albeit being cautious. Still the focus remains more on task performance than on relationships and team joint performance. Climate of cautious progress.*	Community of Tasks, with minor Community of Learning attributes	Emphasis on Identity relationships. *Leader key emphasis on relating personal, team and parish identities to the envisioning (new state of affairs), with many affirmations.*

REACHING STAGE *Definitive advancements away from a "silo" mindset toward acceptance of basic teambuilding dynamics. Emerging attempts at conversation and dialogue. The "elephant" in the room (an obvious truth that is being ignored or goes unaddressed) is being dealt with, albeit with trepidation.*	Community of Tasks, with a better appreciation of behaviors that lead to a steady progress toward Community of Learning	Creating awareness of the need to continue to get things done, but also the value of interpersonal relationships for the pastoral setting. *Leader takes advantage of this stage to envision and assess possibilities of nurturing and transformational relationships.*
AWAKENING STAGE *Awareness of relational values beyond just work, where communications turns into dialogue, co-operation turns into collaboration, and authentic "safe spaces" were created. Climate of sincere mutuality develops.*	An experienced Community of Learning, with some Community of Spirit attributes	Identity and nurturing relationships prevail, with opportunities for trans-formational relationships. *Leader principal emphasis on sustaining identity and nurturing relationships.*
NURTURING STAGE *Relational fulfillment among all in team becomes an enhancer of task performance, and collaboration became a dominant team value. Climate of nurturing inter-relationships.*	Community with Spirit prevails, with effective task fulfillment and continued learning	Sensitivity to transforma-tional relationships, although all other forms of relationship are also present. *Leader seeks moments of prayer, spiritual influence, and practices discernment as a team value.*
TRANSITIONING-OUT *As a new leader is anticipated, instabilities emerge and the team drifts back to the more task oriented stages with increased levels of apprehension, caution, and a sense of loss begins to reappear. Climate of uncertainty and expectancy reappears.*	Regression back to a Community of Tasks	Transactional relationships with opportunities to start re-building assurance and identity relationships. *Leader's foreomost emphasis on willingness to change and the prospects of exploring new possibilities of growth.*

many ways parallel the state of affairs described in each stage. These two influences were primarily directed at *dimensions of community* and *relational* influences. The corresponding *dimensions of community* and *relational influences* to each of the life-cycle stages are summarized in Table 4. What follows is a brief narrative identifying the main behaviors and situations of each stage followed by a commentary characterizing the climate and possible courses of action for the leader using spiritual influences.

Since the activities of the *transitioning-in* stage are oriented toward negotiating potential changes in direction, content or scope of activities triggered by either a new leader or new members in the team, it is essentially a task-driven stage. Under these circumstances, the group (team) behaves primarily as a *community of tasks* and the relational influence that prevails is that of *transactional* relationships. In performing as a *community of tasks,* team members tend to substitute their sense of commitment more toward themselves with a strong commitment to the potential changes to the tasks at hand. Although *transactional* relations are deemed as a portal to "higher" forms of relationships, there is also a risk of setting the stage for isolation from others in the group. As a result, pastoral leaders or group (team) members who tend to see their roles in this stage as *transactional* alone, also tend to give less priority to the relational dimensions of their jobs because they tend to view such an expansion as a transitional complication.

As the conversations continue between the new leader and the members regarding new expectations and changes to task, each member also takes the time to internalize these expectations and convert them into action. This is what we call the *reconfiguring stage*. In this stage, each team member adjusts the work processes, duties and responsibilities, but each one also takes into account the perceived personality image of the leader (e.g., pastor). The overall climate within the team (group) is one of continued negotiations and adjustments, which best relates to a community of tasks. Here, the leader continues to emphasize transactional relationships, but now also seeks opportunities for assurance and identity relationships.

The *reconfiguring* stage was followed by the *validating* stage. Here, each team member is hard at work with first attempts at aligning to the new rules and fulfilling the new expectations, so the focus remains on task performance more than on relationships with others or team performance. Therefore, there is a substantial emphasis on individual member tasks more than on pastoral team relationships, meaning that "individual" spaces are much larger than "team" spaces. Under these circumstances, there is much job stress, delegation is very hard because of possible ambiguities, team conflict and power struggles seem frequent. There is a perceived scarcity of time (e.g., "I don't have time for this…"), a feeling of being overloaded, and a higher risk of isolation (e.g., low degrees of participation) that may lead to burn-out. Because of the realignment efforts, there may also be suppression of sensitive issues that need resolution (e.g., the "elephant" in the room), and where the leader, if not careful, may end up "casting a long shadow" and at risk of micromanaging situations.

These situations suggest the team (group) is behaving as a community of tasks, with minor community of learning attributes since some tasks are inevitably overlapping with other ministries or groups in the parish. In this stage, the leader's emphasis on relating personal, team and parish identities to the envisioning (new state of affairs) with a lot of time on positive affirmations and stress management.

Once expectations and tasks are aligned and stay within reasonable controls, the new prevailing climate of comfort is ripe for a shift of interests from individual performance (silo-syndrome) to team performance (cooperation). There may also be a flourishing of basic team building skills (e.g., effective meetings, team prioritizing, working together, communications, conflict management). In other words, a climate of reassessing the working relationships with others may emerge. We call this the *reaching stage*, in which there is some "reaching out to others" or an emerging acceptance of basic teambuilding and some attempts at conversation and dialogue, albeit very preliminary in nature in which the "elephant" in the room (i.e., an obvious truth that is being ignored or goes unaddressed) is being dealt with, albeit with trepidation. Here is where the team (group) as a well-defined community of tasks starts to develop a better appreciation of behaviors that lead to community of learning. Here is also where the leader creates awareness of the need to continue to get things done but also highlights the value of the interpersonal. This is the juncture in which the leader envisions, assesses and discerns the possibilities of nurturing and transformational relationships.

The movement from the *validating stage* to the *reaching stage* represents a major paradigm shift in team (group) dynamics because it represents a genuine interest in accepting that tasks are relevant, but so are relationships. So far, tasks have been the dominant orientation, but the movement from *validating* to *reaching* signals some interest in harmonizing the understanding of tasks (hard side of leadership) and relationships (softer side of leadership). Here, the biggest risk is complacency within the boundaries of tasks, or "silo-syndrome." Silo-syndrome is when each team member is so entrenched in their own domains that relationships with others remains minimal, trust is fragile, competition is intense, comfort zones are not allowed to be "threatened" and forms of envisioning are limited and unable to overlap. This phenomenon is also typical in major corporations, and in many ways the same techniques use in the for-profit sector to prevent "silo-syndrome" may also enlighten possibilities for the ministry sector. One such resource is the article "Dismantling silos of uncooperative teams" by Diane Katz (2010).

Should the momentum for reaching out to others in the team (group) continue, the team moves into what we call the *awakening stage*. In this stage, members of the team (group) become more aware of the relational values beyond just work, and communications turns into opportunities for deeper dialogue, cooperation turns into collaboration and authentic "safe spaces" are created, respected and used to the benefit of the team. Here is where the team develops experiences that lead toward a full community of learning—and since the team functions within a pastoral setting—prayer and addressing mutual concerns become part of the learning processes. In this stage, the team climate is one of an evolving desire for mutuality, and where *leader* emphasis is on sustaining identity and nurturing relationships.

The team's relational growth within the *awakening stage* leads to the next stage, in which mutuality is able to reach its highest possible degree, given the group and members current circumstances. The relational fulfillment among all in the team becomes an enhancer of task performance, and collaboration among the members and with other entities outside the team (e.g., other ministries, parish, etc.) becomes a dominant team value. The use of "safe spaces" to discuss sensitive issues is well imbedded in the team's performance, and spiritual topics are a natural part of the team's activities. Here is where the team reaches the *nurturing stage*, where they become a *community with spirit* and the leader exercises a keen sensitivity to transformational relationships, although all other forms of relationship are also present. The leader also seeks moments of prayer, spiritual influence and practices discernment within the group until it becomes a team value.

Now by no means are we suggesting that *awakening* and *nurturing* stages require the "perfect team" with "perfect members," because that would be unrealistic. We have actually consulted with parish staffs and pastoral teams that have lived and worked within these stages, and they are all just normal, hard-working laborers in the "Lord's vineyard." In all stages of development, you can find turbulence, conflict, change, tensions, misunderstandings, pressures, frustrations and intense discussions. What matters in these later stages is that relationships among members are sufficiently mature and the team support systems are in place so these pressures can be dealt with in a different manner. At the same time, they are able to "grow while they work" in the pastoral setting.

Eventually, a new leader (or pastor) or new members are incorporated into the team. Therefore, expectations and work processes need to be re-assessed. While the current members or leader is waiting for the replacement—assuming the leader or members do not leave abruptly—some instabilities begin to emerge. We call this the transitioning-out stage, in which there is a tendency to "hold back" and the members seem to drift toward the more task-oriented stages of the life-cycle. With this stage comes increased levels of apprehension, caution and a sense of loss begins. Climate of uncertainty and expectancy re-appears. Consequently, there is a tendency to regress to a community of tasks, where again transactional relationships with opportunities to start re-building assurance and identity relationships exist. Here, the outgoing leader's emphasis is on developing willingness to change and the prospects of exploring new possibilities of growth.

Implications and Conclusions

The findings of this research project make some useful, albeit preliminary, contributions in validating life-cycle modeling and under-standing the nature and development of pastoral teams in religious or-ganizations. The model sheds light on identifying the potential person-al, interpersonal and spiritual relationships as they relate to manage-ment, leadership and performance in the pastoral setting.

In validating life-cycle frameworks within a task-relational spec-trum of pastoral organizational behaviors, it becomes evident that leadership and management styles are contingent upon growth stages. This raises the issues of a pastor-leader's ability to respond in kind with a portfolio of styles, of the value of life-cycle awareness to minis-try leader and pastor training, and of the possibility of accepting lead-ership and managerial functions as a phenomenon embedded in spir-itual practice rather than as an inescapable burden and cause for dis-comfort or eventual burn-out. Similarly, this life-cycle modeling makes evident to the pastoral team and parish organizations that task orientation should lead to spiritual awakening and nurturing, that a need for developing awareness and readiness for growth is essential to parish organizational effectiveness, and that changes brought about by incoming leaders are to be accepted as a natural part of the parish or-ganization's growth.

These findings also benefit the emerging class of management and leadership consultants specializing in pastoral organizations. For example, being able to assess the current stage of an organization's growth in relation to the leadership-life-cycle paradigm allows for the awareness, planning and implementation of concrete sector-specific interventions. Life-cycle language allows for the development of new techniques to recognize and sustain harmony between business practices and spiritual objectives within pastoral organizations. Life-cycle modeling also allows a distinct approach to introducing relational and community competencies. And finally, life-cycle self-assessments may help recognize when consultant services may be sorely needed (e.g., stagnation) and even as a way to promote continued research and continued formation among nonprofit consultants.

Despite these preliminary findings, there is still much to be analyzed, studied and validated in the pastoral sector. Other models, principles, and findings that have already demonstrated validity across nonprofit organizations may also need to be tested in the religious nonprofit sector. Conversely, discoveries from the pastoral sector may also shed light on areas of further development in the general realm of nonprofit organizations, especially along the lines of the task-relational orientation. Nevertheless, this study demonstrates the value of continuing pastoral life-cycle research and possible lines of discourse on parish organizations.

Chapter References

Alexander, J.A, Fennell, M.L., Halpern, M.T. (1993). Leadership instability in hospitals: The influence of board-CEO relations and organizational growth and decline. *Administrative Science Quarterly, 38*(1), 74.

Bowen, W.G. (1994). When a business leader joins a nonprofit board. *Harvard Business Review, 72*(5), 38-43.

Butler, D.M., & Herman, R.D. (1999). Effective ministerial leadership. *Nonprofit Management and Leadership, 9*(3), 229-239.

Cnaan, R. (2007). A primer for pastors and other practitioners. *Nonprofit Management and Leadership, 17*(3), 373-374.

Clifford-Born, C. (2000). *Nonprofit board of director attributes at the stages if the organizational life-cycle.* Ph.D. Dissertation. Los Angeles, CA: California School of Professional Psychology.

Connolly, Paul M. (2006) *Navigating the Organizational Life-cycle: A Capacity-Building Guide for Nonprofit Leaders.* Washington D.C.: Board Source.

Creswell, J.W. (2003). *Research design: qualitative, quantitative and mixed methods Approaches* (2nd ed.). Thousand Oaks, CA: Sage.

Dandridge, T.C. (1979). Children are not little grown-ups: Small business needs its own organization theory. *Journal of Small Business Management, 17*, 53-57.

Dart, R., Bradshaw, P., Murray, V., Wolpin, J. (2006). Boards of directors in nonprofit organizations: Do the follow a life-cycle model? *Nonprofit Management and Leadership, 6*(4), 367-379.

DeLambo, D. (2005). *Lay parish ministers: A study of emerging leadership.* National Pastoral Life Center. National Conference of Catholic Bishops. Bishops' Committee on the Laity: Lilly Endowment. (ISBN: 1881307336 9781881307334).

Dodge, H., & Robbins, J. (1992). An empirical investigation of the organizational life-cycle model for small business development and survival. *Journal of Small Business Management, 30*(1), 27-37.

Duncan, J.B.. & Morris, H.S. (2003). The understanding of internal control principles by pastors. *Nonprofit Management and Leadership, 14*(2), 213-225.

Fernandez, J.J. (2008). Causes of dissolution among Spanish nonprofit associations. *Nonprofit and Voluntary Sector Quarterly*, *37*(1), 113-137.

Fleckerstein, M.P., & Bowes, J.C. (2000). When trust is betrayed: Religious institutions and white collar crime. *Journal of Business Ethics*, *23*(1), 111-115.

Giberson, T., Resick, C.J., & Dickson, M.W. (2005). Embedding leader characteristics: An examination of personality and values in organizations. *Journal of Applied Psychology*, *90*(5), 1002-1010.

Grothe, R. (2008, July). Editorial. *Clergy Journal*. p. 2.

Hernandez, C.M., & Leslie, D.R. (2001). Charismatic Leadership the aftermath. *Nonprofit Management and Leadership*, *11*(4), 493-4-97.

Kamaria, K., & Lewis, A. (2009). The not-for-profit general management responsive capability competencies: A strategic management perspective. *Business Strategy Series, 10*(5), 296-310.

Katz, D.L. (2010). Dismantling silos of uncooperative teams: How to identify and head off damaging information bottlenecks

Kenny-Stevens, S. (2002). *Nonprofit life-cycles: Stage-based wisdom for nonprofits.*

Long Lanke, MN: Stagewise Enterprises.

McLaughlin, T.A. (2001). *Trade secrets for nonprofit managers*. New York, NY: Wiley & Sons.

McMurray A.J., Pirola-Merlo, A., Sarros, J.C., & Islam, M.M. (2010). Leadership, climate, psychological capital, commitment, and wellbeing in a non-profit organization. *Leadership & Organization Development Journal, 31*(5), 436-457.

McNamara, C. (1998, December). Founder's syndrome: How founders and their organizations recover. *Nonprofit World, 16*(6), 38-43.

Milliman, J., Von Glinow, M., & Nathan, M. (1991, April). Organizational life-cycles and strategic international human resource management in multinational companies: Implications for congruency theory. *Academy of Management Review, 16*(2), 318-339.

Murphy, E., Dingwall, R., Greatbatch, D., Parker, S. & Watson, P (1998). Qualitative research methods in health technology assessment. A review of the literature. *Health Technology Assessment, 2*(16).

Quarter, J., & Richmond, B.J. (2001), Accounting for social value in nonprofits and for-profits. *Nonprofit Management and Leadership, 12*, 75-85.

Sharken-Simon, J. (2004). *Five stages of nonprofit organizations: Where you are, where you're going, and what to expect when you get there.* Saint Paul, MN: Amherst.

Schmid, H. (2006). Leadership styles and leadership change in human and community service organizations. *Nonprofit Management and Leadership, 17*(2), 179-194.

Schuh, R.G., & Leviton, L.C. (2006). A framework to assess the development and capacity of nonprofit agencies. *Evaluation and Program Planning, 29*(2), 171-179.

Strauss, A., & Corbin, J. (1990). *Basics of qualitative research: Grounded theory procedures and techniques.* Thousand Oaks, CA: Sage.

Strauss, A., & Corbin, J. (1998). *Basics of qualitative research: Grounded theory procedures and techniques* (2nd ed.). Thousand Oaks, CA: Sage.

Torry, M. (2005). *Managing God's business: Religious and faith based organizations and their management.* Burlington, VT: Ashgate.

Westhead, P., & Cowling, M. (1998), Family firm research: The need for a methodological rethink. *Entrepreneurship Theory and Practice, 23*(1), 31-56.

Framework that guides our choices

Discernment
Envisioning (Worldview)
Spiritual community
Primacy of relationships
Building Character
Your Calling

PASTORAL LEADERSHIP

Goals
Processes
Working together
Getting things done
Exercising influence & power

Framework that guides our actions

"Leadership is a spiritual practice"

304

CHAPTER 10

Moving Forward

It would be an omission if we did not share some of the latest developments and practical techniques we have used in our ongoing pastoral leadership workshops, or share some suggestions for those academics, researchers and consultants interested in continuing a discussion on the topic of pastoral leadership and leadership as a spiritual practice. Therefore, in this last chapter we present some of the preliminary results of a pre-assessment survey we have been administering to the participants of our workshops, followed by some practical techniques we have used to help learn some of the *spiritual influences* we suggest in this book. Next, we consider the possibility of offering a graduate-level course on pastoral leadership and suggest topics of further research. Then we close the chapter and the book with some final remarks.

Pre-workshop Assessments

As we have pointed out many times in this book, most of the ideas and concepts developed here came from experiences over the years of teaching (and preaching) leadership in the pastoral setting. Although these experiences resulted from reflecting on what worked and what did not work for each workshop, we realized that this method of collecting impressions in some ways met the validity criteria for qualitative research (e.g., grounded theory) and therefore would be considered valuable to share. We also realized the need to think about collecting data using quantitative and mixed methods to further our observations and recommendations. In being able to use quantitative and qualitative methods, we hope to take advantages of what both have to offer as we seek to continue expanding the concepts and practice of pastoral leadership, and even the possibility of follow-up editions to this book.

The idea that recently emerged as a quantitative component to our current investigative processes was to develop a survey to collect data on workshop participants before we conducted the workshops. Our hope was to use the data collected to help address specific needs as a workshop was being conducted. The pre-assessment survey would also allow us to establish—with larger sample—the most prevalent and least prevalent forms of spiritual influence being used by pastoral leaders. The assessment would also allow us the prospect of conducting pre- and post-workshop assessments to measure learning.

Consequently, we developed and tested a pre-assessment survey consisting of a demographics section and a 10-question survey (see Appendix B). The demographics section was designed to collect data on variables that we have seen are related to spiritual influences in leadership, such as being clergy or religious, years of ministry service, size of ministry being led and previous experiences in leadership. The survey part of the assessment is in multiple-choice format and addresses each of the spiritual influences presented in this book, but in very simple and somewhat tacit language.

So far, the data collected demonstrates that very few of the spiritual influences we suggest are being used by the laity, whereas they seem to be used much more among clergy and religious (men and women). Of course, our hope is that we can make more discoveries to help the continued efforts of building the pastoral model and the use of spiritual influences.

Workshop Experiences and Learning Activities

Being able to conduct parish workshops for ministry leaders while composing this manuscript has allowed us the chance to validate what we have said about leadership in the pastoral setting and has confirmed the need for more focused activities on leadership as a spiritual practice. But more importantly is the effectiveness of the learning activities we have been using for each module and the shared experiences of many participants, once the workshops are over. Because these learning activities and experiences were so rich, we had to add a section so we could share some of them within the proper context of this book.

One of the opening activities in the first module (Introductory Module) that helps set the tone for what is to follow in the upcoming workshop modules is a group comparison of definitions of leadership. Either we have a handout with various definitions that participants can use to find the best fit for the pastoral sector, or groups are asked to create their own definitions of leadership. Either way, the objective of the exercise is to review some definitions of leadership and start a list of aspects that seem to fit, and don't seem to fit, the pastoral sector. For example, managing by objectives as a leadership technique may be appropriate for pastoral work, but treating volunteers as paid labor (e.g., performance appraisals) may not be appropriate for the pastoral setting. Invariably, this first exercise creates awareness that not all that is readily available regarding leadership in the secular sector would apply to the pastoral sector.

Interestingly enough, the workshop experiences to date have prompted us to change the order of the topics. In the book, the order of topics build on each other as the ideas move from the individual (vocation, character development), to others (relationships and community), to the broader view of ideology and philosophies of life (vision,

307

worldview), then to how pastoral leadership is related to growth within a parish (life-cycles). But in the workshops, we find it more valuable to provide an awareness exercise followed by a brief overview of the spiritual influences and then focus on *discernment* as the first spiritual influence. The objective here is to allow the group to see the value of the discernment skill to leadership, and at the same time ask the participants to discern the next module that should be discussed after the discernment module. This way the discernment module as the first spiritual influence starts as a theoretical presentation, but it also becomes a skills practice session where the participants discern the next module according to their reflection and prayerful dialogue.

Upon completion of the first module on *discernment*, we find another interesting observation worth mentioning. When participants complete the discernment module and discover what they need as the next module, there invariably seems to be a strong preference toward selecting the module on *spiritual community*. This makes sense as a natural next step because for many of the participants, the discernment module was the first time they ever discerned as a group (i.e., a community of parish leaders), and they seemed eager for more along those same lines.

This way of allowing groups of participants to select the order of modules by way of discernment was more difficult than the traditional "linear" method of presenting the topics in the same order as the table of contents of this book. Yet it allowed for a prayerful way of establishing the most immediate needs, and allowed us to use the material as it was needed most. Walking into a workshop without knowing the specific order of the topics was very stressful for us as facilitators, since it meant we had to prepare and carry materials for all of the modules (e.g., presentation, discussion questions, handouts, exercise materials, etc.). Nevertheless, we found this way of conducting the workshops had a more profound impact on the learning processes.

Aside from the changes in the order of presentations that were driven by the participant's discernment outcomes, there were other exercises we have used in the other modules that are worth sharing.

For the *personal vocation* (ontological name) module, using a simple "reverse-engineering" exercise in the group setting followed by a tutorial on focused journaling worked best. We indicated that discovering the personal vocation was an inductive process, in which personal experiences and observations about different major aspects of oneself lead to a conclusion about one's ontological name. So for this module we handed out piece parts of a toy (one at a time), and the groups had to figure out what the toy was based on the parts. The group conclusions were then compared with a picture of the toy (fully assembled), and an analysis of the process ensued. Then we offered an explanation on how each person can collect the "major parts" of our personal realties (e.g., temperament, preferences, talents, significant personality traits, major life events, etc.), and then through a process of reflection and discernment, attempt to find the common threads that lead to "visualizing" the personal vocation. This process seems to work best along with a reflective journaling effort, since there is a lot to discover about oneself and then synthesize into a coherent single idea (or personal mission statement).

For the module on *character* as spiritual influence, there were two exercises, one to be conducted individually and one for a group setting. Because the topic of character strengths consists of such a broad list of possible measurable value, we have decided to use the character attributes that are associated more closely with leadership practice according to formal research and academic literature. As an individual exercise for the topic of character, we relied on a readily available popular assessment tool from the VIA Institute on Character (which can be seen at http://viacharacter.org). The website offers free and in-depth (fee) validated assessments of character along 24 character strengths. The *VIA Inventory of Strengths* takes about 30-40 minutes to complete and prioritizes all 24 strengths, allowing each participant to visualize and then reflect on the impact the top (and bottom) strengths would have in performing the pastoral leadership function. As a group exercise, we ask each group to come up with three character flaws they have seen in other leaders (at work, or elsewhere) and discuss the potential impact of those flaws had they been present in a pastoral leader. The exercise is intended to create awareness of how character strengths and weaknesses affect the leadership function, and help prepare for a discussion that would follow (the training module) on character as a spiritual influence.

The exercise we used most often for understanding the *pyramid of relationships* is experiential sharing. We ask each group to come up with their own definition and one example of each form of relationships (transactional, assurance, identity, nurturing and transformational), which we later share in plenary session. Then, in plenary session we facilitate a discussion on how each one of these forms of relationship are related to the leadership function.

We also conducted an exercise in which we ask the groups of participants to play dominoes, but with a caveat: Each group must "invent" two new and unique rules. After the groups had played dominoes a few times and had become familiar with the new rules, we asked that two players from each group move to another group. Naturally, there was an explanation of the rules to the "newcomers" but it also took a few iterations for the newcomers to adapt to the new rules. As facilitators, we made notes of how the "newcomers" were integrated into the new settings, the tensions that took place and the processes each group used to reach a point of stability. Time allowing, we implemented another rotation of "newcomers" (preferably participants who had not rotated yet) and continued making observations.

Once the exercise was complete, we started a plenary session dialogue analyzing the types of interpersonal relationships that were present throughout the exercise. Some topics that emerged were too much focus on task, poor listening skills, lack of patience, the allowing of the "newcomers" to grow into the new rules, learning to connect with the new-comers (as collaborator, not as a competitor), and comments on how tensions were managed. As facilitators, we checked to see which group took the initiative to think three-dimensional in making their rules. Invariably, most groups remained two-dimensionally in their rules, an observation that allowed us as facilitators to illustrate how hard it is in day-to-day practice to "think beyond" or transcend, an observation that sets the stage for a discussion of multiple forms of relationships and spirituality. With these exercises, we then led the participants into the hierarchy of relationships model and its application as a spiritual influence in pastoral leadership.

Before we delivered the *dimensions of community* module, we had the groups work together in the same room and put together a 50-piece jigsaw-puzzle—but unknowing to the participants—we removed five random pieces from each box and swapped them with other boxes in such a way that no one box had all of its original pieces. As the groups came close to the final stages of completing the puzzle and realized there were parts that did not belong, they also heard the same comments from neighboring groups, which prompted a spontaneous interaction among the groups (groups going beyond just themselves) in search of the missing parts. Typically, there was a participant who enthusiastically yelled out "We won!" to which the facilitator responds, "Not really…" A facilitated discussion then led to the realization that unless all parts in all groups are completed, there is no true winning in the pastoral sense. This allowed a discussion into definitions of "community" and the forces that oppose building true community (e.g., competition). Then we delivered the *dimensions of community* module (community of tasks, practice, with spirit).

One resource that we found extremely valuable to the module on the *dimensions of community*, with a special emphasis on *spiritual community*, is the workbook by Barry Heermann titled *"Building Team Spirit"* (McGraw-Hill, 1997). This workbook contains a model and vocabulary very much congruent with our own, and lays out a series of learning activities that prompt awareness and the building of spiritual teams.

D	B	E	J	D	K	U	B	Q	L	V	W	N	P
E	A	N	G	T	E	R	C	I	N	P	V	B	O
B	N	I	I	N	D	O	A	J	A	C	H	G	P
R	D	L	D	W	I	T	L	P	X	O	O	I	T
A	W	F	U	E	G	Z	E	I	L	N	L	Q	I
L	I	F	Z	N	M	R	I	I	S	L	V	M	E
U	D	O	O	Y	L	H	S	S	Y	Y	A	M	K
N	T	L	I	E	P	T	C	S	N	V	A	B	A
A	H	W	S	H	I	M	U	I	E	W	P	Z	M
R	C	S	O	C	U	S	P	L	R	O	O	X	Z
G	N	I	R	O	E	S	T	H	G	I	R	D	L
N	E	W	E	J	O	N	O	M	Y	Y	A	C	A

Find the following words:
BALLPARK
BANDWIDTH
HOLISTIC
OFFLINE
PAPERLESS
SILOED

The envisioning process is "painting a picture" that is s based on available facts but not all that obvious.

Do you see any other words that may be relevant but not listed above?

Figure 7, Example of Word Search

For the module on envisioning, we used a word game called "Word Search" similar to the one presented in Figure 7. There are websites that can help generate "Word Search" puzzles using words that are particular to a ministry or a parish (see in Appendix C for another example). But what we found valuable from this exercise is the effort to search for words that are "hidden" among the characters, something that a leader is expected to conduct as part of the envisioning process (finding clear meanings among the confusion).

But more importantly was the leader's ability to see beyond the words that are expected to be found just because they are listed. In finding words that are *not* listed, the "leader" is able to guide the group into "new" perspectives previously not envisioned. For example, the Word

Search puzzle in Figure 7 has the word "Jesus" imbedded in the puzzle, but is *not* listed as one of the search words. Can you find it? (See Appendix D for the answer). The objective of the exercise was to offer participants a situation similar to what a leader experiences when composing the vision looking at the set of circumstances and coming up with a perspective that creates a new awareness.

Naturally, there are other possibilities of learning activities for each module, but what we intended to accomplish here was to share some of the more successful exercises that enhanced the understanding of the concepts and carried over the theoretical dialogue into the practice.

Management skill competencies

We have already indicated that this book is about leadership practices intended for the pastoral setting. However, that does not imply that we believe that one should discontinue management training for topics such as team management, strategy tools, project management, financial management, time management, communications skills, managing meetings, conflict management and other management skills.

This would be a big misunderstanding of our purpose. Certainly, those responsible for ministries can benefit from managerial skills training. In fact we would encourage lay ministry leaders, parish staff, religious, clergy, and future pastors to undergo managerial skills training. What we dispute is the tendency to confuse managerial skills and leadership style. Our position is that both leadership and management skills should be adjusted to recognize the uniqueness of the pastoral sector.

A vivid example of our concerns is when management programs intend to portray the parish pastor as a Chief Executive Officer (CEO). Although the acquiring of high-level managerial skills training has value for pastors (and pastors-to-be), these skills should not define the leader-

313

ship style. Being able to perform as a high level manager is a relevant success factor for pastors within the realities and expectations of our society. But training in managerial skills should not take place at the expense of a pastor's true calling, or in a digression from his life-long formation, or as a juxtaposed process to the development of a mature vocation. Being an effective manager should not displace the course of a life-long vocation. Again, everyone engaged in responsibilities for parish life can benefit from management skills training, even if the training comes from the business sector. Our point is to advocate for caution when integrating these training programs into ministry.

As another example, team building skills and project management skills are essential to structuring workflow processes and assessing performance. Parishes have the need for task-driven teams and well-developed project management practices. But we also indicated in earlier chapters that parish ministries are to also emphasize the sense of community that helps make concrete the reality of parish as a community. These highly trained teams will no doubt behave consistently with the leader's performance priorities. But losing sight of the important objective to build a true sense of community by emphasizing task priorities over relationships will likely weaken the main objective of pastoral leadership. If team and group leaders place too much emphasis on task management, then the team will behave as a performance-driven organization and risk undermining relational depth.

Here is a third example. The demand for strategic management tools in a parish setting is another area where caution is warranted. Strategic planning, by definition, consists of providing direction to an organization over a long term, and configuring resources to deal with changing environments, demographics and financial circumstances. But how does the parish leadership account for Divine Providence in setting long term goals and objectives? Isn't the "voice" of God an integral part of parish strategic growth? Furthermore, a parish is connected to the local Church through the Bishop, so it is critical that a parish strategic plan also incorporate what is being envisioned for the local Church. And how does one strategize for a community? An analysis of strengths, weaknesses, opportunities and threats (SWOT) is foundational to the strategic planning framework, yet some of the better formulated strategic plans available on the Web seem to use business language that places more emphasis on the parish as organization than on opportunities to further develop the parish as a community. To be sure, strategic planning, done well, is an invaluable component of parish planning, especially as a way to make the vision and mission come alive. But there are certain significant modifications to consider when using "off the shelf" strategic management resources.

Again, our consistent objective in this book has been to highlight the unique attributes expected of a pastoral leader within the context of leadership as a spiritual practice. But we also recognize that pastoral leaders need managerial competencies, delivered in a way that remains compatible with the uniqueness and demands of the pastoral setting.

A Graduate Course on Pastoral Leadership

One of the most curious findings when evaluating the courses and curricula of Catholic universities in the United States is the lack of a specific course on pastoral leadership. In debating the significance of this omission, we could only hypothesize that the general thinking must have been that what secular leadership modeling had to offer was deemed sufficient for the pastoral setting. Yet when revisiting the programs and challenging our own thinking, we noticed that a significant majority of programs had no leadership courses at all. So the observation was not just that pastoral leadership was lacking; leadership as a discipline was missing.

In similar fashion, we reviewed the curriculum at some seminaries and a few diaconate formation programs only to find a similar omission.

315

This struck us as odd on one hand, and troublesome on the other. Odd, because you would expect that formal academic preparation—especially for lay leaders and clergy—would include specific courses on leadership in general, and leadership is the pastoral setting. The finding was troublesome, because in our consulting experiences, we have found that the most successful parishes are those that have initiated and sustained training programs for their ministry leaders. (Note that we were not able to explore this aspect among communities of religious men or women, so we can't comment on their leadership formation processes.)

Because of this shortfall, one of us took the advantage of teaching as an adjunct at a business graduate school and tailored a leadership course to include discussion and research on spiritual influences. The objective was to explore the possibility of including spiritual influences as part of a graduate leadership course with the expectation that if it would work in a secular institution, it would be easier to implement in a Catholic institution. In doing so, we hoped to start a trend in which pastoral leadership and spiritual influences could become—at least—an elective course.

The course in question was a traditional (face-to-face) doctoral-level class on leadership in which the textbooks were from Quinn, Robert E. (2004). *Building the Bridge as You Walk on It: A Guide for Leading Change.* Jossey-Bass (hardcover; also available in e-book) and Hrebiniak, Lawrence G. (2005). *Making Strategy Work: Leading Effective Execution and Change*. Wharton School Publishing. Because the Quinn textbook was oriented toward the "softer" side of leadership (with hints on spiritual topics) and the Hrebiniak book was oriented toward the "harder" side of leadership, it was easy to introduce the hourglass model of leadership and speak about influences of all kinds (e.g., rational, emotional, power based, etc.) and include a discussion on spiritual influences. In fact, the syllabus was built around the soft and hard sides of leadership, where personal vocation, character strength, the hierarchy of relationships, building true community and envisioning became major topics of discussion and deliverables (assignments). The session-by-session assignments for grading followed this same sequence. There were three sets of deliverables (assignments), and a final exam. The titles of the deliverables for the first group of assignments were:

Option 1-1: An analysis to demonstrate the hard and soft sides of leadership.

Option 1-2: Leadership differences by sector.

Option 1-3: Relationship between identity (personal calling) and leadership.

Option 1-4: What is spiritual intelligence and how does it relate to leadership?

For the second group of assignment deliverables, the topics were:

Option 2-1: Analyze the relationship between character development and leadership.

Option 2-2: Conduct a search for five leadership failures related to character weaknesses.

Option 2-3: Assess the current understanding of relational theory in the business setting as compared to the non-profit setting.

Option 2-4: Discuss how leadership is related to each of the levels of the pyramid of relationships.

For the third group of assignment options, the following topics were addressed:

Option 3-1: Describe the nature of leadership in teams as small "true" communities.

Option 3-2: Describe the nature of leadership in organizations as a community of communities.

Option 3-3: Analyze current leadership models that are worldview based.

Option 3-4: Analyze definitions of "worldview" and indicate their relevance to leadership modeling.

Doctoral students were asked to start a reflective journal at the beginning of the session and were prompted week after week to make entries that related the topics discussed in class to the realities of their own lives wherever they exercised the leadership function. Students were told the final exam consisted of composition of their most significant learning events and the value of this course in relation to the development of their personal leadership styles. The depth of the insights made in the final exam were then a function of how much each student had reflected on the significance of these topics to their personal development as a leader.

Although the class was composed of Catholics, Protestants, Hindu and non-believers, the discussion on the impact of spiritual intelligence on the leadership function became the portal by which each student—in his or her own way—was able to view leadership from an entirely different perspective. The discussions, exercises and deliverables of these students reflected how passionate they became about the softer side of leadership and the spiritual influences presented in class. If fact, their ideas and experiences were so valuable that some of them are incorporated into this book. To them, we owe a debt of gratitude in validating the possibility of using these concepts at the graduate level.

As a result of this class, we were able to suggest a syllabus for a course on pastoral leadership (see Appendix A). The course description reads.

Leading organizations in a contemporary world is increasingly complex, diverse and becoming more "sector" dependent. This course focuses on addressing emerging concepts in leadership and emphasis on comparing and contrasting leadership dynamics as they are enacted in different sectors, with particular emphasis in the pastoral sector. Topics include the evolution and trends in leadership modeling, analysis of leadership effectiveness in sector specific settings, leadership as influence, various forms of influence, and a comprehensive modeling for pastoral leadership with practical emphasis on spirituality as influence.

The books suggested for this course are from Gary Yukl, *Leadership in Organizations*, (latest edition), from Joseph C. Rost, *Leadership for the Twenty-First Century*. (Westport, CT: Praeger) and of course, this book. Each university has its own syllabus format, but we hope the content helps facilitate the justification and implementation of a much needed pastoral leadership course.

Opportunities for Further Research

Formal research is essential to any field of study, and pastoral leadership is no exception. To suggest what we have accomplished to date is a definitive work on pastoral leadership is to not fully understand the dynamics of Church and the workings of the Spirit. In applying spiritual influences to the exercise of leadership in the pastoral setting—and without negating the value that some secular models already add to ministry growth—we realize there are many more possibilities to expand, critique and explore. Leadership is more than just a simple prescription, it seems to depend more on a repertoire of influences that are exercised in different degrees, depending on the internal and external urgencies of the group (team, or community). These conditions set the stage for multiple approaches to formal leadership research applied to the pastoral setting.

One of the more immediate and obvious opportunities for research is in the continued validation of the spiritual influences discussed in this book, and the study of other—maybe even more relevant—forms of spiritual influences in the pastoral setting. If nothing else, an assessment of pastoral leadership needs for clergy and laity alike, as well as an objective assessment of currently available formation programs, should be one of the most immediate–and maybe even urgent—forms of research.

319

Another line of inquiry worth considering is the value of incorporating leadership formation along the lines of multiple forms of intelligence, especially spiritual intelligence. The secular academic literature is generating a lot of enthusiasm with respect to the topic of spirituality (e.g., the Spirituality in the Workplace movement), but many of the aspects of these secularly developed forms of spirituality clash with values, doctrine and expectations of the Church. Formal research available in scholarly and popular publications can assist in providing guidance and minimizing confusion when secular spiritual beliefs and practices seem to infiltrate the pastoral setting.

There are other opportunities for research along the lines of illustrating how the different schools of spirituality and their founders exercise spiritual influences. How are spiritual influences enacted in the traditional schools of spirituality? In this book, we drew insights and examples from a few traditional schools, but what were the unique forms of spiritual influences used by the Benedictine, Franciscan, Dominican, Ignatian, Carmelite, Redemptorist or Monfortian spiritualities? And what forms of spiritual influences are being used by post-Vatican lay movement spiritualities, such as the Charismatic, Schoesntatt, Opus Dei, Focolare or Taize movements? Could not the understanding of how spiritual influences were practiced in these schools of spirituality expand our understanding of a pastoral leadership model safely imbedded within the Church?

A fourth line of study could be in the form of case studies. Well-constructed case studies with probing discussion questions can serve as the basis to share many problems that are similar among parishes and allow opportunities to discuss steps that others have used to manage or correct similar types of problems. Case study analysis also becomes a test of problem-solving skills, a way to engage in problems that otherwise may remain unsolved, and a vehicle to practice collaboration and conflict-management skills. Creating cases based on real scenarios and making them available for use in parish leadership development is a powerful way of sustaining a vigorous leadership momentum in parish life.

There are also possible studies based on replicating pastoral setting leadership research that has been conducted in the for-profit and non-profit settings. There is also value in comparing and contrasting the fit and the shortfalls of prevalent and emerging leadership models in the pastoral setting.

Finally, we mentioned very early in this book there would be a strong focus on spirituality and less emphasis on theology, scripture and tradition. This was a difficult but necessary choice, as it simplified our attempts to effectively integrate and track the evolution of academic (secular) research within the leadership discipline as a foundation to our pastoral leadership modeling. Yet we do believe that theology, scripture and Church teachings are relevant to the emerging forms of effective pastoral leadership, and we encourage pastoral theologians, scripture scholars and parish consultants to continue what this book and others like it have already started.

Closing Remarks

Despite all that we have documented, experienced and presented in this book, we realize our efforts represent only a series of first steps in a long process to establish pastoral leadership as a field of study in its own right. In fact, other first steps have been made by popular and scholarly authors, but maybe the time has come to consolidate these efforts and move forward with more deliberate and coherent energies.

In a very reflective way, we have made what we believe are some valuable discoveries to facilitate the development of pastoral leadership. If we had to devise some "truisms" about pastoral leadership based on all that we had said in this book, they would probably be the following:

1. Leadership in the pastoral setting is fundamentally a spiritual practice.

2. Secular leadership models may not be enough.
3. Pastoral leadership does not come naturally.

4. Relationships and spiritual influences are more appropriate than other forms of power.

5. Discernment is a decisive skill in pastoral leadership.

As a last statement, our hopes are that what is expressed in this book would resonate in parish life, especially among those leaders seeking to use spiritual strengths as the proscenium for the leadership function. We hope that our experiences and insights will motivate others to continue to explore and disseminate in theory and in practice an emerging trend that *leadership is a spiritual practice.*

Appendix A

Pastoral Leadership Course Syllabus
(Generic, graduate level elective)

Pastoral Leadership Course Syllabus
(Generic, graduate level elective)

Course Description:
Leading organizations in a contemporary world is increasingly complex, diverse and "sector" dependent. This course focuses on addressing emerging concepts in leadership with an emphasis on comparing and contrasting leadership dynamics as they are enacted in different sectors, with particular emphasis on the pastoral sector. Topics include the evolution and trends in leadership modeling, analysis of leadership effectiveness in sector-specific settings, leadership as influence, various forms of influence, and a comprehensive modeling for pastoral leadership with practical emphasis on *spirituality* as influence.

Prerequisite:

Required Textbook/Resources:

Yukl, Gary. *Leadership in Organizations*, 5th Edition, 2010. Prentice Hall. (GY)

Rost, Joseph C. Leadership for the Twenty-First Century. Westport, CT: Praeger. (JR)

Rojas, R., R & Alvarez, J.A. (2012). *The Challenges of Pastoral Leadership.* Authorhouse.

Graduate-Level Program Expectations:

1. Research

1.1. **Performing** – Design, conduct and justify applied research in a business context using appropriate methodology

1.2. **Understanding** – Evaluate and apply existing theory and research to current business practice

2. Communication

2.1. **Oral** – Present orally, complex business information that is concise, clear, organized and well supported in a professional manner appropriate to the business context

2.2. **Written** – Present in writing, complex business information that is concise, clear, organized and well supported in a professional manner appropriate to the business context using required format

3. Critical Thinking/Problem Solving

3.1. **Critical thinking** – Evaluate relevance of established theory to current business practice and identify gaps in current literature

3.2. **Problem Solving/Decision Making** – Given a business situation, diagnose the underlying causes of the situation, evaluate possible solutions in relation to underlying business theory, and determine and defend appropriate course of action

3.3. **Information Literacy** - Conduct an exhaustive literature search from a variety of sources, evaluate the credibility of the sources, and apply that information to create new knowledge

4. Team

4.1. **Leadership** - Conduct an team search from a variety of sources, evaluate the credibility of the sources, and apply that information to create new knowledge

4.2. **Collaboration** - Given a case study or business situation, collect, assimilate, and disseminate the views of stakeholders

5. Ethics

5.1. **Ethics** - Given a case study or business situation, evaluate the ethical dimensions of decision situations and personal, social, and corporate responsibility not absolved by market forces

6. Diversity

6.1. **Diversity** - Given a case study or business situation, evaluate the multicultural solutions to business situations

7. Course Outcomes

The over-arching outcomes of this course are to develop a personal understanding of what leaders do to achieve results and what organizational conditions, by sector, favor or hinder organizational performance and leader effectiveness. To achieve these outcomes, graduate students will read and apply ideas from a multidisciplinary perspective, with critical analysis on what makes modeling effective within the common, as well as unique, attributes of each major sector. Most directly, the course will focus on how leaders act, what they do and how they mobilize support and attention in organizations. It will also focus on how they, working with others, accomplish results that achieve significant organizational results in the pastoral setting. Also, grounding in the leadership scholarly literature on leadership is important to prepare leaders for successful implementation of solutions/plans. To achieve these broad, integrative aims, the graduate student will:

1. Examine the characteristics of effective leadership and how leaders impact performance. Demonstrate by reviewing key articles in the literature, both classic and cutting-edge thinking, on leadership effectiveness and leadership theory with special focus on how leaders impact performance. (Program Outcomes include: 4.1, 1.1 and 1.2)

2. Research and analyze the relationships among leadership, followers, organizational performance, and achieving results by sector (Program Outcomes 1.1, 1.2 and 2.2).

3. Analyze and evaluate current literature on leadership modeling, creating awareness of sector differences when applying leadership models, and creating alignment within the organization on goals and strategies to achieve results (Program Outcomes 1.2, 3.1 and 3.2).

4. Research and apply practices to mobilize action and attention to overcome the ineffective use of leadership modeling by sector, with emphasis on the pastoral setting. (Program Outcomes 1.1, 1.2, 2.2, 3.1 and 3.2).

5. Each student will be required to maintain a reflective learning journal throughout the course. A reflective learning journal is required in this course to facilitate your introspection (thought and insights) and to enrich your development and potential for pastoral leadership. Each person's journal is unique, and there is no correct or incorrect response expected. This is a reflective process, not a diary of life activities. You are expected to have at least three journal entries each week. Note that the last day of class you will be graded on the evidence of reflective thought and the quality and consequences of your insights, not the quantity of your narratives. The FINAL EXAM is a composition of your most significant learning events and the value of this course as you find your own experiences of *leadership as a spiritual practice* (Rojas & Alvarez, 2012). The depth of your insights is a function of how much you have reflected during the session on the significance of these topics to your personal development as a pastoral leader. Here I caution you that in trying to complete a 10-12 page reflective paper without the benefit of abundant journaling and reflection during the session will be easy to detect in your final paper and certainly affect your grade. Remember, the final paper is to be completed in the classroom using the insights and observations from your journaling experiences. Again, if you have not kept some form of journal during the session, this final paper will be extremely difficult to compose.

6. For graduate-level assignments, it is expected that you will use credible and reliable citations and references to support your arguments in all your work. This means that all of your supporting sources for this class are expected to come from scholarly databases (see the library) and not from popular sources (such as magazines, newspapers, or the web). This is a crucial component of your course work, since there are also models of leadership that are considered more "fads" than well-researched models. Using scholarly sources will assist in separating true models from any leadership "fads."

7. Since each of your graduate assignments is intended for a scholarly audience, your supporting sources are also expected to be of the highest possible caliber, meaning peer-reviewed journals. Said differently, remember to avoid the use of dictionaries, encyclopedias, websites, newspapers and magazines as much as possible because they tend to be more related to popular literature. The use of scholarly sources increases the reliability and credibility of your claims, so avoid popular sources. Also, many of the discussions in class address topics that may be <u>highly controversial</u>, and consequently, may entail intense discussion. Nevertheless, remember that as a graduate student you are expected to debate with intensity on contentious issues, but at the same time the deliberations are expected to be of high scholarly standards, positive in nature, and focused on the topic (e.g., not on a person, ideology or with a negative attitude). Remember that participation is part of the grade.

8. All students are expected to adhere to the course syllabus and schedule. A session activities worksheet will be distributed each Saturday as a way to plan the session activities. The instructor reserves the right to change or modify the content, should circumstances arise that warrant the changes. Grades will be assigned using the following scale:

A = 95-100	C = 75-79
A- = 90-94	F = Below 75
B+= 86-89	W = Withdraw
B = 83-85	I = Incomplete
B- = 80-82	

Point distributions are based on the following categories of assessments:

Journal Entries & 3DBs	100 points
Assignment 1	200 points
Assignment 2	200 points
Assignment 3	200 points
Final paper	300 points
Total	**1000 points**

9. Although there will be an activities list published for each session, the table below presents the overall structure for the topics to be addressed, the foundational readings for these topics, as well as the classroom activities and assignments (grading deliverables). Remember that as a graduate student, you are not expected to master a book, but you will focus on the topic and the implications of the topic in the broader areas of the disciplines involving leadership. For example, the leadership function affects all major sectors (business, non-profit, government, military, as well as the pastoral sector). So go beyond using the textbooks as sources for your ideas, arguments and supporting evidence.

Weeks	Topics	Assignment
1	Overview of Course/Syllabus; Introductions	GY1-3, RJ1-2
2	Historical Development of Leadership and Perspectives on Effective Leadership Behavior	RJ 3-4
3	Participative Leadership, Delegation, and Empowerment	GY4
4	**Exam 1**	
5	Dyadic Relations, Attributions, and Followership	GY5
6	Power and Influence Managerial Traits and Skills	GY6 GY7, RJ6
7	Early Contingency Theories of Effective Leadership	GY8

331

8	**Exam 2**	
9	Charismatic and Transformational Leadership	GY9
10	Leading Change in Organizations	GY10
11	Leadership in Teams and Decision Groups	GY11
12	Strategic Leadership by Executives	GY12
13	**Exam 3**	
14	Ethical, Servant, Spiritual, and Authentic Leadership	GY14, JR7, RA
15	Leadership as a Spiritual Practice	RA
16	Pastoral Leadership Models	RA
	Exam 4	
	Grades Due	

All assignments are expected to be a "scholarly quality" submission in the university's mandated formatting style (e.g., MLA, APA, other). Each paper is expected to have at least 10-12 pages with a minimum of eight supporting sources. Obviously, these are minimal requirements, but you are encouraged to go beyond the minimum if you want to achieve exceptional work. This includes the final paper, which is composed in the classroom during the final day of class.

Finally, note there is a 5 percent point penalty <u>for each week an assignment</u> is late, so by all means please have your assignments on time.

Make sure that you email your assignments to your instructor using MS Word software.

10. Academic Honesty (Generic)

The university's academic honesty policy is specifically stated in the university catalog. Academic dishonesty is defined as representing another's work or parts of a work as one's own, or acting as an accomplice in such activities, falsifying, or violating test conditions. Plagiarism is the act of stealing and passing off ideas or words of another as one's own. It's essential to see your own work and assess your own learning, not someone else's.

Please use as many scholarly sources (not popular sources) as possible to support your claims you in each assignment, but stay away from just "cutting and pasting" from different sources on the web or other electronic publications. The preference is that you use the information from the source by rephrasing into your own words, and then citing the author and the publication. The instructor will be comparing student deliverables against other published sources within and outside of the university using a variety of software tools (including Turn-It-In) to assess the originality of each student's work as well as the validity of the sources.

11. Americans with Disabilities Act Policy (Generic)

It is the policy of this university to make reasonable accommodations for qualified students with disabilities, in accordance with the Americans with Disabilities Act (ADA). If a student with disabilities needs accommodations, the student must notify the Director of Student Services. Procedures for documenting student disability and the development of reasonable accommodations will be provided to the student upon request. Students will be notified by the Director of Student Services when each request for accommodation is approved or denied in writing via a designated form. To receive accommodation in class, it is the student's responsibility to present the form (at his or her discretion) to the instructor. In an effort to protect student privacy, the Department of Student Services will not discuss the accommodation needs of any student with instructors. Faculty may not make accommodations for individuals who have not been approved in this manner.

12. The University Statement Regarding Diversity (Generic)

This university prepares students to serve populations with diverse social, ethnic, economic and educational experiences. Both the academic and training curricula are designed to provide an environment in which students can develop the skills and attitudes essential to working with people from a wide range of backgrounds.

Appendix B

**LEADERSHIP WORKSHOP PREPARATION
PRE-ASSESSMENT SURVEY**

LEADERSHIP WORKSHOP PREPARATION
PRE-ASSESSMENT SURVEY

Please respond to the following questions to the best of your ability. Preferably, respond to all of the questions listed in the demographics section and in the leadership perceptions section.

GENERAL DEMOGRAPHIC QUESTIONS
GENDER: FEMALE _____ MALE _____

1. Are you clergy (priest, deacon) or religious?
    a. Yes
    b. No

2. How many years have you been a leader in your currently assigned ministry? _____

3. About how many members of this ministry are currently entrusted to you? _____

4. Do you have a spiritual director at this time?
    a. Yes
    b. Not right now.

5. Do you have any formal (academic) education in the theological disciplines?
    a. Yes
    b. No

6. Do you have any formal <u>secular</u> leadership training (workshops, courses, books)?
    a. Yes
    b. No

7. Do you currently occupy a leadership position other than in ministry (e.g., your place of work)?
    a. Yes
    b. No

8. Have you taken any specialized courses on leadership in the parish setting (e.g., LPMI, LIMEX, IPS, etc.)?
    a. Yes
    b. No

LEADERSHIP PERCEPTION QUESTIONS

1. In my experience, leadership models and theories I have learned in the secular world (e.g., at work) apply to the leadership functions I conduct in parish ministry.
    a. All of the time
    b. Most of the time
    c. Sometimes
    d. Less times than often
    e. Seldom

2. Leadership models and theories learned in parish ministry apply when I perform leadership functions in other places, such as work.
    a. All of the time
    b. Most of the time
    c. Sometimes
    d. Less times than often
    e. Seldom

3. How would you rate the effectiveness of your leadership in your currently assigned ministry?
    a. Excellent
    b. Better than average
    c. Average
    d. Maybe less than average
    e. Need lots of help

4. My personal calling (vocation) plays an important role in the leadership functions I currently perform within my assigned ministry.
    a. All of the time
    b. Most of the time
    c. Sometimes
    d. Less times than often
    e. Seldom

5. My <u>character strength</u> plays an important role in the leadership functions I currently perform within my assigned ministry.

     a. All of the time
     b. Most of the time
     c. Sometimes
     d. Less times than often
     e. Seldom

6. Others in my ministry recognize me as…

     a. More of a task oriented than people oriented leader
     b. Equally task oriented and people oriented
     c. More people oriented than task oriented
     d. They haven't clearly expressed themselves one way or the other

7. How would you describe your style of interacting with those entrusted to you? (*Pick only one response that <u>best</u> describes your interaction.*)

     a. It's mostly a "give" and "take" relationship. I say, they do.
     b. I'm finding myself mostly giving out a lot of assurances to make many of them just feel better.
     c. I'm finding myself mostly focusing on dealing with identity issues (who we are, what we do) related to our ministry.
     d. I'm finding myself mostly nurturing them into being better persons.
     e. I'm finding myself mostly offering opportunities for our inner transformation.

8. I consider myself effective in keeping a spirit of "true community" (not only just being a team or a group) among those entrusted to me within my assigned ministry.

     a. All of the time
     b. Most of the time
     c. Sometimes
     d. Less times than often
     e. Seldom

9. In my ministry leadership role, I am constantly developing and applying a clear "picture" of where the ministry should be in the next 3-5 years.

     a. All of the time
     b. Most of the time
     c. Sometimes

d. Less times than often
e. Seldom

10. To what degree is "discernment" a standard practice you as a leader use in your ministry?
        a. All of the time
        b. Most of the time
        c. Sometimes
        d. Less times than often
        e. Seldom

Thank you for sharing with us your experiences as a pastoral leader.

Appendix C

Pastoral Leadership Word Search
(Exercise)

Parish Leadership

STEWARDSHIP
PRAY
JOURNALING
VISION
NURTURE
SPIRIT
PASTOR
PURPOSE
SERVE
GIVE

Y	M	G	I	E	H	I	G	Y	G	P	J	O	Y	V
X	Y	A	I	S	W	B	V	H	I	B	A	F	Z	N
E	V	R	E	S	N	Q	I	H	H	M	J	P	Q	H
Y	W	P	N	Q	U	U	S	Y	E	V	Y	R	L	X
P	M	I	F	D	H	D	D	S	I	C	T	A	D	R
P	A	S	T	O	R	L	O	S	U	U	F	Y	S	N
G	I	V	E	A	Q	P	I	Z	Y	V	K	E	C	D
H	O	N	W	M	R	O	W	Z	R	U	F	I	T	Y
G	W	E	N	U	N	P	S	N	U	R	T	U	R	E
K	T	Y	P	V	S	P	I	R	I	T	S	Z	S	O
S	P	O	N	F	D	Y	M	O	B	I	Q	Y	S	V
W	G	N	I	L	A	N	R	U	O	J	M	O	R	C
C	P	N	T	U	R	H	U	V	K	G	P	D	E	U
R	G	X	J	Y	G	R	A	Z	B	V	M	V	O	Y
W	T	G	N	C	M	L	O	B	S	L	N	H	D	W

Appendix D

Answer sheet to Figure 7

Find the following words:

BALLPARK
BANDWIDTH
HOLISTIC
OFFLINE
PAPERLESS
SILOED

The envisioning process is "painting a picture" that is s based on available facts but not all that obvious.

Do you see any other words that may be relevant but not listed above?

D B E J D K U B Q L V W N P
E A N G T E R C I N P V B O
B N I N D O A J A C H G P
R D L D W I T L P X O O I T
A W F U E G Z E I L N L Q I
L I F Z N M R I S L V M E
U D O O Y L H S S Y Y A M K
N T L I E P T C S N V A B A
A H W S H I M U E W P Z M
R C S O C U S P L R O O X Z
G N I R O E S T H G I R D L
N E W E J O N O M Y Y A C A

344

INDEX

nursery of relationships, 183
nurturing relationships, 154,
    155, 156, 157, 187, 194, 293,
    296

O

ontological name, 78, 79, 80,
    81, 82, 83, 84, 85, 86, 87, 88,
    89, 236, 309

P

pastoral life-cycles, 277
pastors, 11, 12, 103, 107, 128,
    244, 281, 284, 300
personal calling, 55, 71, 76, 77,
    86, 87
personality assessments, 97, 99
personality development, 56,
    95, 236
place of healing, 184
Placemaking, 204
position power, 14, 41, 42
power and influence, 11, 36, 38,
    52, 56, 57, 77, 109, 127
primacy of relationships, 14, 53,
    57, 117, 176, 272

R

rational knowing, 179
reconfiguring stage, 290
relational self, 179
religiosity and ethical behaviors,
    98
Rule of St. Benedict, 240

S

safe space, 184

schools of spirituality, 16, 55,
    81, 85, 201, 238, 239, 242,
    245, 246, 253, 255, 320
self-determination, 105, 106,
    107, 108, 110, 115
self-regulation, 53, 57, 101, 272
softer, 34, 36, 37, 45, 49, 117,
    316
soul role, 84, 88, 89
spiritual communities, 53, 138,
    205, 273
spiritual identity, 151, 153
spiritual influence, 12, 13, 16,
    52, 246, 253, 293, 297, 306,
    308, 309, 311
spiritual intelligence, 169, 174,
    175, 207, 317, 318, 320
spiritual leadership models, 42,
    43, 44, 49
spiritual practice, 12, 13, 14, 16,
    19, 20, 31, 32, 47, 50, 51, 52,
    53, 55, 56, 57, 59, 60, 66, 86,
    94, 103, 106, 107, 108, 109,
    110, 114, 116, 117, 125, 128,
    130, 132, 139, 143, 146, 147,
    148, 154, 161, 185, 189, 198,
    200, 220, 227, 232, 242, 243,
    252, 270, 272, 273, 278, 298,
    305, 307, 322, 329
spiritual voices, 265
spirituality and leadership, 38
stability of character, 96, 97
stewardship, 14, 39, 53, 61, 62,
    159, 160, 161, 270, 273
strength of character, 56, 93, 94,
    95, 96, 97, 98, 101, 103, 104,
    105, 106, 107, 110, 113, 219

347

summative identity, 151, 152, 153, 159
sustaining character, 103, 109, 111
syllabus, pastoral leadership, 315

T

task-sprit connection, 32
team, 169
team, definition, 172
theologians, 11, 17, 30, 181, 321
transactional leadership, 131, 157, 167
transactional relations, 146
transformational leadership, 17, 37, 158
transformational relationships, 157
transforming movements, 236
transitioning stage, 288
types of groups, 171
Tuckman's five stage model, 173

U

Ubuntu, 140

V

values-based leadership, 39, 49
vivencias, 58
vocation, 12, 52, 55, 76, 78, 82, 84, 88, 89, 103, 108, 117, 128, 240, 243, 246, 253, 263, 272, 290, 307, 309, 316, 337

W

way of wisdom, 258
wokshop learning activities, 307
word search exercise, 312
workshop pre-assessment, 306
worldview, 10, 31, 36, 37, 39, 43, 47, 53, 59, 60, 129, 133, 139, 147, 148, 162, 208, 220, 221, 222, 232, 234, 237, 239, 242, 248, 251, 252, 253, 259, 286, 308, 317, 318